Global Staffing

Global Staffing seeks to increase our knowledge and understanding of the nature of staffing issues in an international context and to highlight the importance of international staffing as a critical international HRM issue for multinational companies.

This text critically examines various models and empirical studies on international staffing and reviews the research which examines the key factors influencing the choice between parent country nationals, host country nationals and third country nationals in MNCs. It explores strategic motivations for international transfers and considers international staffing from a subsidiary and a HQ perspective. International recruitment and selection, cross-cultural training, the reasons for shortages of international management talent and the role of women in international management are also analysed.

Global Staffing goes beyond examining traditional expatriate assignments and also considers non-standard forms of international assignments such as commuter assignments, shorter-term contractual assignments and virtual assignments. It is a must-read text for students, academics and practitioners in the field of HRM.

Hugh Scullion is Professor of International Management and Director of the Strathclyde International Business Unit, Strathclyde University Business School, Glasgow.

David G. Collings is Lecturer in Human Resource Management and Organisational Behaviour at the Sheffield University Management School and Visiting Research Fellow at the Strathclyde International Business Unit, Strathclyde University Business School, Glasgow.

Routledge Global Human Resource Management Series

Edited by Randall S. Schuler, Susan E. Jackson, Paul Sparrow and Michael Poole

Routledge Global Human Resource Management is an important new series that examines human resources in its global context. The series is organised into three strands: Content and issues in global human resource management (HRM); Specific HR functions in a global context; and comparative HRM. Authored by some of the world's leading authorities on HRM, each book in the series aims to give readers comprehensive, in-depth and accessible texts that combine essential theory and best practice. Topics covered include cross-border alliances, global leadership, global legal systems, HRM in Asia, Africa and the Americas, industrial relations, and global staffing.

Managing Human Resources in Cross-Border Alliances
Randall S. Schuler, Susan E. Jackson and Yadong Luo

Managing Human Resources in Africa
Edited by Ken N. Kamoche, Yaw A. Debrah, Frank M. Horwitz and Gerry Nkombo Muuka

Globalizing Human Resource Management
Paul Sparrow, Chris Brewster and Hilary Harris

Managing Human Resources in Asia-Pacific
Edited by Pawan S. Budhwar

International Human Resource Management 2nd edition
Policies and practices for the global enterprise
Dennis R. Briscoe and Randall S. Schuler

Managing Human Resources in Latin America
An Agenda for International Leaders
Edited by Marta M. Elvira and Anabella Davila

Global Staffing
Edited by Hugh Scullion and David G. Collings

Managing Human Resources in Europe
A thematic approach
Edited by Henrik Holt Larsen and Wolfgang Mayrhofer

Managing Human Resources in the Middle-East
Edited by Pawan S. Budhwar and Kamel Mellahi

Managing Global Legal Systems
International employment regulation and competitive advantage
Gary W. Florkowski

Global Industrial Relations
Edited by Michael J. Morley, Patrick Gunningle and David G. Collings

Global Staffing

Edited by
Hugh Scullion and David G. Collings

Routledge
Taylor & Francis Group

LONDON AND NEW YORK

First published 2006
by Routledge
2 Park Square, Milton Park, Abingdon, Oxon OX14 4RN

Simultaneously published in the USA and Canada
by Routledge
270 Madison Ave, New York NY 10016

Routledge is an imprint of the Taylor and Francis Group

© 2006 Hugh Scullion and David G. Collings, editorial matter and selection;
the contributors, their individual chapters.

Typeset in Times New Roman and Franklin Gothic by
Keystroke, Jacaranda Lodge, Wolverhampton
Printed and bound in Great Britain by
TJ International Ltd, Padstow, Cornwall

All rights reserved. No part of this book may be reprinted or reproduced or
utilised in any form or by any electronic, mechanical, or other means,
now known or hereafter invented, including photocopying and recording,
or in any information storage or retrieval system, without permission in
writing from the publishers.

British Library Cataloguing in Publication Data
A catalogue record for this book is available from the British Library

Library of Congress Cataloging in Publication Data
Global staffing / [edited by] Hugh Scullion and David G. Collings.
    p. cm.
Includes bibliographical references and index.
1. International business enterprises—Employees. 2. International business
enterprises—Personnel management. 3. Employment in foreign countries.
I. Scullion, Hugh. II. Collings, David G. III. Title.
   HF5549.5.E45G625 2006
   658′.049—dc22   2005018257

ISBN10: 0–415–36936–3 (hbk)
       0–415–36937–1 (pbk)

ISBN13: 9–78–0–415–36936–7 (hbk)
       9–78–0–415–36937–4 (pbk)

Contents

Illustrations

Figures

Tables

Boxes

Contributors

David G. Collings is Lecturer in Human Resource Management and Organisational Behaviour at the Sheffield University Management School and Visiting Research Fellow in the Strathclyde International Business Unit, University of Strathclyde, Glasgow, Scotland. His current research interests centre on human resource management and industrial relations in the multinational firm. He is also a co-editor (with Mike Morley and Paddy Gunnigle) of the *Global Industrial Relations* text in the *Global HRM Series* and has published a number of journal articles on industrial relations and HRM in MNCs.

Wes Harry has a PhD from the University of Strathclyde Graduate School of Business. He has held senior management positions in a variety of international organisations, in Asia and the Middle East, including two banks and two airlines. In his most recent post he has been adviser on Human Resource Management to the oil sector of a Middle Eastern country. He keeps in contact with academia as a member of the adjunct staff of the University of Bradford Management School.

Margaret Linehan is a lecturer in Human Resource Management in the Department of Continuing Education at Cork Institute of Technology, Cork, Ireland and is a Visiting Research Fellow in the Strathclyde International Business Unit, University of Strathclyde, Glasgow, Scotland. She has published eleven academic textbooks and over fifty journal articles. Her main research interest is women in international management.

Michael J. Morley is Assistant Dean, Research in the Kemmy Business School, University of Limerick, Ireland. His current research interests include convergence and divergence in European human resource management, human resource management in MNCs, international assignments and expatriate management.

Emma Parkinson is a teaching and research assistant in the Department of Personnel and Employment Relations, Kemmy Business School, University of Limerick, Ireland. Her current research interests include cross-cultural training and expatriate assignments.

Hugh Scullion is Professor of International Management and Director of the Strathclyde International Business Unit at Strathclyde Business School, Glasgow, having previously worked at Warwick and Nottingham Business Schools. His current research interests include the role of the corporate HR function in the international firm, expatriate psychological contracts, global staffing and further work on female expatriates. He has written over fifty specialist articles in international HRM and his most recent book *International Human Resource Management: A critical text* was published by Palgrave Macmillan in 2005.

Foreword

Global HRM is a series of books edited and authored by some of the best and most well-known researchers in the field of human resource management. This series is aimed at offering students and practitioners accessible, coordinated and comprehensive books in global HRM. To be used individually or together, these books cover the main bases of comparative and international HRM. Taking an expert look at an increasingly important and complex area of global business, this is a groundbreaking new series that answers a real need for serious textbooks on global HRM.

Several books in this series, **Global HRM**, are devoted to human resource management policies and practices in multinational enterprises. For example, some books focus on specific areas of global HRM policies and practices, such as global leadership development, global staffing and global labour relations. Other books address special topics that arise in multinational enterprises across the globe, such as managing HR in cross-border alliances, developing strategies and structures, and managing legal systems for multinational enterprises. In addition to books on various HRM topics in multinational enterprises, several other books in the series adopt a comparative, and within region, approach to understanding global human resource management. These books on comparative human resource management can adopt two major approaches. One approach is to describe the HRM policies and practices found at the local level in selected countries in several regions of the world. This approach utilises a common framework that makes it easier for the reader to systematically understand the rationale for the existence of various human resource management activities in different countries and easier to compare these activities across countries within a region. The second approach is to describe the HRM issues and topics that are most relevant to the companies in the countries of the region.

This book, *Global Staffing* by Hugh Scullion and David G. Collings, focuses on one specific area of global HRM policies and practices. The authors combine their many years of expertise on global staffing into several extremely valuable chapters on global recruiting and selection issues. In four chapters the authors have included Wes Harry, Michael J. Morley, Emma Parkinson and Margaret Linehan because of their special expertise. The first chapter provides the reader with a very extensive contextual appreciation of global staffing. The other chapters then build on specific themes and issues identified in this chapter. All told, their ten chapters form an excellent set of chapters on global staffing and ones that are likely to be much cited in the years ahead. As with all the books in the series, the chapters are based upon the most recent and traditional research and have numerous examples of what multinational enterprises are doing today.

This Routledge series, **Global HRM**, is intended to serve the growing market of global scholars and professionals who are seeking a deeper and broader understanding of the role and importance of human resource management in companies as they operate throughout the world. With this in mind, all books in the series provide a thorough review of existing research and numerous examples of companies around the world. Mini-company stories and examples are found throughout the chapters. In addition, many of the books in the series include at least one detailed case description that serves as convenient practical illustrations of topics discussed in the book.

Because a significant number of scholars and professionals throughout the world are involved in researching and practising the topics examined in this series of books, the authorship of the books and the experiences of companies cited in the books reflect a vast global representation. The authors in the series bring with them exceptional knowledge of the human resource management topics they address, and in many cases the authors have been the pioneers for their topics. So we feel fortunate to have the involvement of such a distinguished group of academics in this series.

The publisher and editor also have played a major role in making this series possible. Routledge has provided its global production, marketing and reputation to make this series feasible and affordable to academics and practitioners throughout the world. In addition, Routledge has provided its own highly qualified professionals to make this series a reality. In particular we want to indicate our deep appreciation for the work of our series editor, Francesca Heslop. She has been behind the series from the very beginning and has been invaluable in providing the needed support and encouragement to us and to the many authors in the series. She, along with her editorial assistant Emma Joyes, has helped make the process of completing this series an enjoyable one. For everything they have done, we thank them all.

Randall S. Schuler, Rutgers University and GSBA Zurich
Susan E. Jackson, Rutgers University and GSBA Zurich
Paul Sparrow, Manchester University
Michael Poole, Cardiff University

Abbreviations

CCT	cross-cultural training
GCC	Gulf Cooperation Council
HCN	host country national
HCR	Human Capital Review
HQ	headquarters
HRM	human resource management
IA	international assignment
IBT	international business traveller
IHRM	international human resource management
IJV	international joint venture
LTDI	Leadership Talent Development Inventory
MBA	Master of Business Administration
MNC	multinational corporations
MNE	multinational enterprise
ORC	Organisational Resource Counselors
PCN	parent country national
ROI	return on investment
SME	small and medium enterprise
TCK	third culture kid
TCN	third country national
TMT	top management team
UNCTAD	United Nations Conference on Trade and Development

Introduction

HUGH SCULLION AND DAVID G. COLLINGS

The major themes of the book

Global Staffing covers a wide range of topics within the rapidly developing field of international staffing. The comprehensive coverage encompasses strategic and operational aspects of global staffing and four major themes run through all the chapters. The first is the need to understand global staffing strategies and practices in relation to the changing strategies of the international firm. The second is the need to explore the links between the implementation of international strategies and staffing policies and practices. Third, there is the need to examine the various global staffing activities in ways that recognise how they link with each other. Finally we are also cognisant of subsidiary perspectives on staffing of subsidiary and headquarter operations and this is reflected in Chapters 2, 3, 7 and 8 in particular. The text is aimed at advanced undergraduate courses, masters' level courses and also as a resource for the reflective practitioner.

This introductory chapter has four main aims. First, it seeks to provide a brief introduction and overview of international human resource management (IHRM) and to consider why international staffing is different from staffing in domestic operations. Second, it examines the main reasons for the growth in importance of international staffing. Third, it outlines the distinctive contribution of this volume and seeks to review important theoretical and empirical developments in the area of global staffing since the mid-1990s. The final section provides a brief summary for each chapter to help the reader identify the main themes and issues covered in each of the chapters.

Staffing in context

The emergence of international HRM

While the primary focus of this book is on *Global Staffing*, in contextualising our later discussions it is important to consider the evolution of IHRM. In this regard, companies operating in the international business environment are faced with a great variety of cultural and institutional variations which make managing in a multinational context particularly complex (Doz and Prahalad, 1986). Significantly, managers of multinational corporations (MNCs) are increasingly realising the importance of HR practices in ensuring the profitability and viability of their business operations, while research suggests that many firms continue to underestimate the complexities of managing human resources across borders which often results in poor performance in international operations (Dowling and Welch, 2004).

Despite some similarities between operating in the domestic and international business environment, there is growing recognition that IHRM is distinctive from HRM (Dowling and Welch, 2004), and there is growing support for the argument of Evans *et al.* (2002: 14) that 'in the global era the most relevant insights into management processes will come from studying human resource management in an international context'.

There are two major factors which differentiate domestic HRM from IHRM. First, the complexities of operating in different countries (and therefore in different cultures), and second, the employment of different national categories of workers. Domestic HRM is involved with employees within only one national boundary, while IHRM, on the other hand, deals with three national or country categories: the parent country where the firm is usually headquartered; the host country where a subsidiary may be located; and other countries which may be the source of labour, finance or research and development. In addition, there are three types of employees of an international firm: parent country nationals (PCNs), host country nationals (HCNs) and third country nationals (TCNs). (For example, Citibank, headquartered in the USA, might recruit some Australian managers to work for them in Japan.) There is no consensus about the definition of IHRM although most studies in the area have traditionally focused on the area of expatriation (Brewster and Harris, 1999). A number of more recent definitions cover a far wider spectrum than the management of expatriates and involve worldwide management of people (Dowling and Welch, 2004). For example, Iles (1995) identifies four key areas in IHRM as recruitment and selection, training and development, managing multicultural teams and international diversity and performance management. Scullion (1995: 352), on the other hand, defined IHRM as 'the HRM issues and problems arising from the internationalization of business, and the HRM strategies, policies and practices which firms pursue in response to the internationalization process.' More recent definitions emphasise a more strategic approach and consider the role and organisation of IHRM functions, the relationship between headquarters and the local units as well as the actual policies and practices adopted. An important contribution defined IHRM as 'the distinct activities, functions and processes that are directed at attracting, developing and maintaining an MNC's human resources. It is thus the aggregate of the various HRM systems used to manage people in the MNC, both at home and overseas' (Taylor *et al.*, 1996: 960). This highlights that IHRM is concerned with identifying and understanding how MNCs manage their geographically dispersed workforces in order to leverage their HR resources for both local and global competitive advantage (Schuler *et al.*, 2002). Globalisation has brought new challenges and increased complexity, for example in the form of changing organisational structures, such as the challenge of managing new forms of network organisation. In recognition of such developments, some writers have developed new definitions where IHRM is seen as playing a balance between the need for control and coordination of foreign subsidiaries and the need to adapt to local environments (Adler and Ghadar, 1990). More recently, definitions have been extended to cover localisation of management, internal coordination, global leadership development and the emerging cultural challenges of global knowledge management (Evans et al., 2002) suggesting that developing future global leaders is a key priority in the management of human resources in the global firm (Scullion and Starkey, 2000).

There are a number of indicators of the rapid development of the field of international HRM since the mid-1990s (Harzing and Van Ruysseveldt, 2004). First, it has been argued that the more rapid pace of internationalisation has led to a more strategic role for HRM and that a more systematic approach to studying international HRM is emerging. One good indicator in this regard is the development of more sophisticated theoretical work in the area including the development of frameworks which identify the main determinants of IHRM policy and practice and the development of models which bring together the strategic and international dimensions of IHRM (De Cieri and Dowling, 1999; Schuler et al., 1993). Another important indicator of the growing importance of IHRM since the mid-1990s is the rapidly growing body of empirical research on IHRM strategies and practices of MNCs taking place outside the United States (Scullion and Brewster, 2001). Research highlights the major differences in approaches to international HRM between US, Asian and European firms (Harzing, 1999; Jung, 1982) and one objective of this book will be to shed light on the differences in international staffing policy and practices employed by MNCs from different regions of the world. Indeed, global staffing is increasingly seen as a primary HR practice used by MNCs to control and coordinate their spatially dispersed global operations (Dowling and Welch, 2004). The next section will examine the reasons for the growing importance of global staffing in the international firm.

The emergence of global staffing as a key area in international HRM

We define global staffing as the critical issues faced by multinational corporations with regard to the employment of home, host and third country nationals to fill key positions in their headquarter and subsidiary operations. Thus our conceptualisation not only concerns the transfer of PCNs to subsidiary operations, as is implied in traditional definitions of expatriation, but also includes staff flows in other directions. Global staffing has emerged as a critical issue in international management for several reasons:

● There has been a considerable increase in the mobility of human resources due to the more rapid growth of internationalisation and global competition since the mid-1990s (Black et al., 2000).

- The effective management of human resources at the international level is increasingly being recognised as a key source of competitive advantage in international business (Dowling and Welch, 2004).
- There is growing recognition that the success of global business depends most critically on recruiting the desired quality of senior management in the MNC (Schuler, 2000).
- Staffing issues are different and more complex in the international environment (Torbiörn, 1997), as in addition to the complexities of operating in different countries, the MNC employs different national categories of workers.
- The performance of expatriates continues to be problematic and the evidence suggests that the costs of poor staffing decisions in international business are often costly in human and financial terms (Dowling and Welch, 2004).
- Many MNCs continue to underestimate the complexities of global staffing and lack of knowledge of labour markets in a variety of countries and how to recruit in these markets is a major challenge for MNCs (Briscoe and Schuler, 2004).
- Shortages of international managers are a growing problem for international firms and the implementation of global strategies are increasingly constrained by shortages of international management talent (Scullion, 1994).
- The rapid growth of the emerging markets such as China and India (cf. UNCTAD, 2003, 2004) implies an increasing need for managers with distinctive competencies and a desire to manage in these culturally and economically distant countries (Garten, 1997). Also, there is greater competition between MNCs and local organisations in the emerging markets for managers with context specific knowledge of how to do business in such countries (Harvey et al., 1999).
- Global staffing issues are becoming increasingly important in a far wider range of organisations partly due to the rapid growth of small and medium enterprise (SME) internationalisation (Anderson and Boocock, 2002). Research has highlighted the importance of staffing and the top management team's international experience to the performance of international SMEs (Monks and Scullion, 2001).
- Recent research highlights the importance of staffing strategies to the successful implementation of the rapidly increasing number of strategic alliances and cross-border mergers and acquisitions (Schuler et al., 2004), particularly as the context of strategic alliances and global business is increasingly shifting from formal, developed and mature markets to informal, emerging and culturally distant markets (Harvey et al., 1999).
- The move towards network multinational organisation and the shift away from traditional hierarchical organisation structure means a more flexible role for staffing in the global network organisation. The development of networks of personal relationships and horizontal communication channels requires a more significant role for global staffing in the network organisation (Boxall and Purcell, 2003; Marschan et al., 1997).
- Research has shown the growing importance of emerging staffing strategies such as inpatriation which reflect the growing need for MNCs to develop a multicultural international workforce (Harvey et al., 1999).

- There is a growing recognition that the source of advantage for multinational firms is derived from the firms' ability to create, transfer and integrate knowledge across borders (Kogut and Zander, 1992). This suggests an increasingly strategic role for international staffing as the role of subsidiary knowledge and the organisational context is increasingly recognised (Foss and Pedersen, 2002; see also Minbaeva and Michailova, 2004).
- Recent studies have highlighted the growing importance of alternative types of international assignment suggesting the emergence of new patterns of global staffing (Fenwick, 2004). Research suggests that long-term expatriate assignments may become a less dominant aspect of international work (Harris, 1999) and that organisations are increasingly using a range of assignment options that were previously only considered within a limited geographical or national context. More employees are 'international' in the sense that they travel widely to other countries on behalf of their organisations on a variety of schedules from brief visits to intermittent expatriates who return home regularly for briefing and do not move permanently to longer term assignments (Mayerhofer et al., 2004).

In evaluating the evolution of the literature on global staffing we can point to a number of key trends. First, much of the early work on international staffing was drawn from research focused on North American MNCs and the main topic of attention was the explanation of expatriate failure, a concept which has received an amount of critical attention (Harzing, 1995). Much of this early work was largely descriptive, prescriptive and lacking in analytical rigour. A notable exception was the work of Tung (1981, 1982) which highlighted that expatriate performance was a particular problem for US MNCs. The management of expatriates continued to be a key issue in international staffing and North American academics 'set the agenda' in this field through exercising a defining influence on research and theory in this field (Scullion and Brewster, 2001). However, there was growing critique that many American based theories implicitly assumed universality despite a large body of empirical research substantiating the cultural diversity of values and the impact of such diversity on organisational behaviour (Hofstede, 1980).

A further critique suggested that staffing policies are often developed in isolation from other corporate policies and companies often fail to connect expatriate selection to the company's international strategy (Brewster and Scullion, 1997). More recently, however, research has shifted towards considering staffing questions in a more strategic context. In an effort to consider the range of possible headquarters – subsidiary relationships, researchers are suggesting more 'variety' (Bonache and Fernandez, 1999) in approaches to staffing and other IHRM activities, and recent work has highlighted the advantages of mixed staffing approaches rather than adhering to a particular policy. Researchers are further drawing attention to the need to consider global strategy as well as local conditions in determining appropriate staffing approaches (Bonache and Cervino, 1997). Drawing on the theoretical notions of the resource based view recent research has attempted to explain the strategic dimensions of expatriate selection (Bonache and Fernandez, 1999). This reflects a new body of work which illuminates the linkage between expatriate assignments and competitive advantage by highlighting the importance of the transfer of tacit knowledge to new markets. It also highlighted the need to pay attention to the international transfer of teams and not just individual managers, which conflicts with the dominant trends in the literature.

Since the mid-1990s there has also been a rapid growth of research on international staffing outside North America, and particularly in Europe which has added to our knowledge of expatriation by contributing to a deeper understanding of the importance of the context in which international staffing takes place. This is an important development as studies suggest that there are major differences between US, Asian and European firms with regard to staffing practices (Kopp, 1994; Ondrack, 1985). This research also highlights the different staffing issues and challenges which firms face during the various stages of the internationalisation process (Scullion and Brewster, 2001). Harzing's (1999) study highlights the importance of country specific factors and reports large differences between European countries in international staffing practices. Also, this study paid attention to the country of location of the subsidiary, the industry and the country of origin of headquarters as well as the characteristics of the subsidiary. While much of the research in this field is less descriptive and more analytical than earlier work, it still has an operational and practical orientation rather than a strategic orientation (Ferner, 1997).

The distinctive contribution of this book

In designing a book, there are difficult decisions as to what to include, and equally importantly, what to exclude. Following the objectives of the book outlined above we have attempted to move beyond traditional cyclical descriptions of the field. In this regard there is a large body of work which considers the expatriate cycle (see Black *et al.*, 1999; or IHRM texts: Briscoe and Schuler, 2004; Dowling and Welch, 2004; Harzing and Van Ruysseveldt, 2004), with a focus on selection, training, adjustment, performance management, compensation and repatriation. In this regard we have decided to exclude two key stages of the expatriate cycle, compensation and performance management. These decisions were made on the basis that there is a companion book in the series titled *Global Compensation* (Milkovich, forthcoming) thus we feel the detailed consideration given to the topic there would render a chapter in this text redundant. The decision to exclude performance management in a global context was a more difficult one. It was based on the premise that there was a large degree of extant and recent literature available (cf. Caligiuri, 2005; Fenwick, 2004; Gregerson *et al.*, 1996; Shen, 2004; Tahvanainen and Suutari, 2005) and further that it did not fit closely with the themes which we develop below. A final potential chapter which was excluded was on staffing issues in international joint ventures. Although this topic does receive some consideration in other chapters, a decision not to include a full chapter was based on the fact that the topic is also the subject of a companion volume in the *Global HRM Series*, *Managing Human Resources in Cross-Border Alliances* (Schuler *et al.*, 2004). Thus we have attempted to focus on issues which were of particular significance in the current business climate and indeed also on topics that may be underrepresented in the extant literature. The exclusion of the aforementioned topics has ensured that we could focus on more contemporary issues which may otherwise have been excluded due to space restrictions. In this regard we point to Chapters 5 and 8 in particular which consider the key issue of shortages of international managerial talent as a key strategic issue for organisations and further consider in detail the alternatives to the traditional expatriate assignment which have emerged since the early 1990s. In a similar vein Chapter 9 on women in international management offers some now important insights into an increasingly important topic in global staffing.

Summary of the distinctive features of the book

Comprehensive

A wide range of topics and themes in global staffing will be covered going well beyond the traditional focus on expatriation. We believe that *Global Staffing* will be the most comprehensive and authoritative text on the subject to date. Strategic and operational dimensions of global staffing will be examined, as well as the links between international strategy, IHRM and global staffing. Also, the links between the different areas of global staffing will be explored in some depth.

Critical research focus

Each chapter has been commissioned from a leading specialist in the field and the excellent research contributions goes well beyond the prescriptive approaches commonly found in the treatment of global staffing in many other texts. Each chapter offers new analysis of key debates in the field.

Integrated

There are a number of key themes running through the wide range of topics covered which gives an overall coherence to the book. This integrated approach helps students make connections among the different concepts and debates.

Global perspective

The authors use examples drawing on research from many countries and students will benefit from the diverse perspectives of the authors and will learn from examples of

MNCs operating in developed and emerging markets and from examples from very different types of international businesses ranging from SME international firms to transnational companies.

Relevance

The latest concepts and models of global staffing are presented throughout the book and are discussed in relation to recent developments in global business to help students relate the material to what is currently happening in the real world.

Who will benefit from reading this book?

The book will also appeal to advanced business and management undergraduates seeking to develop their understanding of specialised topics in international management. In particular, the book will appeal to masters' students majoring in international business and international management. It will also appeal to MBA students seeking to develop a deeper understanding of a topical area of international HRM. The book will help students to better understand the linkages and connections between international strategy, international HRM and global staffing. In particular, it will improve understanding of the role of global staffing strategies in the formation and implementation of international strategies.

Finally, while the book does not offer international HR managers the quick-fix solutions to their complex problems, the frameworks presented in the book should help managers develop a better understanding of the dynamic nature of global staffing in relation to the changing nature of the international firm, and also offers insights into the strategic and operational aspects of global staffing.

Before outlining the content of our volume, it is important to mention three key themes under which the content is structured.

The first part, 'Global staffing: theory and practice', is intended to introduce the reader to the field of global staffing. In the two chapters in this part we introduce some of the key theoretical contributions in the field and set the context for our later chapters. Further we attempt to introduce a more dynamic understanding of the concepts underlying staffing in a global context. In contrast to much of the literature in the field, which assumes a top-down perspective, we also attempt to give subsidiary perspectives a reasonable degree of consideration in this opening part.

The second part is titled 'Global staffing: composing the international staff'. This part consists of four closely related chapters. Chapter 4 addresses the issue of recruiting and selecting in the international context. Chapter 5 examines the strategic staffing issue of shortages of international management talent. Chapter 6 looks at the key role played by cross-cultural training in preparing international assignees for their assignments. Finally

Chapter 7 examines an often neglected aspect of global staffing, localisation. Here again we focus on one of our key themes and examine the creation of employment opportunities for HCNs.

The final part of our text, 'Global staffing: emerging themes', looks at a number of key emerging research themes in the context of global staffing. Chapter 8 examines the increasing emergence of alternatives to the traditional expatriate assignment. An area which is receiving increasing interest from academic and practitioners alike in the context of drives to reduce the costs of international assignments while ensuring the overall success of international business operations continues. In expanding on this challenge, Chapter 9 looks at the key issue of women in international management, or more correctly the lack of women in international management. This is significant given the shortages of suitable candidates for international assignments identified above. The final chapter closes the cycle on the role of expatriation. Although repatriation has long since been a key theme in the international assignment literature, we include it as a key emerging theme as it has until recently continued to be neglected by a large number of organisations. Thus we consider it to remain a key challenge in the context of global staffing. We will now outline the key issues to be covered in the chapters in the book.

Part 1: Global staffing: theory and practice

Chapter 2, 'Approaches to international staffing', expands on Chapter 1 and further develops the context for our later discussions on staffing by considering the various orientations that multinational firms' headquarters can have toward subsidiary operations. In this regard we draw on the classical theoretical studies of Perlmutter (1969) and Heenan and Perlmutter (1979). We also consider the implications of various options with regard to staffing on the operation of the MNC. Further we attempt to elaborate on these early studies and develop a more nuanced understanding of staffing issues, where the limits of Perlmutter's model will be discussed and studies which propose a more differentiated approach to staffing will be considered. Finally, we examine models which examine the factors influencing the choice between employees of different nationalities within the MNC. We will focus in particular on the impact of country of origin on these decisions and attempt to develop a more nuanced understanding of the factors impacting on international staffing decisions in MNCs.

While Chapter 2 considers the factors which influence the composition of management teams in subsidiary operations, Chapter 3, 'Strategic motivations for international transfers', focuses on the reasons why MNCs use expatriate assignments. In this regard we provide an introduction to the reasons why MNCs use expatriates. We then consider some antecedents of staffing orientations in MNCs. Finally we examine the relative benefit of international assignments to organisations through a discussion on the return on investment of expatriate assignments.

Part 2: Global staffing: composing the international staff

Chapter 4, 'International recruitment and selection', begins with a discussion of expatriate failure and then links expatriate failure to adjustment. Various models of expatriate adjustment are examined. Having established the significance of the selection of suitable individuals for expatriate assignments, appropriate selection criteria for expatriate management positions in theory and practice are discussed. We then examine alternative resourcing strategies and the different recruitment methods companies use to attract international managers. Finally, we consider methods of selecting international managers.

Chapter 5, 'International talent management', discusses some of the major international staffing challenges and constraints faced by international firms who seek to develop a pool of global managers. It will highlight the strategic importance of these constraints in relation to the implementation of global strategies. These issues are becoming more significant as the shortage of international management talent has emerged as a critical strategic issue for many international firms and often constrains the implementation of global strategies (Evans *et al.*, 2002). We begin by examining constraints on the supply of international managers. We then examine the role of the HR function with regard to international talent management and the management of the talent pipeline in the international firm. In expanding this discussion we consider the competencies required by the IHRM function and what these may be in the future. The challenges of developing global managers and the development of the global mindset will then be considered.

Chapter 6, 'Cross-cultural training' (CCT), examines in detail the topic of CCT, a topic which is increasingly emerging as an important element of the landscape of international business. Specifically this chapter, defines cross-cultural training and distinguishes between pre-departure and post-arrival training and highlights some cited advantages and disadvantages of each approach. It further identifies different forms of cross-cultural training, namely cognitive, experiential and integrated and associated techniques. Finally it reviews a number of key studies that have been conducted in the area in an attempt to assess the role and value of CCT in preparing assignees for international assignments.

Chapter 7, 'Localisation: societies, organisations and employees', considers the often neglected debate around the localisation of human resources. The chapter begins by considering the changing meaning of local responsiveness in international business. The benefits and barriers of the localisation of human resources are then considered in detail. Finally the chapter discusses the nature of localisation in practices with a particular focus on the role played by expatriates in the localisation process.

Part 3: Global staffing: emerging themes

Chapter 8, 'Alternative forms of international assignments', examines the emergence of non-traditional international assignments and alternative forms of international working.

It considers the reasons for the growth in alternatives to traditional expatriate assignments such as commuter assignments (frequent flyers), rotational assignments and short-term contractual assignments. The growth of virtual global assignments is discussed and the staffing challenges of creating and developing global teams are examined. The chapter highlights that the capacity to develop and maintain trust based relationships is critical to the performance of virtual organisations in the international context. Role conflict, dual allegiance, identity issues and establishing trust have been identified as important areas for future research with respect to the management of virtual teams (Clases *et al.*, 2004)

Chapter 9, 'Women in international management', examines the limited participation of women in international management and discusses the reasons for the low participation of women in international management in different countries. It considers the impact of gender on women's managerial careers and the related issues of work–family conflicts. The chapter also considers the main barriers to women developing international management careers and considers various international HRM strategies to increase the participation of women in international management.

Chapter 10, 'Repatriation: the frequently forgotten phase of an international assignment', focuses on the repatriation of managers which has been identified as a major strategic staffing problem for multinational companies in Europe and North America (Black *et al.*, 1999); research shows that the failure by many companies to address this issue impacts adversely on the supply of international managers. There is growing awareness that potential expatriates will be more reluctant to accept the offer of international assignments in companies which fail to handle repatriation issues effectively (Scullion, 1994). The chapter considers the key challenges associated with the repatriation of managers and also discusses the additional difficulties faced by female international managers in this context.

References

Adler, N.J. and Ghadar, F. (1990) 'Strategic human resource management: a global perspective', in R. Pieper (ed.) *Human Resource Management: An International Comparison*, Berlin: De Gruyter.

Anderson, V. and Boocock, G. (2002) 'Small firms and internationalisation: learning to manage and managing to learn', *Human Resource Management Journal* 12(3): 5–24.

Black, J.S., Gregerson, H.B., Mendenhall, M.E. and Stroh, L.K. (1999) *Globalizing People through International Assignments*, Reading, MA: Addison-Wesley.

Black, J.S., Morrison, A.J. and Gregerson, H.B. (2000) *Global Explorers: The Next Generation of Leaders*, New York: Routledge.

Bonache, J. and Cervino, J. (1997) 'Global integration without expatriates', *Human Resource Management Journal*, (7)3: 89–100.

Bonache, J. and Fernandez, Z. (1999) 'Expatriate compensation and its link to the subsidiary strategic role: a theoretical analysis', *International Journal of Human Resource Management*, 8: 457–75.

Boxall, P. and Purcell, J. (2003) *Strategy and Human Resource Management*, Basingstoke: Palgrave Macmillan.

Brewster, C. and Harris, H. (eds) (1999) *International HRM: Contemporary Issues in Europe*, London: Routledge.

Brewster, C. and Scullion, H. (1997) 'A review and an agenda for expatriate HRM', *Human Resource Management Journal*, 7(3): 32–41.

Briscoe, D.R. and Schuler, R.S. (2004) *International Human Resource Management*, 2nd edn, London: Routledge.

Caligiuri, P.M. (2005) 'Performance measurement in a cross-national context: evaluating the success of global assignments', in W. Bennett, D. Woehr and C. Lance (eds) *Performance Measurement: Current Perspectives and Future Challenges*, Mahwah, NJ: Lawrence Erlbaum Associates.

Clases, C., Bachmann, R. and Wehner, T. (2004) 'Studying trust in virtual organizations', *International Studies of Management and Organization*, 33(3): 7–27.

DeCieri, H. and Dowling, P.J. (1999) 'Strategic human resource management in multinational enterprises: theoretical and empirical developments', in P.M. Wright, L.D. Dyer, J.M. Boudrea and G.T. Milkovich (eds) *Research in Personnel and Human Resource Management: Strategic Human Resources in the Twenty-First Century*, Supplement 4, Stamford, CT: JAI Press.

Dowling, P. and Welch, D. (2004) *International Human Resource Management: Managing People in a Global Context*, 4th edn, London: Thomson Learning.

Doz, Y. and Prahalad, C.K. (1986) 'Controlled variety: a challenge for human resource management in the MNC', *Human Resource Management*, 25: 55–71.

Evans, P., Pucik, P. and Barsoux, J.L. (2002) *The Global Challenge: Frameworks for International Human Resource Management*, New York: McGraw-Hill.

Fenwick, M. (2004) 'International compensation and performance management', in A.W.K. Harzing and J. Van Ruysseveldt (eds) *International Human Resource Management*, 2nd edn, London: Sage.

Ferner, A. (1997) 'Country of origin effects and HRM in multinational companies', *Human Resource Management Journal*, 7(1): 19–37.

Foss, N.J. and Pedersen, T. (2002) 'Transfering knowledge in MNCs: the role of subsidiary knowledge and organizational context', *Journal of International Management*, 8: 49–67.

Garten, J. (1997) *The Big Ten: The Emerging Markets and How They Will Change Our Lives*, New York: Basic Books.

Gregersen, H.B., Hite, J.M. and Black, J.S. (1996) 'Expatriate performance appraisal in US multinational firms', *Journal of International Business Studies*, 27: 711–38.

Harris, H. (1999) 'The changing world of the expatriate manager', research paper, Centre for Research into the Management of Expatriation, Cranfield: Cranfield School of Management.

Harvey, M., Speier, C. and Novicevic, M.M. (1999) 'The role of inpatriation in global staffing', *International Journal of Human Resource Management*, 10: 459–76.

Harzing, A.W.K (1995) 'The persistent myth of high expatriate failure rates', *International Journal of Human Resource Management*, 6: 457–75.

Harzing, A.W.K. (1999) *Managing the Multinationals: An International Study of Control Mechanisms*, Cheltenham: Edward Elgar.

Harzing, A.W.K. and Van Ruysseveldt, J. (eds) (2004) *International Human Resource Management*, 2nd edn, London: Sage.

Heenan, D.A. and Perlmutter, H.V. (1979) *Multinational Organizational Development*, Reading, MA: Addison-Wesley.

Hofstede, G.H. (1980) *Culture's Consequences: International Differences in Work-Related Values*, Beverly Hills, CA: Sage.

Iles, P. (1995) 'International HRM', in C. Mabey and G. Salaman (eds) *Strategic Human Resource Management*, Oxford: Blackwell.

Kogut, B. and Zander, U. (1992) 'Knowledge of the firm's combinative capabilities and the replication of technology', *Organization Science*, 3: 383–97.

Kopp, R. (1994) 'International human resource policies and practices in Japanese, European and United States multinationals', *Human Resource Management*, 33: 581–99.

Marschan, R., Welch, D. and Welch, L. (1997) 'Control in less hierarchical multinationals: the role of personal networks and informal communication', *International Business Review*, 5: 137–50.

Mayerhofer, H., Harmann, L.C., Michelitsch-Riedl, G. and Kollinger, I. (2004) 'Flexpatriate assignments: a neglected issue in global staffing', *International Journal of Human Resource Management*, 15(8): 1371–89.

Milkovich, G.T. (forthcoming) *Global Compensation*, London: Routledge.

Minbaeva, D.B. and Michailova, S. (2004) 'Knowledge transfer and expatriation in multinational corporations: the role of disseminative capacity', *Employee Relations*, 26: 663–79.

Monks, K. and Scullion, H. (2001) 'An empirical study of international HRM in Irish international firms', *Personnel Review*, 30(5): 536–53.

Ondrack, D. (1985) 'International human resource management in European and North American firms', *International Studies of Management and Organization*, 15(1): 6–32.

Perlmutter, H.V. (1969) 'The tortuous evolution of the multinational corporation', *Columbia Journal of World Business*, 4: 9–18.

Schuler, R.S. (2000) 'The internationalization of human resource management', *Journal of International Management*, 6: 239–60.

Schuler, R.S., Dowling, P.J. and DeCieri, H. (1993) 'An integrative framework of strategic international human resource management', *Journal of Management*, 19: 419–59.

Schuler, R.S., Budhwar, P.S. and Florkowski, G.W. (2002) 'International human resource management: review and critique', *International Journal of Management Reviews*, 4: 41–70.

Schuler, R.S., Jackson, S.E. and Luo, Y. (2004) *Managing Human Resources in Cross-Border Alliances*, London: Routledge.

Scullion, H. (1994) 'Staffing policies and strategic control in British multinational', *International Studies of Management and Organization*, 4(3): 18–35.

Scullion, H. (1995) 'International human resource management', in J. Storey (ed.) *Human Resource Management: A Critical Text*, London: Routledge.

Scullion, H. and Brewster, C. (2001) 'Managing expatriates: messages from Europe', *Journal of World Business*, 36: 346–65.

Scullion, H. and Starkey, K. (2000) 'The changing role of the corporate human resource function in the international firm', *International Journal of Human Resource Management*, 11: 1061–81.

Shen, J. (2004) 'International performance appraisals: policies, practices and determinants in the casc of Chinese multinational companies', *International Journal of Manpower*, 25: 547–63.

Tahvanainen, M. and Suutari, V. (2005) 'Expatriate performance management in MNCs', in H. Scullion and M. Linehan (eds) *International Human Resource Management: A Critical Text*, Basingstoke: Palgrave.

Taylor, S., Beechler, S. and Napier, N. (1996) 'Towards an integrative model of strategic international human resource management', *Academy of Management Review*, 21(4): 959–85.

Torbiörn, I. (1997) 'Staffing for international operations', *Human Resource Management Journal*, 7(3): 42–51.

Tung, R.L. (1981) 'Selection and training of personnel for overseas assignments', *Colombia Journal of World Business*, 23: 129–43.

Tung, R.L. (1982) 'Selection and training procedures of US, European and Japanese multinationals', *California Management Review*, 25(1): 57–71.

UNCTAD (2003) *World Investment Report 2003: FDI Policies for Development: National and International Perspectives*, Geneva: UNCTAD.

UNCTAD (2004) *Prospects for FDI Flows, Transnational Corporation Strategies and Promotion Policies: 2004–2007*, GIPA Research Note 1, Geneva: UNCTAD.

Part 1

Global staffing: theory and practice

2 Approaches to international staffing

DAVID G. COLLINGS AND HUGH SCULLION

Introduction

In the previous chapter we outlined the importance of staffing as a concern for management in MNCs and introduced the concept of staffing in an international context. In this chapter we will: further develop the context for our later discussions on staffing by considering the various orientations that multinational firms' headquarters can have toward subsidiary operations; consider the implications of various options with regard to staffing on the operation of the MNC; attempt to elaborate on these early studies and develop a more nuanced understanding of staffing issues, where the limits of Perlmutter's model will be discussed and studies which propose a more differentiated approach to staffing will be considered; examine models which examine the factors influencing the choice between employees of different nationalities within the MNC. We will focus in particular on the impact of country of origin on these decisions and attempt to develop a more nuanced understanding of the factors impacting on international staffing decisions in MNCs.

Models of staffing the multinational enterprise

Without doubt the orientation of a MNC's top management team toward the staffing of the organisation's foreign subsidiaries will have a significant impact on the nature of the international human resource management policies introduced within the firm which will in turn impact on the final configuration of the management teams in subsidiary operations. This has however often been overlooked in the literature and it has recently been argued that most studies of international assignments fail to analyse the relationship between a firm's international strategy and its expatriation policies (Bonache *et al.*, 2001). Thus we will begin our discussion of global staffing by looking at an empirical model of multinational staffing.

Perlmutter's study

Discussions on the orientation toward staffing in MNCs are generally traced to the work of Howard Perlmutter and his work represents the seminal theoretical contribution to the field. In developing a model of the *multinationality* of international firms, he argued that no single criterion of multinationality was enough, nor were quantifiable measures such as percentage of foreign equity enough in themselves. Rather 'the orientation toward "foreign people, ideas, resources" in headquarters and subsidiaries, and in the host and home environments, becomes crucial in estimating the multinationality of a firm' (Perlmutter, 1969: 11). Thus key to his measure of multinationality is the orientation toward 'foreign people' and this is of particular interest to our discussion. Perlmutter introduced a classification of multinationals which differentiated between firms based on their attitude toward the geographic sourcing of their management teams. Initially he identified three approaches to the staffing of MNCs, namely *ethnocentric*, *polycentric* and *geocentric* (Perlmutter, 1969) while in later work he classified a fourth approach, the *regiocentric* approach (Heenan and Perlmutter, 1979). We also point to linkages between Perlmutter's typology and some important literature on international strategy (cf. Bartlett and Ghoshal, 1989).

The ethnocentric orientation

Ethnocentric organisations are primarily home-country orientated. Key positions in the headquarters (HQ) and subsidiaries are filled by parent country nationals or citizens of the country where the HQ is located. Perlmutter notes that, in these organisations home based policy, practice and even employees are viewed as superior and foreigners can be viewed as, and feel like second class citizens. Subsidiaries are controlled directly through PCNs in key positions and there are rarely opportunities for host employees to be promoted beyond their subsidiary operation or even to be promoted to key positions in the subsidiary operation. Ethnocentric staffing policies are most appropriate during the early stages of set-up of a foreign subsidiary when the need for control is greatest. They may also be used where there is a perceived lack of qualified host country nationals. It has also been argued that ethnocentric policies are appropriate strategies after international acquisitions in ensuring the acquired firm complies with corporate policy (Dowling and Welch, 2004). It has been argued in a European context that ethnocentric policies are likely to prevail due to a number of factors (Mayrhofer and Brewster, 1996: 766–7). The most significant of these are first, a unique mix of having a common basis of cultural understanding alongside peculiar cultures increases the opportunities for the expatriates to broaden their perspective in a relatively short time frame; and second, the geographic situation means that working in a given country does not necessitate living there. The ethnocentric orientation is most consistent with Bartlett and Ghoshal's (1989) conceptualisation of global companies. In this regard global companies are characterised by standardisation and the promotion of organisational efficiency. They are focused on the integration of production and the production of standardised products in a cost-effective manner. In global companies most key functions tend to be centralised and the role of subsidiaries is limited.

The ethnocentric staffing policy has for some time been subject to a large degree of critical attention. For instance, since the early 1990s, a growing body of literature has highlighted the headquarter concern that: 'if American [and firms of other nationalities] corporations fail to integrate an international perspective into their human resource policies and practices, their ability to compete successfully in the global marketplace will continue to be encumbered' (Tung and Miller, 1990). In this vein many authors have called for the development of a 'global mindset' among managers in global corporations (cf. Kedia and Mukherji, 1999). Quite clearly the ethnocentric orientation does not fit well with the concept of a global mindset. In fact managers in ethnocentric organisations would perceive home country knowledge and personnel as hegemonic and superior and thus would have little interest in the views of those of other nationalities. In Schuler *et al.*'s words (2002: 49): 'ethnocentric forces can compromise the MNE's [multinational enterprise] ability to identify and benefit from cultural synergies in their operating units'. Thus the homogenous mindset of the management team in an ethnocentric organisation can retard the MNC's international development. Other disadvantages of ethnocentric policies from a HQ point of view resonate with the emerging critical literature on expatriate assignment. These include the cost implications of expatriate assignments, the possibility of failure and the difficulty in getting PCNs to accept assignment in non-traditional destinations, among others (cf. Banai, 1992; Harvey *et al.*, 2001; Scullion and Brewster, 2001).

From a subsidiary point of view there are also a number of disadvantages of the ethnocentric orientation. First, it retards development opportunities for high-performing host country nationals, as there is no opportunity for their advancement within the corporation, as key positions in the subsidiary are filled by PCNs and the possibility of transfer to the HQ is generally limited in these firms. Pay disparities between home and host nationals may lead to perceptions of injustice and inequality and thus result in reduced motivation or increased turnover of HCNs. PCNs may be resented by host country employees who may feel that their allegiance is to the HQ and not to the subsidiary and their perception may be overly focused on HQ desires and thus may not always be in the subsidiary's best interest (Banai, 1992). Also empirical research on Japanese transplants in Britain indicated deep tensions between PCNs and indigenous managers. Specifically, Broad (1994) found that while the former enjoyed authority through their position as agents of HQ, the HCNs maintained considerable power and influence in the subsidiary through informal networks which provided them with information that the PCNs could not access. In particular this power was used to resist and ultimately dilute the practice of 'high performance management' introduced by the Japanese in the subsidiary. Thus it is important to note that the use of PCN expatriate managers is not a panacea for solving organisational control problems.

The polycentric orientation

Polycentric organisations on the other hand are primarily host country orientated. Foreign subsidiaries are primarily staffed by host country nationals or managers from the subsidiary location. Perlmutter has compared these organisations, to confederations, or as 'loosely connected group[s] with quasi-independent subsidiaries as centres' (1969: 12). Subsidiaries are allowed to develop with minimal interference from HQ and generally controlled through good financial monitoring and procedures. Thus while polycentric organisations provide ample opportunity for promotion within foreign subsidiaries, the opportunity for advancement beyond the subsidiary is also limited in organisations of this type. Polycentric staffing policies are most likely to be evident where organisations serve heterogeneous product markets and where products and services must be adapted and marketed to suit specific national tastes. They may also be evident where organisations have low levels of production integration between foreign operations and thus subsidiaries may be relatively autonomous and have little impact on production in other subsidiaries or operations. Indeed even organisations primarily categorised as ethnocentric are likely to fill senior marketing and HR positions with HCNs as these are the most likely functions to be country specific and thus most likely to require adaptation to the local environment. The polycentric orientation is consistent with Bartlett and Ghoshal's (1989) multidomestic organisation model. The multidomestic companies are characterised by a decentralisation of decision making and manufacturing driven by a desire for local responsiveness. The differentiation of products and services to accommodate local tastes and requirements is more important than the standardisation which is characteristic of global firms.

Polycentric staffing policies also have a number of further advantages from a HQ point of view. Many of these again closely resonate with the literature on the expatriation. Specifically language and cultural barriers that may exist through the use of PCNs are reduced if not eliminated through the use of HCNs. The MNC will not have to pay the premiums usually associated with expatriate assignments to HCNs, and thus they may represent a cheaper option. In contrast to the perception that HCNs who manage subsidiaries may act in accordance with their personal short-term goals which may not always be congruent with the best interests of the subsidiary, HCNs are more likely to take a long-term view of the subsidiary's operation. The employment of HCNs in key positions is also likely to be well received by host governments and employees in general. For instance, it has been argued that the employment of HCNs in key positions in Chinese MNCs may be particularly well received by host authorities. Selmer (2004) postulates that this localisation of staff may be perceived as an illustration of commitment to the host economy by central and regional authorities. Finally, politically, the option of employing HCNs may reduce the overt perception of foreignness in volatile or politically sensitive areas (see Boyacigiller, 2000: 127 for a discussion). From a subsidiary point of view, we can point to increased career opportunities for HCNs which may increase their motivation and attachment to the organisation.

The polycentric approach is not without its disadvantages however. Specifically as pointed to above, there are limited career paths for both PCNs and HCNs. Specifically

PCNs find it difficult to gain experience outside their home country as there are few opportunities abroad, while HCNs are generally limited to career opportunities within the subsidiary operation (Dowling and Welch, 2004). Also, more specifically, the organisation may find it difficult to fully integrate the subsidiary operation into the corporation as HCNs will generally have little experience of working in the corporation and will not be socialised into the organisation. To combat this MNCs often utilise expatriate PCNs in key positions in the early stages of setting up of foreign operations. Alternatively the company may attempt to socialise new HCNs into the corporation prior to the actual opening of the new subsidiary by getting them to spend some time working in the HQ operation, a process termed reverse expatriation (Mendenhall and Stahl, 2000) or more commonly inpatriation (Harvey and Buckley, 1997). The reaction of HCNs to these PCNs in subsidiary operation is also likely to have a significant impact on their adjustment and performance in their new roles. There is a growing amount of research emerging in this regard. Earlier work in this area has pointed to the importance of HCNs as socialising agents, sources of support, friendship and assistance to expatriates, particularly in the early stages of assignment (Black *et al.*, 1991; Caligiuri and Casco, 1998). More recently, Toh and DeNisi (2002) and DeNisi *et al.* (2003) have developed the research base in this area.

The geocentric orientation

Geocentricism involves filling positions at both HQ and subsidiary level with the 'best person for the job' regardless of nationality. Nationality and superiority are not related concepts. 'The skill of the person is more important than the passport' (Evans *et al.* 2002: 25). Geocentricism aims to produce a truly global approach to the management of MNCs. It has been argued that geocentric organisations represent the most complex form of organisational structure, thus requiring high levels of communication and integration across borders, the aim of the structure is to de-emphasise national culture and to emphasise an integrating corporate culture (Edström and Galbraith, 1997; see also Caligiuri and Stroth, 1995). Geocentric organisations are consistent with Bartlett and Ghoshal's (1989) transnational model of organisation. The transnational is characterised by flexible organisational strategy which can respond to emerging developments in the business environment. The MNC is conceptualised as an integrated network of sub-units within which expertise and resources are neither centralised nor completely decentralised.

Geocentric staffing policies are most likely to be seen in organisations where production is integrated to a large extent across subsidiaries. Organisations which have a large percentage of their operations outside the home country or where a large percentage of sales are outside the home country are also potentially more likely to pursue a geocentric staffing policy. Obviously organisations pursuing a geocentric approach are more likely to have managers with global mindsets, as referred to above, than organisations with an ethnocentric or polycentric orientation. This is likely to aid the organisation in competing in the global marketplace as decisions and top management action are underscored by a deep understanding of the international business environment. An example of a company which pursues this approach is Gillette, where only 15 per cent of the company's expatriate managers are from the home country, while the remaining 85 per cent are drawn from the other 27 countries in which the company operates (cited in Gooderham and Nordhaug, 2003). This approach also provides unbridled career opportunities for highly performing employees, not only in the home and host country but also those from other countries. The approach also facilitates the sharing of knowledge and best practices across the multinational as employees bring these practices with them when they transfer from one operation to another.

The disadvantages of the geocentric approach again are closely linked to the traditional drawbacks identified in the expatriation literature. Obviously there would be cost implications of having a large percentage of your management team categorised as international assignees. This additional cost would not be limited to additional premiums attached to expatriate assignments, but could include relocation costs, costs associated with the relocation of spouse and family, cultural adjustment training etc. As Dowling and Welch (2004) note, organisations would require a large cohort of PCNs, TCNs and HCNs to be sent abroad in order to develop and maintain the international team required to support a geocentric organisation. Roberts et al. (1998) have termed these career assignees *aspatial careerists*. These *aspatial careerists* operate in a borderless workplace and typically work in multiple countries in the course of their working lives. Empirical evidence in the UK context however indicates that the idea of an international manager is largely a myth. Specifically, Forster (2000) found in his study of UK MNCs that, while, multinationals were becoming increasingly international, their managers were not. He found that in contrast to generally accepted definitions, international managers in his study were little more than individuals who were proposing to or had spent time abroad on a once-off international assignment. Indeed while there is cohort of managers who find the notion of *aspatial careers* appealing, the reasons why managers may prefer more traditional career structures are pervasive. As Forster (2000) notes it is psychologically impossible for most people to cope with the dislocation and upheaval that would be caused by regular international assignments. Dowling and Welch (2004) further note that developing the large cohort of *aspatial careerists* required to staff a geocentric organisation will require more central control over the staffing process and longer lead times in terms of socialising employees into the organisation, which may in turn impact on the perceived autonomy of the subsidiary and may result in subsidiary resistance to this perceived loss of autonomy (see also Welch, 1994). Finally organisations may be faced with legislative constraints in transferring managers across national borders. Immigration laws can be used to protect the employability of a country's citizens and these laws would impact on foreign firms operating in these countries (Welch, 1994).[1]

---

1 It is important to note that this is not a constraint for Europeans travelling within the European Union (EU), as freedom of movement of individuals is one of the principles underpinning the European free market. Thus any citizen of the EU has the right to be employed in any member state of the Union.

The regiocentric orientation

Finally *regiocentric* organisations are conceptualised on a regional basis and managers are generally selected on the basis of 'the best in the region' with international transfers generally being restricted to regions. Under this structure subsidiaries within a region may have a relatively large degree of autonomy. Corporate policies and communication are generally mediated through the regional HQ. This strategy has become more popular in recent years with many MNCs choosing to organise operations regionally. This approach reduces the need for costly duplication of support services when an organisation has a significant presence in a region. For example a MNC may have a regional HR services centre where all HR related queries in a region are handled by trained operators in a central location. Likewise sales and customer support services may be handled centrally on a regional basis. The approach promotes localisation of policy as key positions in subsidiaries are generally filled by HCNs or TCNs with reasonable knowledge of the host context. HCNs may also feel more allegiance to the corporation as regional staff will be viewed as the face of the corporation and their views may not be perceived as alien as their corporate counterparts.

The regiocentric approach however may constrain the organisation in developing a truly global mindset as staff transfers and management know-how will generally be restricted to a regional level. Thus while the company may have regional experts, it will be restrained in developing global expertise. This will also mean that career opportunities for key personnel will be limited to regional structure. So while high calibre employees may successfully rise through the subsidiary and indeed may be promoted to regional level, there is limited opportunity for development beyond this.

The proceeding discussion of management orientations with regard to the orientation of international business is useful in highlighting the various options with regard to staffing the global enterprise (the model does of course have limitations and we will return to these below). Significantly the majority of the extant literature in the field of global staffing has focused on PCN expatriate employees and when this is considered in the context of Schuler *et al.*'s (1993) argument that a mix of PCNs, HCNs and TCNs can impact significantly on an MNC's ability to achieve learning, innovation and corporate integration, this represents a significant deficit in the literature. Thus, in the following section, we will briefly discuss the advantages of filling positions with these various nationalities of managers.

Nationality and staffing

As was demonstrated above, top management's attitude toward the orientation of their global business operation can have a significant impact on the direction of the corporate staffing configuration. In this section we will briefly consider the advantages and disadvantages of employing PCNs, HCNs and TCNs in multinational corporations. In developing on much of the extant literature, we will differentiate between the advantages and disadvantages from the point of view of the subsidiary and the headquarter operation. (Table 2.1 summarises the advantages and disadvantages from a corporate point of view, while Table 2.2 does likewise from a subsidiary point of view.)

A headquarter perspective

While some of the material covered above in relation to the advantages and disadvantages of the orientation of MNCs' management towards the geographic sourcing of their management teams may be replicated in summary form in Table 2.1 and Table 2.2, it will not be included in the accompanying text to avoid unnecessary duplication, thus this section should be read in conjunction with the preceding one.

Parent country nationals

Most of the advantages and drawbacks of utilising PCNs to staff foreign operations have been discussed in detail in the preceding discussion on ethnocentric MNCs and thus merit limited discussion here. It is worth reiterating however that the PCN is particularly useful in the early stages of multinational operation as a means of direct control over subsidiaries and indeed as a means of engraining corporate philosophy and culture into subsidiaries at an early stage. On the other hand the most significant drawbacks are those associated with the high cost of expatriate assignments and further expatriate failure particularly when poor performance while on assignment is taken into account. Finally due to the relatively short-term nature of expatriate assignments, it is possible that PCNs may take a relatively short-term view of the subsidiary operation and thus may not always act in the best interest of the subsidiary (see Mayrhofer and Brewster, 1996 for a full discussion on the use of PCNs in subsidiary operations).

Host country nationals

We turn next to the use of HCNs in key positions in subsidiary operations. Again this is covered extensively above in our discussion on polycentric organisations so we will simply reiterate some key issues which emerge from a corporate perspective. The most significant benefits of filling key positions with HCNs include an in-depth knowledge of the local business environment and understanding of local culture and traditions. They are also likely to increase motivation in the subsidiary as other colleagues will realise that there are career opportunities for high performing employees. It will generally also represent a cheaper option than staffing with PCNs or TCNs as HCNs will not be paid the premiums associated with international assignments.

There are of course a number of drawbacks associated with utilising HCNs in key positions in subsidiary operations. Not least of these are the difficulties associated with

Table 2.1   Nationality and staffing: a corporate view

Nationality	Advantages	Disadvantages
PCNs	• Direct and personal control over subsidiary • Help to transfer and establish organisational culture in early stages of establishment • Provides a career ladder for high performing HQ employees	• Can be an expensive option • Risks associated with expatriate failure • May create tensions with host government • Supply and demand issues for assignments in volatile areas and assignees with families – dual career • Limited awareness of local culture, legislation and market • HCNs may take a short-term view of subsidiary operations; interested only in what happens when they are there • May result in discontinuity in host management team, particularly with shorter term assignments • May be work permit and other legislative restrictions
HCNs	• Knowledge of local culture, legislation and market • Provides career path for high performing local employees • Generally cheaper option than PCNs • Ensure continuity in host management team, as opposed to frequent managerial changes associated with expatriates • Perceived well by local government and employees • More likely to take a long-term view of subsidiary operation due to fact that appointment is long term	• More difficult to exercise control: rely on formal procedures and organisational culture • Reduced career opportunities for PCNs • Possible lack of familiarity or network with HQ personnel – may make communication more difficult
TCNs	• Even though TCNs may be just as socialised into corporation as PCNs they may not be as threatening to host employees – a neutral alternative • Salary and relocation costs may be lower than PCNs • May reduce language barriers, e.g. a Spanish employee of a US MNC transferred to a new Mexican operation • Significantly expand recruitment pool within MNC • May be more willing to accept international assignments than PCNs due to limited labour market opportunities in their country of origin	• TCNs may take a short-term view of subsidiary operations; interested only in what happens when they are there • May be work permit and other legislative restrictions • Possible national cultural difficulties, e.g. Greece and Turkey • Overuse of TCNs may result in the MNC 'losing control' of its foreign operations • Repatriation problems as there may be no similar position for manager on return to their home country • May be selected on basis of language competency rather than technical or managerial ability

Table 2.2 Nationality and staffing: a subsidiary view

Nationality	Advantages	Disadvantages
PCNs	• Increased expertise means learning opportunities for HCNs • Eases transition to MNC for HCNs • Experienced technical expertise for problems which may arise in operation • Provides a lead time for HCNs to reach the required standard of performance • A direct and immediate contact with HQ	• Lack of career opportunity for HCNs • Resentment due to possible differences in reward packages between PCNs and HCNs
HCNs	• Career opportunities for high performing employees • Perceived autonomy for subsidiary operations	• A lack of technical and managerial competence may lead to poor performance and demise of subsidiary • May result in political conflicts within the subsidiary over key appointments
TCNs	• Increased expertise means learning opportunities for HCNs • TCNs more likely to appreciate legal and cultural idiosyncrasies of host country due to likely international career experience • Lower level TCNs are generally perceived as short-term assignees and thus not perceived as a threat to HCN's career paths	• Higher level TCNs seen as an alternative to PCNs and viewed as blocking career opportunities for HCNs • Lack of career opportunity for HCNs • May be cultural biases if TCNs come from a country with a history of conflict, e.g. India and Pakistan

coordination and control which result from the spatial dispersion of MNC subsidiaries. Without the presence of PCNs in key positions, the MNC will require sophisticated formal procedures and financial control systems to monitor subsidiary performance and ensure adherence with corporate standards and requirements. In the short term, the HCNs' lack of familiarity with the overall corporation and lack of networks within the MNC may make communication more difficult. Finally by removing the option of transferring PCNs to subsidiary operations the corporation is severely restricting the career and management development opportunities available to high performing employees in the home country.

Third country nationals

Finally we look at the use of TCNs in staffing key subsidiary positions from a headquarters' point of view. This is the category of employee which receives the least attention in our above discussion and thus we can point to a number of key trends in this regard. It is important to note however that with a few notable exceptions (cf. Reynolds, 1997; Selmer, 2002; Zeira and Harari, 1977) there is a paucity of research on the use of TCNs in MNC and there is ample scope for future study in this area. It has been argued that TCNs are more likely to successfully adjust to new environments as they are generally transferred within a geographic region, and, thus due to their spatial proximity to the country in which they are assigned they will have a greater knowledge of the host culture (Reynolds, 1997). Empirical evidence however fails to support this argument and indeed Selmer (2002) found in his study on the adjustment of Western PCNs and Asian and Western TCNs in the Chinese context that Asian TCNs were less well adjusted than the Western PCNs and TCNs. It is however clear that TCNs do offer a useful alternative to PCNs in certain circumstances. Specifically they provide a useful option when a subsidiary is established in a country where the national language is different to the parent country. For example an American MNC which has a subsidiary in Portugal may use Portuguese employees who are already socialised into the company through their experience in the subsidiary to set up a Brazilian subsidiary. This may reduce language barriers and aid in the case of transferring corporate culture. It has also been argued that some TCNs may be more inclined to accept international assignments than PCNs because of smaller labour markets and lack of job opportunities in their home countries. Thus they may view the MNC as a means of advancing their careers to a level greater than possible in their home countries. This however may create a difficulty peculiar to this group of expatriate employees. Specifically, the very reason these TCNs may accept an international assignment is due to a lack of opportunities in their home country, thus when they are eventually repatriated to their home country there may be no comparable position for them to return to (Evans et al., 2002). Indeed the reparation of TCNs in MNCs represents a fruitful avenue for future research. Finally there is little doubt that by utilising high performing TCNs, a MNC may significantly increase their recruitment pool for staffing their organisation (see Reynolds, 1997 for a full discussion of the issues surrounding TCNs and staffing in MNCs).

Third culture kids

Finally, a newly emerging pool of expatriate candidates who are closely related to TCNs are so-called *third culture kids* (TCKs) (Selmer and Lam, 2004). TCKs have been defined as

> individuals who, having spent a significant part of their adolescence years in cultures other than the culture of their parents, [and who] develop a sense of relationship to all of the cultures they have been exposed to while not claiming full ownership of any of them.
>
> (Selmer and Lam, 2004: 432)

It has been argued that TCKs offer international firms a potentially fruitful recruitment pool for international assignments as these TCKs may desire international mobility and careers, and due to their socialisation into a number of cultures they may also be more international in their outlook, and thus more adaptable to new cultural contexts. The concept of TCKs is however in its infancy and there is need for further empirical work in the area.

A subsidiary perspective

While there has been a large degree of debate in the literature as to the impact of nationality on performance from a HQ perspective, with some notable exceptions (cf. DeNisi *et al.*, 2003; Toh and DeNisi, 2003), the subsidiary perspective has been generally neglected and thus there is great scope for further studies in this area. Even allowing for the limited literature base in the area we can however point to a number of implications of different staffing options from a subsidiary perspective.

Parent country nationals

We look first at the implications of utilising PCNs in key positions from this perspective. First, given the commonly advanced reason of technical expertise for utilising PCNs, particularly in the early stages of internationalisation, it is clear that host employees will benefit from increased expertise. This will result in easing any technical or administrative problems which emerge in the early stages of the subsidiary's operation and also provides a valuable learning opportunity for HCNs. It is important to note however that some emerging research evidence in the Chinese context points to the unwillingness of expatriates to transfer their knowledge and indeed may even abandon their responsibilities as soon as it becomes apparent that they are going to be moved on from their current position (Furst, 1999; Selmer, 2004) and this represents a challenge for top management in multinationals (this will be discussed in greater detail in Chapter 4 on localisation). Key to avoiding these kind of situations is linking the objective of developing local management and an efficient transfer of portfolio on leaving to the expatriate's performance appraisal or bonus payments (Selmer, 2004). Nonetheless it is equally clear that the use of PCNs in key positions in the early stages of establishment provides a lead-time for HCNs to be socialised into the parent company and reach the standard of performance required by the HQ. An alternative strategy for assisting HCNs to become socialised into the organisation and aid in ensuring their performance is to the standard required by the HQ is through transferring them to the HQ for a period of time, a process termed inpatriation which we will discuss in detail in Chapter 8. Finally the use of PCNs will ensure that the subsidiary will have direct and immediate communication channels with the HQ at an early stage. This will assist in managing complex issues and in helping to secure HQ trust of the subsidiary operation.

The use of PCNs in key positions is not without its drawbacks however. Most significant in this regard are perceptions of inequality between host employees and their foreign counterparts. This is manifest in two ways, first, the perceived lack of career opportunity for host employees as key positions are filled by PCNs, and second, a perceived lack of equality in pay terms between HCNs and PCNs due to the subsidies attached to expatriate assignments. These perceived inequalities are likely to be more explicit in more developed host countries (see DeNisi *et al.*, 2003; Toh and DeNisi, 2003). This is because traditionally expatriate assignments were used to transfer technical and managerial expertise that was not available in the host context. Thus local employees generally accepted that these PCNs were more technically competent and thus deserving of the premiums associated with their expatriate assignment (see also Smith and Meiskins, 1995 on the notion of economic dominance and the transfer of management practices). Increasingly the perceived and actual disparity between home and host countries, particularly in terms of technical and managerial expertise, is decreasing and thus HCNs are becoming more likely to resent the inequalities in pay policies (Toh and DeNisi, 2003). This is significant as a growing body of research points to the importance of HCNs in aiding in the successful adjustment and performance of PCN expatriates in subsidiary operations (cf. DeNisi *et al.*, 2003 for a discussion).

Host country nationals

We turn next to the implications of the use of HCNs in key positions from a subsidiary perspective. In this regard the most obvious benefits are increased career opportunities for high performing host employees within the subsidiary operation. This may result in increased motivation and performance among subsidiary employees. While good organisation and financial reporting procedures will ensure that the HQ will keep the subsidiary under close scrutiny and aid in controlling foreign operations, the lack of large numbers of PCNs may aid in the subsidiary perceiving a sense of autonomy and may lead to innovative behaviours at the subsidiary level.

From a negative viewpoint the use of large numbers of HCNs in key positions may result in a lack of technical and managerial know how and expertise and thus poor performance and ultimately perhaps the demise of the subsidiary operation. Empirical evidence in the Chinese context has pointed to the danger of promoting or recruiting HCNs too quickly and at the last minute throwing them into positions vacated by expatriates. These studies pointed to disastrous results for both the firms and the individual managers (Furst, 1999; Worm *et al.*, 2001). Competition for a limited number of desirable positions within the subsidiary may lead to undesirable competition and conflicts within the subsidiary operation, which could potentially result in poor performance within the subsidiary operation. Further nepotism or selecting people for positions based on friendship or criteria other than 'best candidate for the job' may mean that the most appropriate candidate is not chosen for a position. If positions were filled from outside the firm this may reduce these tensions and help to minimise political influences. HQ input in the selection process for key positions is also critical to help minimise political implications if HCNs are to be used.

Third country nationals

Finally in this section we take a subsidiary perspective on the use of third country nationals in key positions in the subsidiary operation. In a similar vein to the use of PCNs, TCNs may bring valuable technical and managerial competence to the subsidiary operation. This results in valuable learning opportunities for HCNs and further provides them with a lead time to reach the standard of performance expected by the MNC. Further as TCNs generally appear to be transferred within regions they are more likely to understand the legal and cultural idiosyncrasies of the host environment. Finally TCNs who occupy lower level positions may not be perceived as a threat to the long-term career opportunities of HCNs as they may be perceived to be on short-term assignments.

TCNs also present disadvantages from a subsidiary perspective. Most acute of these is that they may often be perceived as no more than substitutes for PCNs and thus host employees will equally perceive a lack of career opportunities. A further and more significant consideration however is the possibility that long histories of racial difficulties and animosities in certain areas of the world may mean that representatives of some nationalities may find it difficult to interact smoothly with representatives of other nationalities (Dowling and Welch, 2004; Reynolds, 1997). For instance long running animosities between India and Pakistan or Arabs and Israelis are prominent examples of the type of conflicts that need to be considered.

What the above discussion highlights is that the utilisation of different nationalities of employees in staffing multinational subsidiaries brings with them their own advantages and drawbacks. The weakness of a staffing policy which overly relies on any single nationality in fulfilling their staffing requirements should also be apparent. Thus we argue for the importance and benefits of a differentiated approach to staffing in MNC. Box 2.1 illustrates some of the key issues.

Box 2.1   Foodco International

Background

Foodco International (a pseudonym) is a UK based multinational employing 40,000 staff worldwide. This company was operating with an international rather than a global strategy and was still in the relatively early stage of internationalisation; 12 per cent of staff were employed outside the UK, mainly in Europe. International growth has been entirely through direct investment in subsidiaries. A change of strategic direction in the mid-1990s resulted from a strategic decision to concentrate international activities in Europe. There followed a major disposal of non-strategic businesses and all Far East subsidiaries were sold off.

Ethnocentric staffing policy

The company's strategy was to use senior parent country nationals to run operations abroad. In practice, the two most senior subsidiary positions were usually held by PCNs, while HCN managers held the other managerial positions.

The advantages of this approach for the company were twofold: it facilitated communication between the centre and the subsidiaries and it was easier to pass on the corporate culture to the local units

This highly decentralised MNC operated without a group HR director and no group-wide international HR planning. Unlike some of its competitors, international assignments were not used specifically for management development purposes.

A key problem for the firm was the severe shortage of managers for top positions in subsidiaries. There was an insufficient supply of UK managers with the international experience to run the subsidiaries and a major weakness of the company's ethnocentric staffing policy was the failure to develop local managers to move into these senior subsidiary positions. The lack of promotion opportunities for the high potential HCN managers resulted in the company losing some of its best young talent to competitors.

Thus since the early 1990s the company has had to re-evaluate its staffing orientation and we have witnessed a shift towards the promotion of host country nationals to key positions in subsidiary operations.

We will develop this argument in the next section and further explore some of the key factors which impact on the configuration of the staffing mix in MNCs.

Toward a more dynamic understanding of global staffing

As noted above, while Perlmutter's model is useful as a starting point in our discussions on staffing, it is important to remember that this typology is primarily concerned with staffing policies for key positions within MNC, and thus its focus is on top management team (TMT) positions at HQ and subsidiary locations (Harzing, 2004). Lower level positions are almost inevitably filled by HCNs in MNCs. Further the typology represents a number of ideal types of organisation and it is unlikely that many MNCs will exactly fit any of the ideal types, and indeed most organisations will display elements of more than one type. Indeed this is acknowledged by Heenan and Perlmutter (1979: 21) when they note that 'all four attitudes [ethnocentric, polycentric, regiocentric and geocentric] are usually displayed to varying degrees [in MNCs]', however their underlying thesis remains that firms evolve from an ethnocentric to a geocentric orientation. While there is support for the argument that as a firm passes through the different stages of internationalisation, there will be implications for its international staffing strategy (cf. Scullion, 1996), on balance the empirical evidence however does not support a linear evolution (as suggested by Perlmutter) and suggests more heterogeneous tendencies within MNCs. For example based on a study of Chinese MNCs, Shen and Edwards (2004: 831) argue that the firms in their study adopted 'an ethnocentric approach, but with a strong polycentric tendency'. Thus, they argue, Chinese MNCs adopt firm-specific approaches, drawn from the four ideal types rather than any specific type (see also Welch, 1994). Harzing (2001b) also found that less than 10 per cent of the companies in her study had a uniform staffing policy (only HCN or PCNs). Thus in practice it appears that the 'torturous evolution' from ethnocentric to geocentric orientation may not be as predictable as Perlmutter initially expected. Nonetheless what is clear is that organisations appear to staff key positions with employees of a number of nationalities in their global operations. Thus, having discussed the advantages and disadvantages of PCNs, HCNs and TCNs above we will now explore the factors which influence the balance of HCNs, PCNs and TCNs in filling key positions in MNCs.

In this regard we identify a number of broad characteristics which impact of the use of different nationalities in filling key positions within MNCs and we will discuss them briefly in turn. These factors include: the host country; the nationality of the parent organisation; cultural distance between the host and home country; type of ownership of foreign operation; the age of the subsidiary operation; and industry. The most consistent predictor of PCN presence or otherwise in foreign subsidiaries is the HQ country of origin. At one extreme Japanese organisations are consistently identified as the most likely to utilise PCNs in key positions in subsidiary operations (Harzing, 1999; Oddou *et al.*, 2001; Tung, 1982). For example Kopp (1994) found that 75 per cent of Japanese owned multinational subsidiaries in his study had PCNs as directors. The figures for European and US owned subsidiaries were significantly lower at 54 and 51 per cent respectively (Kopp, 1994). Perhaps surprisingly given that it has been argued that ethnocentrism is inherent in US based organisational theory and management education (Boyacigiller and Adler, 1991) the general trend in the use of PCNs in US organisations is at the other extreme and they are generally considered to have lower levels of utilisation than their Japanese and European counterparts (Harzing, 1999; Tung, 1982). While it has been argued that the majority of European firms rely heavily on PCN presence (Mayrhofer and Brewster, 1996; Scullion, 1996) it is important to note that the European case is one of heterogeneity with empirical evidence suggesting that German firms are closer to the Japanese model while UK firms are more akin to their American counterparts (cf. Brewster and Scullion, 1997; Harzing, 1999). It has also been argued that pragmatic rather than strategic consideration influence staffing patterns in European MNCs (Torbiörn, 1994). Harzing (2004) points to the significance of cultural orientations in explaining this divergence. She posits that multinationals from countries which score highly on Hofstede's uncertainty avoidance index, which indicates the extent to which members of cultures feel threatened by unknown situations, are more likely to employ a PCN in the subsidiary managing director position.

The host country also emerges as a significant moderating factor on the use of PCNs. In this regard, the extant research points to a lack of suitably qualified HCNs, particularly in developing countries as a significant predictor of the presence of PCN in key positions (Boyacigiller, 1990; Harzing, 2001a) however it is also important to note that if the knowledge and skills required are generic, MNCs may train HCN relatively easily and thus may not be required to utilise PCNs (Gong, 2003a). Thus a differentiation between generic technical knowledge and corporate, context specific resources such as corporate culture and managerial process may emerge as a key variable in exploring staffing orientations in MNCs. In the case of the latter, the use of PCNs or TCNs is called for because of their socialisation into the company and also the potentially smaller shared knowledge base in developing countries (ibid.). Educational level also emerges as a significant factor, with low levels of education pointing to increased levels of PCNs (Gong, 2003a; Harzing, 2004).

The cultural distance between the home and host country is also positively correlated to the use of PCNs in key positions in subsidiary operations (Boyacigiller, 1990; Gong, 2003a) although cultural distance raises a number of issues with regard to the willingness of PCNs to accept assignments. Building on the earlier work of Feldman and Thompson (1993) and Fish and Wood (1997) among others, Harvey et al. (2001) argue that assignments in developing countries may represent particularly challenging assignments for PCNs, particularly in terms of cultural adjustment and quality of life issues. Thus they call on MNCs to focus on the potential of hiring HCNs and TCNs and socialising them into the MNC through assignments in the HQ, a process they term inpatriation. This, they argue, is a means of increasing subsidiary performance and minimising the risk of expatriate failure. We argue elsewhere (Collings and Scullion, 2005) that this use of PCNs in culturally diverse subsidiaries could be related to a lack of trust in host employees. We propose that this represents a potentially fruitful avenue for future study. Studies could focus on measures of trust or a proxy measure of confidence in subsidiary managers while controlling for cultural distance.

Although the literature is not consistent, the age of the subsidiary also appears to impact on the nationality of staff in key positions. While Boyacigiller (1990) found no relationship between the age of the subsidiary and the penetration of PCNs, emerging research points to an inverse relationship between the age of the subsidiary and the presence of PCNs in key subsidiary positions (Gong, 2003a; Harzing, 2001a). For instance based on their study of 235 cases, Downes and Thomas (2000) found that younger subsidiaries have proportionately larger expatriate populations than do those which have been longer established. Thus the longer the subsidiary is in operation the lower the penetration of PCN although it is important to note the potential impact of other factors such as cultural distance of this finding. It is also important to note that Downes and Thomas (2000) found that expatriate presence tended to pick up in 'much older' subsidiaries. Thus they argue that the relationship between expatriate presence and the age of a subsidiary conforms to a 'U-curve' approach. Thus expatriate presence is greater in newly established subsidiaries, presence then reduces as the subsidiary matures but ultimately begins to increase again in 'much older' subsidiaries. While the higher level of expatriate presence in newly established firms is discussed above, as is the consequent reduction in numbers, the increase in older subsidiaries is explained by the fact that technological innovations combined with product/service innovations may render subsidiary knowledge outdated and thus push expatriate transfers to update subsidiary learning (Downes and Thomas, 2000). While this explanation is certainly plausible, an equally plausible explanation could be that as MNCs mature, they develop higher levels of international mobility as a means of developing high potential employees and sharing knowledge within the organisation.

Other variables which have been found to impact on the staffing composition in subsidiary operations include; size of the foreign operation. While Gong (2003a) found an inverse relationship between size and PCN penetration in subsidiaries, Boyacigiller (1990), Harzing (2004) and Richards (2001) point to a positive correlation between size and PCN presence.

The factors which influence the choice between HCNs and PCNs have been summarised nicely by Harzing (2004). In adapting Harzing's model we include an ad hoc variable to reflect the fact that not all decisions are as strategically planned as the literature may suggest. Indeed Torbiörn (2004: 64) posits, based on Harzing's (2001a) study, that: 'a proportion of at least 25 per cent of the variation [between HCNs and PCNs] in staffing, taken at a firm level, remain unexplained'. While allowing for the possibility that some of this variation may be explained by variables not included in the analysis, he posits that it leaves room for a complementary ad hoc reactivity hypothesis. Where 'Ad hoc reactivity taken as a determinant of staffing should reflect occasional or unsystematic outcomes of staffing decisions where priorities are governed by available options in specific situations' (Torbiörn 2004: 64). This appears to be confirmed by Brewster *et al.* (2002) who found that in 40 per cent of cases international vacancies were filled on an ad hoc basis. Thus decisions with regard to international staffing may not always be underscored by strategic orientations as is often implied in some prescriptive literature, rather pragmatic reasons may drive staffing decisions in certain albeit limited circumstances (see Figure 2.1).

Conclusion

This chapter has continued to set the context for our later discussions on global staffing. We further develop the context for our later discussions on staffing by introducing some of the key theoretical contributions to the field and considering the various orientations that multinational firms' headquarters can have toward subsidiary operations. Further we consider the implications of various options with regard to staffing on the operation of the MNC. In this regard we adopt a broader understanding of the impact of the orientation adopted with a particular focus on, often neglected, subsidiary perspectives on the orientation. We have attempted to elaborate on these early contributions and developed a more nuanced understanding of staffing issues through acknowledging the limits Perlmutter's model and discussing other studies which propose a more differentiated approach to staffing. In this regard we examined models which examine the factors influencing the choice between employees of different nationalities within the MNC. We focused in particular on the impact of country of origin on these decisions and attempt to develop a more nuanced understanding of the factors impacting on international staffing decisions in MNCs.

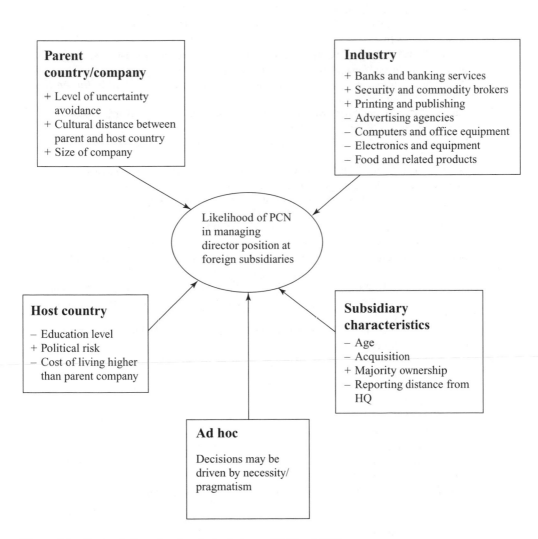

Figure 2.1   Factors influencing the choice between HCN and PCN

Source: adapted from Harzing (2004: 257).

References

Banai, M. (1992) 'The ethnocentric staffing policy in multinational corporations: a self-fulfilling prophecy', *International Journal of Human Resource Management*, 3(3): 451–72.

Bartlett, C.A. and Ghoshal, S. (1989) *Managing across Borders: The Transnational Solution*, Boston, MA: Harvard Business School Press.

Black, J.S., Mendenhall, M. and Oddou, G. (1991) 'Toward a comprehensive model of international adjustment: an integration of multiple theoretical perspectives', *Academy of Management Review*, 16: 291–317.

Bonache, J., Brewster, C. and Suutari, V. (2001) 'Expatriation: a developing research agenda', *Thunderbird International Business Review*, 43(1): 3–20.

Boyacigiller, N. (1990) 'The role of expatriates in the management of interdependence, complexity and risk in multinational corporations', *Journal of International Business Studies*, 21: 265–73.

Boyacigiller, N. (2000) 'The international assignment revisited', in M. Mendenhall and G. Oddou (eds) *Readings and Cases in International Human Resource Management*, 3rd edn, Cincinatti, OH: South-Western.

Boyacigiller, N. and Adler, N.J. (1991) 'The parochial dinosaur: organizational science in global context', *Academy of Management Review*, 16(2): 262–90.

Brewster, C. and Scullion, H. (1997) 'A review and an agenda for expatriate HRM', *Human Resource Management Journal*, 7(3): 32–41.

Brewster, C., Harris, H. and Sparrow, P. (2002) *Globalizing HR: Executive Brief*, London: Chartered Institute of Personnel and Development.

Broad, G. (1994) 'The managerial limits to Japanisation: a manufacturing case study', *Human Resource Management Journal*, 4(3): 52–69.

Caligiuri, P.M. and Cascio, W.F. (1998) 'Can we send her there? Maximising the success of western women on global assignments', *Journal of World Business*, 33: 394–416.

Caligiuri, P.M. and Stroth, L.K. (1995) 'Multinational corporation management strategies and international human resource practices: bringing IHRM to the bottom line', *International Journal of Human Resource Management*, 6(3): 494–507.

Collings, D. and Scullion, H. (2005) 'Global staffing', in G.K. Stahl and I. Björkman (eds) *Handbook of Research in International Human Resource Management*, Cheltenham: Edward Elgar.

DeNisi, A.S., Toh, S.M. and Colella, A. (2003) 'Expatriate success and the host country national: an unexplored link', in proceedings of Seventh Conference on International HRM, Limerick, 4–6 June.

Dowling, P.J. and Welch, D.E. (2004) *International Human Resource Management*, 4th edn, London: Thomson Learning.

Downes, M. and Thomas, A.S. (2000) 'Knowledge transfer through expatriation: the U-curve approach to overseas staffing', *Journal of Managerial Issues*, 12(2): 131–52.

Edström, A. and Galbraith, J.R. (1977) 'Transfer of managers as a coordination and control strategy in multinational organizations', *Administrative Science Quarterly*, 22: 248–63.

Evans, P., Pucik, P. and Barsoux, J.L. (2002) *The Global Challenge: Frameworks for International Human Resource Management*, New York: McGraw-Hill.

Feldman, D. and Thompson, H.B. (1993) 'Expatriation, repatriation and domestic relocation: an empirical investigation of adjustment to new job assignments', *Journal of International Business Studies*, 24(4): 75–100.

Fish, A. and Wood, J. (1997) 'Cross cultural management in Australian business enterprises', *Asia Pacific Journal of Human Resource Management*, 35: 37–52.

Forster, N. (2000) 'The myth of the "international manager"', *International Journal of Human Resource Management*, 11(1): 126–43.

Furst, B. (1999) 'Performance management for localization', in J. Lee (ed.) *Localization in China: Best Practice*, Hong Kong: Euromoney.

Gong, Y. (2003a) 'Subsidiary staffing in multinational enterprises: agency, resources and performance', *Academy of Management Journal*, 46: 728–39.

Gong, Y. (2003b) 'Toward a dynamic process model of staffing composition and subsidiary outcomes in multinational enterprises', *Journal of Management*, 29: 259–80.

Gooderham, P.N. and Nordhaug, O. (2003) *International Management: Cross-Boundary Challenges*, Oxford: Blackwell.

Harvey, M.G. and Buckley, M.R. (1997) 'Managing inpatriates: building a global core competency', *Journal of World Business*, 32: 35–52.

Harvey, M., Speier, C. and Novecevic, M.N. (2001) 'A theory-based framework for strategic global human resource staffing policies and practices', *International Journal of Human Resource Management*, 12: 898–915.

Harzing, A.W.K. (1999) *Managing the Multinationals: An International Study of Control Mechanisms*, Cheltham: Edward Elgar.

Harzing, A.W.K. (2001a) 'An analysis of the functions of international transfer of managers in MNCs', *Employee Relations*, 23: 581–98.

Harzing, A.W.K. (2001b) 'Who's in charge? An empirical study of executive staffing practices in foreign multinationals', *Human Resource Management*, 40: 139–58.

Harzing, A.W.K. (2004) 'Composing and international staff', in A.W.K. Harzing and J. van Ruysseveldt (eds) *International Human Resource Management*, 2nd edn, London: Sage.

Heenan, D.A. and Perlmutter, H.V. (1979) *Multinational Organizational Development*, Reading, MA: Addison-Wesley.

Kedia, B.L. and Mukherji, A. (1999) 'Global managers: developing a mindset for global competitiveness', *Journal of World Business*, 34(3): 230–50.

Kopp, R. (1994) 'International human resource policies and practices in Japanese, European and United States multinationals', *Human Resource Management*, 33(4): 581–99.

Mayrhofer, W. and Brewster, C. (1996) 'In praise of ethnocentricity: expatriate policies in European MNCs', *International Executive*, 38(6): 749–78.

Mendenhall, M.E. and Stahl, G. (2000) 'Expatriate training and development: where do we go from here?' *Human Resource Management*, 39(2–3): 251–65.

Oddou, G., Gregersen, H.B., Black, J.S. and Derr, C.B. (2001) 'Building global leaders: strategy similarities and differences among European, U.S., and Japanese multinationals', in M.E. Mendenhall, T.M. Kühlmann and G.K. Stahl (eds) *Developing Global Business Leaders: Policies, Processes, and Innovations*, Westport, CT: Quorum.

Perlmutter, H.V. (1969) 'The tortuous evolution of the multinational corporation', *Columbia Journal of World Business*, 4: 9–18.

Reynolds, C. (1997) 'Strategic employment of third country nationals: keys to sustaining the transformation of HR functions', *Human Resource Planning*, 20(1): 33–40.

Richards, M. (2001) 'US multinational staffing practices and implications for subsidiary performance in the UK and Thailand', *Thunderbird International Business Review*, 43: 225–42.

Roberts, K., Ernst Kossek, E. and Ozeki, C. (1998) 'Managing the global workforce: challenges and strategies', *Academy of Management Executive*, 12(4): 93–106.

Schuler, R.S., Dowling, P.J. and DeCieri, H.D. (1993) 'An integrative framework of strategic international human resource management', *Journal of Management*, 19: 419–58.

Schuler, R.S., Budhwar, P.S. and Florkowski, G.W. (2002) 'International human resource management: review and critique', *International Journal of Management Reviews*, 4(1): 41–70.

Scullion, H. (1996) 'Food and drink international: International staffing policy and practice', in J. Storey (ed.) *Blackwell Cases in Human Resource and Change Management*, London: Blackwell.

Scullion, H. and Brewster, C. (2001) 'Managing expatriates: messages from Europe', *Journal of World Business*, 36: 346–65.

Selmer, J. (2002) 'Adjustment of third-country national expatriates in China', *Asia Pacific Business Review*, 19(20: 101–17.

Selmer, J. (2004) 'Expatriates hesitation and the localisation of Western business operations in China', *International Journal of Human Resource Management*, 15(6): 1094–107.

Selmer, J. and Lam, H. (2004) 'Third-culture kids: future business expatriates?', *Personnel Review*, 33(4): 430–45.

Shen, J. and Edwards, V. (2004). 'Recruitment and selection in Chinese MNEs', *International Journal of Human Resource Management*, 15: 814–35.

Smith, C. and Meiskins, P. (1995) 'System, society and dominance effects in cross-national organizational analysis', *Work, Employment and Society*, 9(2): 241–67.

Toh, S.M. and DeNisi, A.S. (2003) 'Host country national reactions to expatriate pay policies: a model and implications', *Academy of Management Review*, 28(4): 606–21.

Torbiörn, I. (1994) 'Operative and strategic use of expatriates in new organisations and market structures', *International Studies of Management and Organization*, 24(3): 5–17.

Torbiörn, I. (2004) 'Staffing policies and practices in European MNCs: strategic sophistications, culture-bound policies or ad hoc reactivity?', in H. Scullion and M. Linehan (eds) *International Human Resource Management: A Critical Text*, Basingstoke: Palgrave Macmillan.

Tung, R.L. (1982) 'Selection and training procedures of US, European and Japanese multinationals', *California Management Review*, 25(1): 57–71.

Tung, R.L. and Miller, E.L. (1990) 'Managing in the twenty-first century: the need for global orientation', *Management International Review*, 30: 5–18.

Welch, D.E. (1994) 'Determinants of international human resource management approaches and activities: a suggested framework', *Journal of Management Studies*, 31: 139–64.

Worm, V., Selmer, J. and deLeon, C.T. (2001) 'Human resource development for localization: European multinational corporations in China', in J.B. Kidd, X. Li and F-J. Richter (eds) *Advances in Human Resource Management in Asia*, Basingstoke: Palgrave.

Zeira, Y. and Harari, E. (1977) 'Managing third-country nationals in multinational corporations', *Business Horizons*, 20(5): 83–9.

3

Strategic motivations for international transfers: why do MNCs use expatriates?

DAVID G. COLLINGS AND HUGH SCULLION

Introduction

While the previous chapter considered the factors which influence the composition of management teams in subsidiary operations, this chapter will focus on the reasons why MNCs use expatriate assignments. As noted earlier there is an increasing realisation among academics and practitioners alike that people are the key to successfully competing in the global economy (Black *et al.*, 1999). In Doz *et al.*'s (2001:1) words companies must 'innovate by learning from the world'. In this regard expatriate employees generally play a key role in implementing a multinational company's global strategy. Further, as the approaches to and strategies associated with international business have become more complex so too have the staffing options for the firms involved (Briscoe and Schuler, 2004), thus the discussions in this chapter should be considered in companion to later discussions on inpatriation. In this chapter we will examine the rationale for utilising expatriate assignments primarily from a headquarters' point of view. This is significant for three reasons. First, empirical research has shown that the reasons why expatriates are sent on assignment may impact on job performances, adjustment and roles performed (Shay and Baack, 2004), although it is important to not that there may be few 'pure' cases whereby assignments have a singular purpose. Rather many assignments generally have more than one rationale (Sparrow *et al.*, 2004). Second, while it has been argued that traditionally global assignments were not used for strategic purposes, but rather to carry out specific tasks due to a lack of confidence in local managements' competence to perform same, more recently leading MNCs are realising the strategic importance of international assignments (Black *et al.*, 1999). Third, as organisations are increasingly monitoring the costs associated with expatriate assignments, and exploring alternatives to the traditional long-term assignment, the purposes of assignments will need to be clearly articulated and justified. We begin our discussion by considering a further seminal work in the field of international staffing, Edström and Galbraith's (1977) study.

Motives for using expatriates

Edström and Galbraith (1977) identified three key motives for utilising international transfers.

1 When qualified local country nationals were not available, particularly in developing countries, expatriates were used to fill positions.
2 Organisations use international assignments (IAs) as a means of management development. This type of assignment is aimed at developing the global competence of the individual manager and indeed organisations utilising this type of assignee are likely to do so regardless of the competence of employees in the host environment.
3 IAs could be utilised as a means of organisational development, control and coordination. In this instance IAs are used to transfer knowledge between subsidiaries and to modify and sustain organisational structure and decision process.

The significance of Edström and Galbraith's study is reflected in the fact that since its publication it has formed the basis of almost all research on the functions of international assignments. It has been argued however that a body of foreign language literature had largely been neglected in the debate and we will now briefly review some of this literature.

A missing literature base

Harzing (2001c) has identified a significant body of German language literature which has largely been neglected in the study of this area to date. In synthesising this literature she points to two key additions to the English language literature. First, these German language studies tend to define organisational development more broadly and in contrast to Edström and Galbraith's typology, incorporate both control and increasing organisational capability or competence to compete successfully in the global market place under this heading. Thus she argues that 'organizational development is not a goal of international transfers as such, but is rather the result of knowledge transfer, management development, and the creation of a common organizational culture and effective informal information network' (Harzing, 2001c: 368) and further that Edström and Galbraith's organisational development function may be more accurately labelled 'coordination and control'. Second, these studies appear to conceptualise organisational control more broadly and include direct control in addition to the informal control posited by Edström and Galbraith. Thus, Harzing calls for an examination of the different forms of control and coordination that can be achieved through international assignments.

Empirical evidence on the purpose of expatriate assignments

As Edström and Galbraith's (1977) study is now nearly 30 years old, it is important to examine if the typology proposed by them is still useful in the twenty-first century. In this regard a study by Sparrow *et al.* (2004) is informative. Sparrow and his colleagues identified six primary organisational reasons for sending expatriates on assignments, the results of this study are summarised in Table 3.1. When we categorise the objectives identified according to Edström and Galbraith's reasons for using expatriates, it becomes clear that developing a cadre of international managerial talent (95.3 per cent of respondents) and organisational development and control (81.2 per cent of respondents) emerge as the key objectives of international assignments in the organisations studied by Sparrow and his colleagues with lack of qualified host country nationals emerging as the third most significant reason at 56.3 per cent. Thus while there are few cases where there is only a single reason for using expatriate assignments, based on this study it could be argued that the reasons expatriates are used differs depending on the strategy perused by a given organisation. Thus Edström and Galbraith's study does appear to remain appropriate in examining the nature of expatriation in the current business environment although it is important to note that the nature and types of international assignments currently utilised by MNCs are far more complex and varied than they were at the time of Edström and Galbraith's study (see Chapter 8 in this volume).

Table 3.1 Main organisational reasons for sending expatriates on assignment

Reason	*Percentage*
Management development	
Career development	57.8
Creating international cadre of managers	37.5
Lack of qualified HCNs	
Local expertise not available	56.3
Organisation development and control	
Transfer of expertise	53.1
Control of local operations	20.3
Coordination of global policy	7.8

Source: adapted from Sparrow *et al.* (2004: 138).

* Total does not add up to 100 per cent due to the fact that assignments may have multiple objectives.

The purposes of expatriate assignments: theoretical insights

In developing on Edström and Galbraith's (1977) typology, Pucik (1992) differentiates between demand driven and learning driven motives for expatriation. Assignments for the purposes of position filling or control are generally classified into the former category while assignments for the purposes of individual or organisation development fit the latter. Drawing on Pucik's earlier work, and also taking account of the duration of international assignments, Evans *et al.* (2002) have, without empirical support, developed a useful framework for classifying the duration and purposes of international assignments and this is presented in Figure 3.1. This differentiation is important because as Shay and Baack (2004: 218) postulate: 'managerial development reasons for the assignment will foster expatriate personal change and role innovation, whereas control reasons will focus attention on the expatriate making personal changes and on role innovation in the subsidiary'. Thus in learning driven assignments, the expatriate adapts his/her frame of reference to adapt to the new environment and indeed adapts his/her behaviour to meet the requirements of the new environment. While in control driven assignments, subordinates are expected to absorb the new demands of the expatriate manager and change their frames of reference, and further role requirements are adapted to meet the transferred manager's expectations (Shay and Baack, 2004). In a similar vein Delios and Björkman (2000) have argued that under control driven assignments the expatriate strives to align the operations of the subsidiary with those of the parent organisation. In contrast under knowledge-sharing driven assignments the expatriate's focus is on transferring the parent company's knowledge to the host subsidiary under conditions where the parent is considered to have greater proprietary knowledge. Further, empirical research by Harris (2002: 2) confirms the significance of the duration of assignments on skill transfer, managerial control and management development while short-term assignments are more generally used for skill transfer and sometimes management development.

	Demand driven	Learning driven
Long	**CORPORATE AGENCY** Control/knowledge transfer	**COMPETENCE DEVELOPMENT**
Short	**PROBLEM SOLVING**	**CAREER ENHANCEMENT**

Assignment duration (left axis: Long / Short)

Demand driven   Learning driven

Assignment purpose

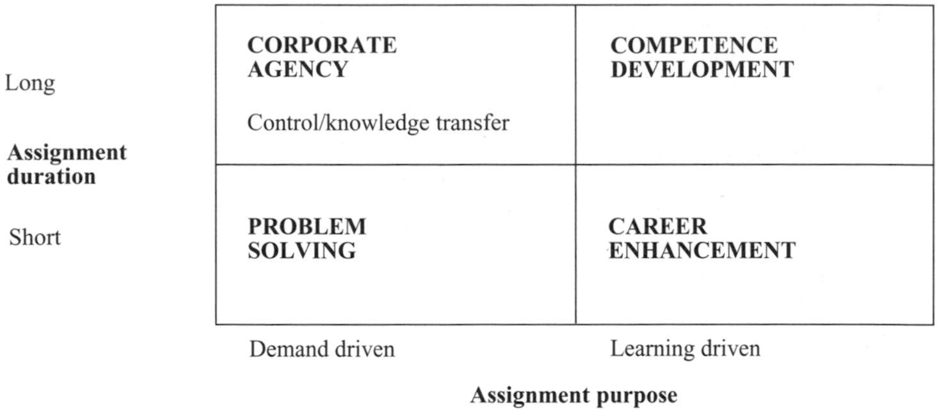

Figure 3.1 The purpose of expatriation

Source: Evans, P., Pucik, V. and Barsoux, J.L. (2002) *The Global Challenge: Frameworks for International Human Resource Management*, New York: McGraw-Hill, p. 119. Reproduced with permission of the McGraw-Hill Companies.

Demand driven assignments

Evans *et al.* (2002) posit that traditionally expatriate assignments were predominately demand driven. Assignees of this type were considered either position fillers who acted as corporate agents by transferring knowledge or assisting in controlling newly established subsidiaries, or problem solvers. These assignments tend to be longer term (i.e. over three years' duration). Problem solving expatriates perform similar type roles but they are categorised as such by the singular purpose and duration of their assignment, which is determined by the length of time required to complete a specific task. These assignments are generally driven by short-term or start-up problems. Demand driven assignments are usually utilised where there is a lack of suitably qualified HCNs and are teaching driven.

Learning driven assignments

As the name would suggest, learning driven assignments focus on learning rather than teaching. These assignments become more common as subsidiaries develop local managerial and technical capability, and the initial skills gap experienced by the firm reduces. Again learning driven assignments can be categorised by duration and purpose. Assignments whose purpose is to increase cross-national, organisational coordination capabilities are generally longer-term assignments with the focus on developing a global mindset within the organisation. A lack of this global orientation has been identified as a key challenge facing organisations operating on a cross-national basis in the twenty-first century (cf. Tung and Miller, 1990) and thus the use of this type of international assignment is likely to increase in the future. Finally organisations are increasingly identifying high potential employees who as part of fast track career programmes are provided with the opportunity to gain international experience through short-term foreign assignments. Indeed a study by Petrovic *et al.* (2000) reported that 66 per cent of the companies in his study expected to increase the number of employees sent on short-term assignments over a five year period. These assignments are aimed at enhancing the careers of the employees concerned.

Expatriates and knowledge transfer

It has been argued that exposure to new ideas, business practices, foreign cultures and markets through international assignments can aid in the creation of knowledge within MNCs and further can aid in building and sustaining competitive advantage (Tallman and Fladmoe-Linquist, 2002). Since the late 1990s there has been a growing body of research which has focused specifically on the role of expatriate employees in transferring knowledge within MNCs (cf. Downes and Thomas, 1999; Minbaeva and Michailova, 2004). In contrast with much of the early work in the field these studies tend to move beyond ethnocentric prescriptions of knowledge transfer and recognise the potential for knowledge to be created in subsidiaries as well as in the headquarter operations. The knowledge transfer function of expatriates is congruent to the traditional coordination and control function discussed above (Minbaeva and Michailova, 2004). While the research is not conclusive, for example Björkman *et al.* (2004) found no relationship between expatriate presence and the extent of knowledge transfer in MNCs, there is a growing acknowledgement of the role of expatriate managers in transferring knowledge originating within subsidiaries in MNCs. These knowledge flows can happen during the expatriate assignment and also on repatriation thus further emphasising the requirement for and benefit of appropriate repatriation programmes for MNCs. Further more recent work has attempted to illuminate how organisations can successfully capture and utilise knowledge and competencies gained by international assignees on repatriation (cf. Blakeney *et al.*, 2006). This is likely to become a very significant avenue for further research in coming years.

Bears, bumble bees and spiders

A further study which developed a useful typology of international management assignments was Harzing's (2001c) study. Harzing identified three control specific roles of expatriates, namely the bear, the bumble bee and the spider. This study is significant and merits discussion because it goes beyond the basic question of why MNCs use expatriates and sheds light on the more significant question of whether these roles are equally important in different situations. This stands in contrast to much of the North American literature which often assume universality despite the burgeoning literature substantiating the cultural diversity of values (cf. Hofstede, 2001) and the diversity of business systems as a constraint on management behaviour (cf. Whitley, 1999) and the impact of such diversity on organisational behaviour. Harzing (2001c) identified three forms of personal/cultural control which could be effectuated by expatriate managers. She also differentiates between direct and indirect control.

1 Managers can act as a means of replacing the centralisation of decision making in MNC and provide a direct means of surveillance over subsidiary operations. She labels assignees based around these purposes as *bears*, highlighting the degree of dominance these assignees have over subsidiary operations.
2 Expatriates can be used to control subsidiaries through socialisation of host employees and the development of informal communication networks. These assignees are termed *bumble bees*, which reflects the bees 'flying "from plant to plant" and creat[ing] cross-pollination between the various offshoots' (Harzing, 2001c: 369).
3 *Spiders*, as the name suggests, control through the weaving of informal communication networks within the MNC.

A more significant contribution of Harzing's (2001c) study is the consideration of the applicability of the different roles of expatriate assignees in different circumstances. In this regard she argues that although expatriates generally appear to perform their role as *bears* regardless of the situation, the study suggests that their role as *spiders and bumble bees* tend to be more context specific. Specifically, the *bumble bee and spider* roles appeared to be more significant in longer established subsidiaries (longer than fifty years) while the *bumble bee* role appeared to be important in newly established subsidiaries also. Significantly the level of localisation of subsidiary operations and further lower levels of international integration, in that the subsidiary was not greatly reliant on the HQ for sales and purchases, were positively related to the likelihood of expatriates performing the *bumble bee and spider* roles. Perhaps unsurprisingly *bumble bees* and *spiders* were also more prevalent in greenfield than brownfield acquisitions.

Purposes of expatriate assignments: the empirical evidence

While the above studies are significant in identifying a number of important control functions of expatriates it is important to note that there has been little in terms of empirical testing of the effectiveness of expatriate managers in terms of controlling foreign operations. A notable exception is the work of Paik and Sohn (2004). Based on their study of Japanese multinationals operating in four countries (Korea, Taiwan, Singapore and the United States) they point to the significance of expatriates' cultural knowledge of the host country in determining their effectiveness as agents of control in foreign subsidiaries. In other words expatriates with significant cultural knowledge of the host country are more likely to be effective in controlling foreign subsidiaries while expatriates with low levels of cultural knowledge of the host country not only may be less effective in terms of controlling subsidiaries, but also may in fact be harmful to the MNC's ability to control. This study is significant as it is the first that we are aware of which attempts to illuminate the debate about the effectiveness of expatriate managers as agents of control in MNCs. This area is however an area where the potential for further study abounds. For example Paik and Sohn's study could be replicated in other countries, or the effectiveness of managers as control agents, dependent on the type of control mechanism favoured by the HQ could be examined. Further the effectiveness of the different types proposed by Harzing (2001c) could be empirically tested.

Since the early 1990s a growing body of literature in Europe and North America has attempted to fill this void (e.g. Harzing, 2001a; Scullion, 1994; Shay and Baack, 2004). Looking first at demand driven assignments, Harzing (2001a) found a clear and consistent link between home and host countries and the purpose of expatriate assignment. Specifically she found that US and UK MNCs were most likely to utilise parent country nationals in position filling roles, and thus IAs were demand driven in these companies. The use of PCNs as position fillers was also more common in developing countries where local expertise was not available. Control and coordination driven assignments emerged as the more significant in Japanese and German MNCs.

Looking next at learning driven assignments, there is a growing emphasis on developing a global mindset in managers of MNCs in the IHRM literature. This global mindset is achieved primarily through learning driven assignments. Thus these learning driven assignments are gaining increasing research attention in the literature. Learning driven assignments were most common in German, Swiss and Dutch firms in Harzing's (2001b) study, where the emphasis was on individual management development. Learning driven assignments have however recently received some critical attention in the literature. Indeed based on their empirical study Shay and Baack (2004: 228–9) argue: 'it is not apparent that making an expatriate assignment for managerial development reasons results in any additional benefits than are already delivered by an assignment made for control reasons'. Thus, they postulate that expatriate assignments should be made 'primarily, if not exclusively, for control reasons' (ibid.). They argue that linking expatriate assignments to control objectives, helps to identify a link between the assignment and operational effectiveness of the firm, and thus, debates about the need and value of these assignments may be reduced or even eliminated. Indeed recent research has indicated that expatriates place greater emphasis on the relevance of self-learning than their employers, perhaps indicating that firms are increasingly aware of the requirement to justify the bottom-line benefit of expatriate assignments (Hocking *et al.*, 2004). We will develop this discussion below. See Box 3.1.

Box 3.1   The changing pattern of global staffing in an international bank

Background information

Bankco (a pseudonym) was a UK based international bank operating in over 20 countries with overseas operations mainly in Europe, the United States, the Caribbean and South America. International growth came mainly through acquisitions and organic growth. It employed over 100,000 employees worldwide, 40 per cent of whom were employed outside the United Kingdom.

Staffing

Historically there was very heavy reliance on senior British expatriates to manage foreign operations. The career expatriate system was heavily utilised until the mid-1990s (i.e. the system whereby a senior expatriate would move direct from one major assignment to another). For example an expatriate might work four years in a senior capacity in the United States, three years in Mexico and three years in Argentina.

Changes

Since the late 1990s there has been a shift of policy to reduce the numbers of expatriates and to develop local managers. There has been a significant shift to using HCNs in most foreign markets. However, in practice, in the two major markets, the US and German, senior UK expatriates are used to run the business. Trust is the key factor here – 'HQ likes to have the confidence of using one of our own people' (HR Director). A further significant variable is the fact that these markets represented two of the company's biggest foreign markets, thus the operations were particularly significant in the company's overall portfolio.

In explaining the evolution of the staffing policy within Bankco we point to three key factors: (1) cost; (2) a reduced emphasis of the career expat system – huge repatriation problems with this approach; (3) recognition of the need for HCN development.

Expatriate assignments: value for money?

Having outlined why MNCs use expatriate employees in staffing their foreign subsidiaries, we will now consider the question of whether expatriate assignments represent value for money. This is a significant debate as despite anecdotal evidence which posits the decline of the expatriate assignment and the rise of alternatives to long-term assignments, traditional expatriate assignments remain an important consideration in the management of MNCs. Indeed one study found that 80 per cent of organisations studied had identified cost reduction in expatriate assignments as either 'important' or 'very important' in the development of international assignment practices (PricewaterhouseCoopers, 2002: 10). A second study (GMAC Global Relocations Services, 2003) found that while a high percentage of companies were concerned about measuring return on investment (ROI) of international assignments, ROI was not only generally poorly calculated in these firms, but also not widely used as a means of reducing expatriate costs. When this is considered in the context of the long-standing debates about expatriate performance and expatriate failure, combined with recent drives to reduce the costs of expatriate assignments, the importance of ensuring value for money becomes apparent.

Darned expensive to be taken for granted

Given the preceding discussion on the costs associated with expatriate assignment and failure one could reasonably expect that organisations would have placed significant emphasis on the measurement of expatriate performance from an early stage. However, as Tahvanainen and Suutari (2005) note, very often the focus in the strategy process, in this context the staffing strategy pursued by the MNC, has been on strategy formulation, with a lack of consideration for the implementation phase. Thus we often witness a failure of strategic planning at the operational level, reflected in a failure to develop personnel policy and practices aimed at ensuring congruence between employees' work behaviours and the organisational strategy (see also Torraco and Swanson, 1995). So while organisations may have a well-designed and articulate strategy with regard to staffing their foreign operations, they have often failed to adequately monitor international assignees to measure their performance and contribution to the bottom line. Thus one could plausibly argue that organisations for many years failed to monitor the relative value of expatriate assignments to subsidiary performance and even their level of performance when on assignment. As Peak (1997: 9) notes however, expatriate assignments are 'darned expensive to take for granted'. Nonetheless the apparent lack of emphasis traditionally placed by organisations on the repatriation process is one illustration of the apparent lack of emphasis placed by organisations on the evaluation of the utility of the expatriation process. As Dowling and Welch (2004: 159) note 'attention to this aspect of international assignments [repatriation] has been somewhat belated'. Indeed Linehan and Mayrhofer (2005) argue that many organisations still do not consider this aspect of the international assignments until after the assignees return home (see also Chapter 10 in this volume). This lack of preparation for the return of international assignees represents a significant anomaly given the significant cost of the assignment and the potential additional expertise which the expatriates may bring with them on return from the assignment. Further it is an illustration of the lack of strategic attention paid to measuring the effectiveness of international assignments.

In this section we will attempt to outline some approaches which management can use in assessing the monetary value of expatriate assignments. We will not be concerned with managing the performance of the individual expatriate but rather the focus will be on measuring the relative return achieved by MNCs through expensive expatriate assignments.

Measuring returns on expatriate assignments

While the preceding discussion illustrates the apparent lack of emphasis placed by organisations on monitoring the value of expatriate assignments, even those organisations which did attempt to monitor expatriates' performance while on assignment did so in a limited way. Traditionally these organisations measured the worth of expatriate programmes against one of four criteria:

- early return of expatriated employees – generally termed expatriate failure
- turnover of assignees following repatriation
- financial costs associated with the assignment
- performance of the individual expatriate.

Although a full discussion of all the issues surrounding this area is beyond the scope of this chapter, a summary outline will help to contextualise our discussions in this section.

Early return of expatriated employees

Expatriate failure is generally defined as the premature return of international assignees to their home countries. Traditionally practitioners and academics alike used the level of expatriate failure as a measure of the effectiveness of expatriate assignments. In the earlier literature in the field failure rates of 10 to 45 per cent were commonly cited. To this day failure rates in this range are commonly cited in the North American literature (cf. Black *et al.*, 1999; Thomas, 2002). In contrast reported failure rates in European and Japanese MNCs tend to be lower. For instance Brewster (1991) reported failure rates of below 5 per cent in 72 per cent of his sample. Likewise Scullion's (1991) study of UK and Irish multinationals found that only 10 per cent of these firms had failure rates over 5 per cent. Nonetheless any significant level of expatriate failure is likely to result in significant cost implications for the organisation concerned and also has the potential to considerably impact on the subsidiary operation. Hence this was a metric commonly utilised by MNCs in evaluating the utility of expatriation programmes.

Turnover of assignees following repatriation

Repatriation, the reintegration of international assignees into their original home operation following an expatriate assignment, is a key but often neglected element of the expatriate cycle. However, turnover of expatriates on repatriation is a second measure traditionally used by organisations in measuring the usefulness of expatriate programmes. In an era where international managerial expertise and the coveted 'global mindset' are scarce commodities which are in great demand the turnover of expatriate employees on, or soon after, their return to the home organisation represents a key challenge to the global competitiveness of any MNC. Based on a number of studies Black *et al.* (1999) posit that in US firms approximately 20 per cent of managers leave their organisation within one year of completing an international assignment. Figures from the GMAC (2002: 52) confirm this trend. Respondents to this survey indicated that 22 per cent of expatriates left within one year of completing their assignment, while a further 22 per cent left within the second year. When this loss of expertise is considered in combination with the financial costs associated with the international assignment, organisations have traditionally used levels of turnover as a means of measuring the cost effectiveness of international assignments.

Financial costs associated with the assignment

The financial cost of expatriate assignments had long since represented a key measure in the evaluation of the use of expatriate employees. Absolute costs of assignments have also emerged as a key challenge in the staffing of key positions in subsidiaries of MNCs. This is because in addition to the costs associated with relocating the assignee, and often their family, expatriate assignees generally receive a premium for accepting the assignment. Further, 85 per cent of companies base expatriate salaries on home country remuneration levels (GMAC, 2003). This is particularly significant when the assignment is in a lower cost economy where the cost differential between foreign expatriates and HCNs can be very large. Black *et al.* (1999) estimate the average costs associated with sending US expatriates on assignment to be between US$150,000 and US$250,000 per year while citing figures up to US$816,000 for one company.

Performance of the individual expatriate

The issue of managing the performance of individual expatriate employees represents a key challenge for MNCs. In this context Mendenhall and Oddou (1985) point to the complexity added to this process by the fact that expatriates must meet the often conflicting expectations of HQ management and subsidiary colleagues. Designing performance management systems for international assignees involves considering a number of key factors including the impact of exogenous factors such as foreign exchange fluctuations on the performance of business operations (Black *et al.*, 1999), the clear articulation of the performance objectives of the assignee and ensuring that the appraisal measures same, and identifying the persons best placed to evaluate the performance of the assignee. Taking these challenges into account, the measurement of performance still represents an important means of measuring the utility of the individual expatriate.

These methods of measurement have been subject to a number of criticisms. In particular the topic of expatriate failure had been subject to a large degree of critical attention since the mid-1990s. Most notably Harzing (1995: 458) posits that: 'there is almost no empirical foundation for the existence of high failure rates when measured as premature re-entry'. Harzing's criticisms are based primarily on the fact that assertions of high levels of expatriate failure were for the most part based on a misinterpretation of the work of a single researcher (Tung 1981, 1982). In challenging the traditional assertion high failure rates, Harzing also points to a number of European studies which indicated that failure rates are significantly lower than figures cited in the mainstream literature.

Boudreau and Ramstad (1997) further note that the above indicators provide only a measurement of the expatriate's past performance, often only after the assignment has ended. This does not aid the MNC in controlling the costs of the assignment during the assignment. Thus since the mid-1990s researchers have attempted to develop more business-focused methods of measuring the relative benefit of expatriate assignments. We will review one of the key ones, return on investment, here (other options include transition cost analysis: cf. Benito *et al.*, 2005).

Expatriate return on investment

The concept of return on investment has only relatively recently began to be applied to the monitoring of expatriate assignments. While traditionally ROI developed as an accounting term to describe the ratio between profit and investment (cf. Flamholtz, 1985) more recently economists have pointed to the limits of utilising traditional accounting methods in calculating ROI and have expanded the definition to include both current (lagging) and future (leading) returns and further to include both financial and non financial returns (see McNulty and Tharenou, 2004 for a discussion). This is a more pertinent definition for measuring the ROI of expatriate assignments as international assignments provide many non-financial outcomes, such as global management development, coordination of a MNC's global operations and the transfer of know-how and expertise within the MNC (cf. Harzing, 2001c; Minbaeva and Michailova, 2004). Further the value of expatriate assignments may not only add financial value to a firm's performance but also add to the strategic orientation of the firm (Dyer and Reeves, 1995; McNulty and Tharenou, 2004). This strategic value may, for example, be reflected in the localisation of managerial roles within a foreign subsidiary whereby expatriate managers play a role in developing the competence of local managers (see Chapter 7 in this volume). Thus ROI may help managers to effectively evaluate the utility of expatriate assignments through illuminating the contribution of expatriates to firm performance by looking beyond traditional historical cost analyses and measurements of failure and turnover on repatriation.

Measuring ROI on expatriate assignments

McNulty and Tharenou (2004) and Johnson (2005) point to the limited usefulness of a single best ROI formula which expects identical costs and benefits to be calculated for each assignment. This is because the ROI calculation would differ from one assignment to another due to the fact that the strategic objective of each assignment is likely to be different (see above and Kamoche, 1997). The timing of the calculation may also differ depending on the nature of assignments. For example whether repatriation was a key objective of the assignment or not would determine whether repatriation related criteria were included in the ROI calculation (McNulty and Tharenou, 2004).

At a minimum there are two areas of focus which need to be considered in measuring the ROI of expatriate assignments. First, the cost of the assignment must be quantified (the *investment*), and second, what defines the success of the assignment must be established (the *return*) (Johnson, 2005).

Costs: the investment   In measuring the cost of the international assignment (the I) accurate cost tracking emerges as a key concern. This represents a significant challenge to IHRM practitioners due to the lack of clarity associated with defining assignment costs. While the expenses associated directly with the assignment (salary, taxes, housing, relocation etc.) may be relatively easy to quantify, the administrative costs of running the international assignment programme represent a significant variable which may be more difficult to quantify for an individual assignment. It has been argued however that technological advancements combined with trends towards outsourcing parts of or entire relocation programmes are assisting organisations in managing their relocation programmes (Johnson, 2005). More complex measures of investment may also attempt to factor in costs associated with 'getting up to speed' following the transfer, although

Johnson (2005) posits that it is rare to find such variables measured. This is understandable given the complexity associated with trying to quantify such criteria. Nonetheless such an approach would aid organisations in justifying the costs associated with pre-departure training and 'settling in' support (Johnson, 2005). This is significant because these policies are often considered soft and thus are difficult to justify when cost-saving efforts are introduced within organisations, however if their value could be quantified in terms of benefits associated with them, IHRM managers could more plausibly argue for their continuance.

Benefits: the return   The second step in measuring ROI is measuring the return associated with the assignment. In this regard defining critical success criteria emerges as a key concern. This is significant as the return can be realistically measured only in the context of the overall objectives of the assignment. While this may be a straightforward exercise, in practical terms it may not be as simple as expected. First, as was noted above most assignments have more than one objective. Thus in successfully measuring the return, various outcomes will have to be weighted to reflect their respective importance. Second, not all objectives lend themselves easily to measurement. Specifically assignments which call for knowledge transfer or the development of business relationships are by their nature nebulous and thus difficult to quantify. Assignments whose purpose is to gain international experience and to develop a global mindset are also difficult to measure in terms of success due to the difficulty in quantifying the quality of international experience. In attempting to overcome these and other challenges Johnson (2005: 53) calls for companies to 'establish a base line of global competencies that are part of the performance management process for the assignment'. Box 3.2 outlines examples of these competencies.

Box 3.2   Examples of global competencies associated with managing the performance of expatriate employees

- Learning the local language up to a professional level
- Understanding the complexities of managing in an international marketplace
- Ensuring decisions are made in the context of a global business environment
- Networking in another country to build a new client base
- Providing effective feedback to subordinates in a manner appropriate to the local culture
- Making effective presentations to an international audience

Source: draws from Johnson (2005).

The way forward

In developing a sound theoretical foundation for the consideration of expatriate
ROI McNulty and Tharenou (2004) call for a strategic approach to calculating ROI
on expatriate assignments, an approach which ensures that items included in the ROI
calculation are based on a link between the costs and benefits of the assignment and
the objective of the assignment itself. Further they posit that, when an international
assignment has clearly defined objectives and is carefully planned, the MNC is likely
to display a set of congruent HR policies to support the assignment. Specifically the
MNC is more likely to have a selection process that recruits an appropriate candidate,
a training and development programme that supports the particular cross-cultural needs
of the assignee, and a compensation system that is consistent with the assignment's goals
(McNulty and Tharenou, 2004).

Thus they argue the link between the assignee's performance and the objectives of the
assignment are easier to determine. Further it is proposed that by examining the effect
of the entire bundle of IHRM practices used during the assignment, organisations will
by able to more accurately determine rates on return on the costs of expatriate
assignments. This is outlined in Figure 3.2. In expanding on the simple consideration of
return and investment outlined above, McNulty and Tharenou (2004) present a four-step
approach for the calculation of ROI.

1 Identify financial and non-financial costs and benefits associated with the assignment.
2 Link the costs and benefits to the purpose of the international assignment.
3 Identify the appropriate antecedents of ROI from a systems (integrated) perspective.
4 Conduct the calculation at an appropriate time within the context of the assignments
  purpose.

Conclusion

In this chapter we have examined the reasons why firms use expatriate assignments.
This chapter is significant because – as the approaches to and strategies associated with –
international business have become more complex so too have the staffing options for
the firms involved (Briscoe and Schuler, 2004). We have attempted to outline the
differing factors which influence these key decisions. In moving beyond simply
considering the alternatives, through a discussion of Harzing's (2001c) work we have
attempted to illustrate the debate as to whether the roles performed by expatriates are
equally important in different situations. Our discussions then focused on the empirical
effectiveness of expatriate assignments. Finally we consider the key question as to
whether expatriate assignments represented value for money.

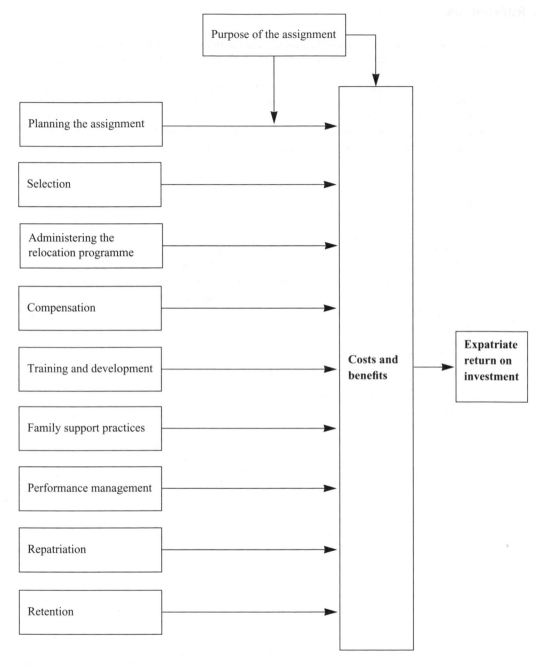

Figure 3.2 A model of expatriate return on investment

Source: McNulty, Y.M. and Tharenou, P. (2004) 'Expatriate return on investment: a definition and antecedents', *Journal of International Studies of Management and Organisation*, 34(3): 68–95, Figure 1 (p. 74). Reprinted with permission of M. E. Sharpe.

References

Benito, G.R.G., Tomasen, S., Bonache-Perez, J. and Pla-Barber, J. (2005) 'A transaction cost analysis of staffing decisions in international operations', *Scandinavian Journal of Management*, 21: 101–26.

Björkman, I., Barner-Rasmussen, W. and Li, L. (2004) 'Managing knowledge transfer in MNCs: the impact of headquarters control mechanisms', *Journal of International Business Studies*, 35(5): 443–55.

Black, J.S., Gregersen, H.B., Mendenhall, M.E. and Stroth, L.K. (1999) *Globalizing People through International Assignments*, Reading, MA: Addison-Wesley.

Blakeney, R.N., Oddou, G. and Osland, J.S. (2006) 'Repatriate assets: factors impacting knowledge transfer', in M. Morley, N. Heraty and D. Collings (eds) *International HRM and International Assignments*, Basingstoke: Palgrave.

Boudreau, J.W. and Ramstad, P.M. (1997) 'Measuring from intellectual capital: learning from financial history', *Human Resource Management*, 36: 343–56.

Brewster, C. (1991) *The Management of Expatriates*, London: Kogan Page.

Briscoe, D.R. and Schuler, R.S. (2004) *International Human Resource Management*, 2nd edn, London: Routledge.

Delios, A. and Björkman, I. (2000) 'Expatriate staffing in foreign subsidiaries of Japanese multinational corporations in the PRC and the United States', *International Journal of Human Resource Management*, 11(2): 278–93.

Dowling, P.J. and Welch, D.E. (2004) *International Human Resource Management*, 4th edn, Thomson Learning.

Downes, M. and Thomas, A.S. (1999) 'Managing overseas assignments to build organisational knowledge', *Human Resource Planning*, 22(4): 33–49.

Doz, Y., Santos, J. and Williamson, P. (2001) *From Global to Metanational: How Companies Win in the Knowledge Economy*, Boston, MA: Harvard Business School Press.

Dyer, L. and Reeves, T. (1995) 'Human resource strategies and firm performance: what do we know and where do we need to go?', *International Journal of Human Resource Management*, 6: 656–70.

Edström, A. and Galbraith, J.R. (1977) 'Transfer of managers as a coordination and control strategy in multinational organizations', *Administrative Science Quarterly*, 22: 248–63.

Evans, P., Pucik, V. and Barsoux, J-L. (2002) *The Global Challenge: Frameworks for International Human Resource Management*, New York: McGraw-Hill.

Flamholtz, E. (1985) *Human Resource Accounting: Advances in Concepts, Methods and Applications*, San Francisco, CA: Jossey-Bass.

GMAC Global Relocation Services (2003) *Global Relocation Trends: 2002 Survey Report*, Warren, NJ: GMAC.

Harris, H. (2002) 'Strategic management of international workers', *Innovations in International HR*, 28(1): 1–5.

Harzing, A.W.K. (1995) 'The persistent myth of high expatriate failure rates', *International Journal of Human Resource Management*, 6(2): 457–74.

Harzing, A.W.K. (2001a) 'An analysis of the functions of international transfer of managers in MNCs', *Employee Relations*, 23(6): 581–98.

Harzing, A.W.K. (2001b) 'Who's in charge? An empirical study of executive staffing practices in foreign multinationals', *Human Resource Management*, 40: 139–58.

Harzing, A.W.K. (2001c) 'Of bears, bees and spiders: The role of expatriates in controlling foreign subsidiaries', *Journal of World Business*, 26(4): 366–79.

Hocking, J.B., Browne, M. and Harzing, A.W. (2004) 'A knowledge transfer perspective of strategic assignment purposes and their path-dependent outcomes', *International Journal of Human Resource Management*, 15: 565–86.

Hofstede, G. (2001) *Culture's Consequences*, 2nd edn, London: Sage.

Johnson, L. (2005) 'Measuring international assignment return on investment', *Compensation and Benefits Review*, 37(2): 50–5.

Kamoche, K. (1997) 'Knowledge creation and learning in international HRM', *International Journal of Human Resource Management*, 8: 213–25.

Linehan, M. and Mayrhofer, W. (2005) 'International careers and repatriation', in H. Scullion and M. Linehan (eds) *International Human Resource Management: A Critical Text*, Basingstoke: Palgrave.

McNulty, Y. and Tharenou, P. (2004) 'Expatriate return on investment', *International Studies of Management and Organization*, 34(3): 68–95.

Mendenhall, M. and Oddou, G. (1985) 'The dimensions of expatriate acculturation', *Academy of Management Review*, 10: 39–47.

Minbaeva, D.N. and Michailova, S. (2004) 'Knowledge transfer and expatriation in multinational corporations: the role of disseminative capacity', *Employee Relations*, 26(6): 663–80.

Paik, Y. and Sohn, J.D. (2004) 'Expatriate managers and MNC's ability to control international subsidiaries: the case of Japanese MNCs', *Journal of World Business*, 39: 61–71.

Peak, M. (1997) 'Darned expensive to be taken for granted', *Management Review*, 86(1): 9.

Petrovic, J., Harris, H. and Brewster, C. (2000) 'New forms of international working', Centre for Research into the Management of Expatriation, Cranfield: Cranfield School of Management.

PricewaterhouseCoopers (2002) *International Assignments: Global Policy and Practice, Key Trends 2002*, PricewaterhouseCoopers.

Pucik, V. (1992) 'Globalizing human resource management', in V. Pucik, N.M. Tichy and C.K. Barnett, *Creating and Leading the Competitive Organization*, New York: Wiley.

Scullion, H. (1991) 'Why companies prefer to use expatriates', *Personnel Management*, 23: 32–5.

Scullion, H. (1994) 'Staffing policies and strategic control in British multinationals', *International Studies of Management and Organization*, 4(3): 18–35.

Shay, J.P. and Baack, S.A. (2004) 'Expatriate assignment, adjustment and effectiveness: an empirical examination of the big picture', *Journal of International Business Studies*, 35: 216–32.

Sparrow, P., Brewster, C. and Harris, H. (2004) *Globalizing Human Resource Management*, London: Routledge.

Tahvanainen, M. and Suutari, V. (2005) 'Expatriate performance management in MNCs', in H. Scullion and M. Linehan (eds) *International Human Resource Management: A Critical Text*, Basingstoke: Palgrave.

Tallman, S. and Fladmoe-Linquist, K. (2002) 'Internationalization, globalization and capability based strategy', *California Management Review*, 45(1): 116–35.

Thomas, D.C. (2002) *Essentials of International Management: A Cross Cultural Perspective*, London: Sage.

Torraco, R.J. and Swanson, R.A. (1995) 'The strategic role of human resource development', *Human Resource Planning*, 18(4): 10–12 .

Tung, R.L. (1981) 'Selection and training of personnel for overseas assignments', *Colombia Journal of World Business*, 16: 68–78.

Tung, R.L. (1982) 'Selection and training procedures of US, European and Japanese multinationals', *California Management Review*, 25: 57–71.

Tung, R.L. and Miller, E.L. (1990) 'Managing in the twenty-first century: the need for global orientation', *Management International Review*, 30: 5–18.

Whitley, R. (1999) *Divergent Capitalisms: The Social Structuring and Change of Business Systems*, Oxford: Oxford University Press.

Part 2

Global staffing: composing the international staff

4

International recruitment and selection

HUGH SCULLION AND DAVID G. COLLINGS

Introduction

The focus of this chapter is on recruitment and selection in an international context and in this context we consider how recruiting and selecting staff for international assignments plays an important role in enabling international firms to compete effectively in international business. First, we will examine expatriate failure and adjustment which is an important area in international recruitment and selection because the high cost of failure in international assignments in both economic and human terms highlights the importance of effective recruitment and selection. Second, we will discuss the core competencies of the global manager and will consider the three main research streams which have contributed to our knowledge in this area. Third, we will examine three broad alternative approaches to resourcing. Fourth, we will evaluate some important methods which international companies use to source and attract international managers, and in particular consider to what extent selection techniques can be adapted for use in the international context. A summary of the issues which will be addressed in the chapter are outlined below:

- expatriate failure and adjustment
- the core competencies of the international manager
- alternative resourcing strategies
- different approaches to attracting and sourcing international managers
- methods of selecting international managers.

Expatriate failure

An important issue in the international staffing literature is that of expatriate failure. Research highlights the complexity of the expatriate selection process and suggests that predicting future performance potential when hiring staff to work in foreign markets is particularly challenging (Dowling and Welch, 2004). The failure to select the 'right' people is a major reason for poor performance or failure in international assignments.

The costs of expatriate failure are both direct (salary, training costs, travel and relocation expenses) and indirect (damaged relations with host country organisations, loss of market share and requests that parent country nationals be replaced with host country nationals). It has been argued that the latter should be considered as the most significant costs by multinationals, as damage to reputation in key strategic foreign markets or regions could be terminal to the prospects of successfully developing international business in that region.

The notion of a high expatriate failure is a very common one in the literature with figures in the region of 15–50 per cent for developing countries commonly cited in the literature (Harzing, 1995). Success or failure for expatriates is often defined as the premature return of an expatriate (i.e. return home before the assignment is completed). But it has been argued that success or failure is a more complex issue than this (Briscoe and Schuler, 2004) and some research has questioned the wisdom of defining expatriate failure so narrowly (Dowling and Welch, 2004). A study of European multinationals provided considerable support for using a broader definition of expatriate failure and added ' underperformance' to its definition of assignment failure (Price Waterhouse, 1997). This study concluded:

> The rates for employees currently underperforming on assignment as a result of difficulties in adapting to their cultural surroundings are even higher. 29 % of companies report a rate in excess of one in twenty, with 7 % reporting a rate over one in ten.
>
> (cited in Dowling and Welch, 2004: 87)

This suggests that expatriate success or failure might be better defined in terms of wider criteria such as:

- overall performance in the foreign assignment
- personal satisfaction with the experience
- lack of adjustment to local conditions
- lack of acceptance by local nationals
- the inability to identify and train a local successor.

Also, the degree of expatriate failure is influenced by a number of factors (adapted from Dowling and Welch, 2004, and Briscoe and Schuler, 2004):

- length of assignment
- focus on technical skills rather than wider criteria in selection
- lack of preparation for international assignment.

The main reasons for expatriate failure have been summarised in Box 4.1 by Briscoe and Schuler (2004).

The failure rate of expatriates in US multinationals (figures of around 30–40 per cent are commonly cited) is considerably higher than their European or Japanese counterparts, who rarely experience expatriate failure rates in excess of 10 per cent (Björkman and Gertsen, 1989; Harzing, 1995; Scullion and Brewster, 2001; Tung, 1981). A number of reasons have emerged as significant in explaining this:

- Europeans have more exposure to differing cultures and languages.
- There is a longer-term perspective on international assignments particularly in Japanese multinationals.
- Longer assignments and longer adjustment periods are common in Japanese international assignments.
- In European multinationals it was felt that closer attention was paid to the selection of expatriates, and that higher calibre managers went abroad.
- Research suggests that European managers were more international in their orientation and outlook than US managers reflecting the importance of international markets relative to domestic markets (Scullion and Brewster, 2001).

Box 4.1 Reasons for expatriate failure

- Inability of spouse/partner to adjust or spouse/partner dissatisfaction
- Inability of expatriate to adjust
- Other family-related problems
- Failures in expatriate selection
- Expatriate's personality or lack of emotional maturity
- Expatriate's inability to cope with larger responsibilities of overseas work
- Expatriate's lack of technical competence
- Expatriate's lack of motivation to work overseas
- Dissatisfaction with quality of life in foreign location
- Dissatisfaction with compensation and benefits
- Lack of cultural and language preparation
- Lack of support for expatriate and family while on overseas assignment.

Source: adapted from Briscoe and Schuler (2004: 244).

Family-related problems, particularly the inability of the spouse to adapt to the new culture, have emerged as the major reason for poor performance in international assignments in European multinationals (Brewster, 1991; Scullion and Brewster, 2001). This finding is consistent with previous research on US multinationals (Tung, 1982). Some research has highlighted the importance of considering the family in the selection and training practices of multinationals, yet many multinationals fail to take this factor into account in their selection decisions (Briscoe and Schuler, 2004; Dowling and Welch, 2004). Several studies have highlighted that there were considerable national differences in the reasons cited for expatriate failure (Scullion and Brewster, 2001; Tung, 1981) (see Table 4.1). In Japanese multinationals, for example, the inability of the spouse to adjust was not regarded as a significant factor affecting expatriate performance. This was related to the role and status of the spouse in Japan (Tung 1981, 1984). Dowling *et al.* (1994) suggest that wider social factors may also contribute to this finding. They

Table 4.1 Reasons for expatriate failure (in descending order of importance)

American	Japanese	Europe
1 The inability of spouse to adjust	1 Inability to cope with larger overseas responsibility	1 The inability of the spouse to adjust
2 Manager's inability to adjust	2 Difficulties with new environment	2 Other family problems
3 Other family problems	3 Personal or emotional problems	3 Concerns over re-entry
4 Manager's personal or emotional maturity	4 Lack of technical skills	
5 Inability to cope with larger overseas responsibility	5 Inability of spouse to adjust	

Sources: American and Japanese: adapted from Tung (1982: 55–71), cited in Dowling and Welch (1988); Europe: Scullion (1994); Scullion and Brewster (2001).

argue that, because of the highly competitive nature of the Japanese education system, the spouse commonly opts to remain in Japan with the children. Also Tung (1981) suggests that the longer-term orientation of the Japanese companies allows the Japanese expatriate more time to adjust to the foreign situation. One weakness of the expatriate failure literature is, surprisingly, the relative failure to consider the effects of poor performance from the perspective of the expatriates themselves. Poor performance or failure in the international assignment or early recall, may lead to loss of self-esteem, self-confidence and prestige among peers. In addition, the expatriate's family relationship might be threatened (Dowling and Welch, 2004).

There has been considerable debate over the magnitude of the expatriate failure problem. Harzing (1995, 2002) notes that most publications in expatriate management – and in particular those dealing with cross-cultural adjustment or cross-cultural training – assume that expatriate failure rates (measured as the premature return of the expatriate) are very high, with commonly cited figures in the region of 16–50 per cent. Harzing (1995, 2002) however questions the reported high expatriate failure rates in the US literature and she shows that there has been little reliable empirical work in this area for a decade and a half. She posits that there is little empirical evidence for the claims of high expatriate failure and claims that the myth of high expatriate failure rates has been perpetuated by careless and inappropriate referencing. Harzing also argues that this may have a negative impact on the effectiveness of expatriate management by focusing companies on avoiding the premature return of expatriates to the detriment of other more fundamental issues. Harzing's arguments are generally supported in the more solidly research based studies where reported expatriate failure rates are considerably lower (Brewster and Scullion, 1997; Scullion, 1994).

Further, one review provides some support for the suggestion of a declining expatriate failure rate (Dowling and Welch, 2004). One global survey of 300 multinationals

(European and US) conducted by Organizational Resource Counselors (ORC 2002) reported that less than 10 per cent of international assignments ended in early recall. A second survey by GMAC Global Relocation Services (2003) indicated failure rates of around 17 per cent. However, perhaps of even more interest was that in the first survey 54 per cent of respondents did not know the return rate of expatriates and 39 per cent of respondents in the second survey also did not have the figures. Briscoe and Schuler (2004) highlight three key summary points on the debate on expatriate failure:

● It is important to broaden the discussion of expatriate failure beyond that of premature return used in earlier studies.
● The emergence of expatriate failure as a high profile issue has stimulated research attention towards expatriation and the management of expatriation.
● The evidence on expatriate failure rates is inconclusive. High expatriate failure rates have not consistently been reported outside North America. Research on European and Japanese MNCs suggests much lower expatriate failure rates.

Linking expatriate failure and adjustment

Tung's (1981) pioneering study highlighted that expatriate failure is often due to the inability of the expatriate or the expatriate spouse to adjust or the expatriate's inability to cope with larger international responsibility. Harzing (2004) suggests that addressing expatriate failure involves paying more attention to many of the same factors indicated under adjustment and these are outlined below:

● recognising that expatriate adjustment involves adjustment to another job, to the interaction of host nationals as well as a more general adjustment to living in a foreign country
● having a more sophisticated approach to selection using techniques such as cross-cultural competence and language fluency
● implementing rigorous organisational support systems
● providing appropriate job design
● including the spouse in training and support programmes.

Expatriate adjustment

In the previous section we commented on the importance of expatriate adjustment and the links with recruitment and selection. In this section we will discuss two important models of expatriate adjustment and will link this to the discussion of expatriate failure and consider the implications for international recruitment and selection.

Mendenhall and Oddou (1985) argue that there is insufficient knowledge about the relevant dimensions of expatriate acculturation which they claim can lead to the use of inappropriate selection procedures. They developed a taxonomy of acculturation profiles which outlines four personality dimensions which are seen to facilitate the successful adjustment of international managers:

- self-oriented dimension
- others oriented dimension
- perceptual dimension
- cultural toughness dimension.

Self-oriented dimension

The self-oriented dimension (personal skills) can be subdivided into three sub-factors: reinforcement substitution, stress reduction and technical competence.

Reinforcement substitution relates to the individual's ability to substitute other actions and activities in the host country for those usually undertaken at home. Research suggests that international managers who manage to find substitute activities in the new culture (e.g. willingness to adapt to changes in food, eating habits and hobbies) are more likely to adjust to the new environments (Torbiörn, 1982).

Stress reduction: research has highlighted that the transfer to an international assignment can be stressful for a variety of reasons including: inability to adapt to the new culture; feelings of isolation and alienation; separation from family and friends; failure to communicate with host nationals (e.g. Enderwick and Hodgson, 1993). In this context Coyle and Shortland (1992) demonstrated that a person's ability to handle stressful situations should be assessed during the selection process and that an inability to handle stressful situations may lead to expatriate failure.

Technical competence or technical expertise may be used as a basic measure to identify potential expatriates but empirical research suggests that many companies overemphasise the importance of technical ability as a key determinant in the selection process (Anderson, 2005; Mendenhall and Oddou, 1988; Tung, 1981). This point is well made by Mendenhall and Oddou (1988: 82): 'Technical competence has nothing to do with one's ability to adapt to a new environment, deal effectively with foreign co-workers, or perceive and if necessary imitate the foreign behavioural norms.'

Others oriented dimension

The others oriented dimension refers to the expatriate's desire and ability to interact with host country nationals and comprises of two elements, namely relationship development and a willingness to communicate.

Relationship development refers to the willingness of the expatriate and family to develop relationships with host country nationals. Research suggests that the expatriate's tendency to form friendships with host country nationals may have a strong influence on the level of adjustment (Torbiörn, 1982). Also, the degree of social activity with host nationals has a greater impact on the adjustment of the spouse than it has on the expatriate (Brewster and Pickard, 1994).

A willingness to communicate is another key factor which includes the expatriate's desire to use the host national language and a willingness to understand and work with host country nationals.

Perceptual dimension

The perceptual dimension refers to the expatriate's ability to understand and accept the 'different' behaviour of the host country nationals. Mendenhall and Oddou (1985) identified four approaches to acculturation:

- Assimilation occurs when an expatriate wants to become immersed in the new culture and does not wish to maintain the old identity and culture.
- Integration takes place if the expatriate is interested in maintaining his/her own cultural identity as well as integrating with locals.
- A separatist mode of acculturation takes place when the expatriate does not want to integrate with the host country nationals and is keen to keep his/her cultural identity.
- Marginalisation comes when the expatriate has little interest in the new culture or the maintenance of his/her identity.

Cultural toughness dimension

In culturally tough countries (countries which are culturally very different from the home country), the first three dimensions become even more important than in culturally similar countries.

* * *

Mendenhall and Oddou (1985) suggest that the expatriate selection process should focus explicitly on the strengths and weaknesses of the applicant on the above mentioned dimensions which will focus attention on cross-cultural adaptability which complements the assessment of technical ability. Further, it has been argued that the expatriate's ability to understand the reasons for the host nationals' behaviour will enable him/her to predict future behaviours and respond accordingly (Mendenhall *et al.*, 1987). This taxonomy of acculturation styles may prove useful in categorising how expatriates with specific skill combinations will fare in terms of future acculturation (Mendenhall and Oddou, 1985: 75). Ideally a candidate selected for an expatriate position should possess the necessary skills and attributes in each of the three dimensions of self-orientation, others orientation and perceptual orientation. It follows that individuals who possess none of these skills should not be selected for expatriate assignments. However, there is also the need to consider other criteria when selecting international managers as we will see when examining a comprehensive model of expatriate adjustment below.

Black, Mendenhall and Oddou's (1991) model of expatriate adjustment

This comprehensive model of expatriate adjustment integrates perspectives from theoretical work in both the domestic and international adjustment literature. Black *et al.* (1991) argue that expatriate adjustment includes two principal components: anticipatory adjustment and in-country adjustment.

Anticipatory adjustment

Anticipatory adjustment can have an important positive impact on in-country adjustment and is positively influenced by cross-cultural training and previous international experience, both of which help create more realistic expatriate expectations. International firms can positively influence anticipatory adjustment by providing cross-cultural training.

In-country adjustment

This part of the Black *et al.* (1999) model was tested by Shaffer *et al.* (1999), who introduced two moderating variables, previous assignments and language fluency. The model identifies three dimensions of adjustment:

- adjustment to work
- adjustment to interacting with host nationals
- general adjustment to living conditions abroad.

Role clarity and role discretion were positively related to work adjustment while role conflict and role novelty did not show the expected negative relationship to work adjustment. On the other hand, support from co-workers and logistical support were positively related to interaction adjustment. Cultural novelty and spousal adjustment had a strong impact on general adjustment and a significant impact on interaction adjustment.

The number of previous assignments and language fluency had a significant positive direct effect on interaction adjustment, and previous experience also moderated the relationship between supervisor and co-worker. The empirical work of Shaffer *et al.* (1999) suggests that experienced expatriates have learned to rely more on host country management than parent country management.

The conceptual model of Black *et al.* (1991) has generally been verified by the empirical work of Shaffer *et al.* (1999). The implications of this work highlight the importance of job design, organisational support systems and the inclusion of the spouse in any training or development programmes designed to make expatriate adjustment more effective. It also draws attention to the importance of language skills as selection criteria.

Having reviewed the topics of expatriate failure and adjustment, we will now examine the debate over the competencies required to be an effective global manager as these will be significant in designing appropriate selection interventions.

The core competencies of international managers

For organisations to survive, let alone flourish in the future, increasingly their perspective must be global. It has been argued that global skills and perspectives cannot be viewed as a speciality or segment of business but should be an integral part of an enterprise (Pattison, 1990). A key question concerns, what the successful international business organisation will look like in 2100 and what competencies and qualities will be needed by managers and executives to run these international organisations? Effective global managers see the need to manage cultural differences and develop the skills necessary to participate effectively in the global environment. However, given the growing costs of international assignments for many international organisations the first basic question in international recruitment and selection is 'Do we really need an international manager?' Further in terms of sourcing international managers, it may be very difficult for international organisations to find candidates who are willing to go to abroad and organisations are forced to consider alternatives to traditional forms of expatriation (see Chapter 8, this volume). In this regard, there may be alternatives to sourcing an international manager such as using a local national manager to manage subsidiary operations (see Chapter 7, this volume).

There is a lack of consensus in the academic literature about what an international manager or a global manager actually is (Forster, 2000). Likewise for many organisations there is confusion about what is meant by the ' international manager'. Some international managerial roles may require people to relocate with their families to another country; others such as international commuters may involve extensive international business travel while others may involve communication with people from other countries. Some argue that what makes an individual a 'global manager' is more a state of mind (global mindset) which involves a willingness to cross-geographic and cultural borders (Baruch, 2004). Indeed Evans *et al.* (2002) note that while expatriates are defined by location, global managers are defined by their state of mind, or their capacity to work effectively in varied cultural, organisational and functional situations. This notion of the global mindset will be discussed in Chapter 5.

Sparrow (1999a) identified several different role specifications of international managers:

- home-based managers with a central focus on international markets
- multicultural team members who work on international projects
- internationally mobile managers who undertake frequent short trips to international locations
- employees in specialist non-management roles which involve international activity or knowledge transfer

- expatriates who undertake a number of lengthy international assignments in a limited number of host countries
- transitional managers who move across borders on behalf of the organisation but who are relatively detached from any single organisational HQ.

While it is generally understood that the role specification and resourcing strategies are different for every organisation, it is sometimes assumed that the same selection and assessment criteria are valid across the board. However, this is not supported by the research evidence which suggests that the role of the international manager varies significantly across sectors of the economy (Sparrow, 1999b). For example, Scottish and Newcastle International and Rolls Royce require different skills from managers working in greenfield sites compared to managers working in international joint ventures or in mature businesses. Many companies also differentiate between technical roles which essentially involve engineering competencies and networking roles which focus more on customer relationships and marketing through networking.

Thus a key question which emerges in this debate is if there is a different set of competences required for each of these roles? In addressing this question, early research linked high expatriate failure rates to lack of pre-departure training and spouse adjustment problems (Tung, 1982) perhaps suggesting generic requirements regardless of the nature of assignment or individual. More recently, however our knowledge about skills and competencies related to international job changes has increased and attempts have been made to understand the more complex psychological processes involved (Bognanno and Sparrow, 1995).

Various studies have identified comprehensive lists of the competencies required for the international manager. The main problem is that various studies produce lists with very large dimensions of competency for the international manager. For example, two leading specialists in the field of cross-cultural management, Harris and Moran (1996) cited almost seventy dimensions of competency, of which over twenty are seen as most desirable. Other studies identify similarly large lists (Barham and Wills, 1992). The practitioner literature also contains many lists of apparently predictive factors, many of which are of questionable validity. There is a consensus between practitioners that there is a range of specific competencies linked with effective performance in international roles. However, it was noted that the approach of some organisations was to continue to create lists of potentially relevant dimensions rather than engage with the more challenging task of defining the key generic attributes which include both personality characteristics and management competencies (Sparrow and Hiltrop, 1994). The main reason for this problem is that three main research streams have contributed to our knowledge about effective performance in an international setting (Sparrow, 1999a): expatriation studies, international joint venture (IJV) research and research into the socialisation process for international managers. The research evidence on each will be examined below.

Expatriation studies

Studies of expatriation highlight the costs of selection errors in expatriate selection and the costs of expatriate failure. They focus on three sets of competencies: individual attributes, cross-cultural people skills and perception skills (Mendenhall and Oddou, 1985). Research has identified a number of behaviours that are most important for effective international assignments (Abe and Wiseman, 1983; Black *et al.*, 1999) and include the following:

- the need to be flexible
- the need to be able to tolerate ambiguity
- the need to have a clear goal orientation
- the need to be sociable and people oriented
- the need to be empathetic and non-judgemental
- the need to have good communication skills.

Analysis of the criteria actually used for selection of international managers by European firms suggests the following factors, in rank order (Brewster, 1991):

- technical competence
- previous track record in the home country
- motivation
- language skills
- stress resistance
- independence
- goal-oriented personality
- communication skills.

This supports the view that many organisations undervalue the importance of the 'soft skills' of international management – such as relational and intercultural abilities. Often, domestic track record is not the best indicator of success abroad (Mendenhall and Oddou, 1985; Miller, 1972). Research examining personality traits relevant for international managers has highlighted the need for managers to be:

- open and non-judgemental
- interested in the ideas of others
- capable of building relationships based on trust
- sensitive to the feelings and perspectives of others.

Further, research examining the links between personality attributes and successful international assignments has focused on three principal areas:

- *Openness to experience* is a personality variable and a trait which can be reliably assessed and which is often cited in studies of international managers (Hays, 1974; Jordan and Cartwright, 1998).
- *Being strongly extrovert* has often been found to be negatively associated with success (Hays, 1971). Introvert individuals are often more in tune with their environment and more sensitive to subtle changes in it (Smith, 1989).

● *Low anxiety, coupled with emotional stability*: the ability to deal effectively with unexpected change has been linked to success in high-stress professions such as expatriation (Furnham, 1990).

When selection decisions in practice are examined it would seem that judgements made about people are often based on unreliable techniques and there are still considerable weaknesses in our knowledge of how to source and assess people on a reliable and valid basis (Jordan and Cartwright, 1998).

International joint venture research

IJV research examines the role of managers in situations where there is a premium placed on the ability to work through partnerships and collaborative working. Clearly this requires a different skill set from that of the traditional expatriate. We have argued above that a number of factors influence the competency requirements for international managers. It has also been argued that competency demands differ significantly depending on the nature of the assignment. For example, studies of German–Japanese international joint ventures found that German managers needed a different set of skills in comparison to expatriates working in wholly owned subsidiaries. The managers working in the joint venture needed more self-control, patience and group orientation and a less strong individual goal orientation (Stahl, 1998, cited in Sparrow, 1999a). However, there is no consensus about the relative skill levels needed to operate effectively in an IJV role compared to the traditional expatriate role. It has been claimed that the IJV role is characterised by:

● more complexity
● higher levels of role ambiguity
● lower power and lower trust environment.

On the other hand, others claim that the IJV managerial role is a more positive one for the following reasons:

● the challenge of combining at least two organisational cultures
● less need to conform and impose parent company culture
● higher level of autonomy to design strategies to suit the overall objectives of the IJV (Black *et al.*, 1992).

In practice, the managerial skills required to operate in an IJV depend to a considerable degree not only on the organisational politics that surround the venture but also on the level of maturity in the relationship between partners. The competency requirement would be altered by the level of seniority of the appointment and by the new job content. If the appointment is seen as a promotion to a senior position, senior managers would have greater power to innovate and act as change agents (Feldman, 1994).

Indeed Schuler *et al.* (2004: 65) posit that in maximising knowledge flow, sharing and transfer in IJVs, employees should possess the following characteristics:

- openness
- systemic thinking
- creativity
- self-confidence
- empathy.

Socialisation research

Research into the socialisation process for international managers examines the skills that managers need to learn about and cope with in new jobs. A key challenge for international managers is the need to be trusted by other cultural groups. The increased use of international assignments has radically changed the socialisation process in global organisations. A key issue on research on socialisation had been to understand the way in which organisations induct new employees in order to ensure they fit in with organisational demands. More recently, research has focused on the proactive skills and strategies that newcomers need in order to cope in their new environment (Anderson and Thomas, 1997). Research has only recently begun to address the 're-socialisation' of employees as they move through the organisation and change countries of employment. Research has focused on the cross-cultural job transitions made by international managers and their work adjustments (Feldman and Thomas, 1992). This research identifies two specific career-transition problems faced by the international manager: first, international managers face more challenges coping with the social aspect of their role, as they need to build up trust in a foreign culture. Second, due to the lack of a shared organisational culture it is more difficult to interpret and deal with uncertainties in a foreign environment and access to information is more restricted. Socialisation research highlights the importance of:

- information-seeking skills in order to reduce uncertainty
- collecting the required information about social norms as different cultures have different norms associated with the creation of trust.

Research shows that coping strategies are strongly predictive of expatriate adjustment (Feldman and Tompson, 1992).

The selection of international managers in practice

As we briefly discussed above, in practice the majority of international firms continue to rely on technical skills and domestic track record as the most important selection criteria. There are a number of reasons for this:

- the majority of international assignments are concerned with filling a position
- there is the difficulty of identifying and measuring the relevant interpersonal and cross-cultural skills

● selectors will seek to minimise the personal risk involved in selecting a candidate who might fail on the job (Miller, 1972).

Earlier research highlighted the importance of personal recommendations and informal methods for expatriate transfers and the suggestion was that the outcome of selection interviews may often be predetermined before the actual interview (Brewster, 1991). Harris and Brewster (1999) develop this notion of informality in expatriate selection further in an important article 'The coffee-machine system: how international selection really works'. They provide a typology of expatriate selection systems based on the distinction between open and closed systems and formal and informal systems. The closed/informal system was the dominant one used in the UK organisations studied by Harris and Brewster (1999). The typology of selection systems is shown in Table 4.2 and helps to explain variations found in the way expatriate selection is conducted. They show that expatriate selection, in practice, is often an ad-hoc process and they suggest that the selection process can be started through a casual conversation about an assignment between executives chatting around the coffee machine:

'How's it going?'

'Oh, you know, overworked and underpaid.'

'Tell me about it. As well as all the usual stuff, Jimmy in Mumbai has just fallen ill and is being flown home. I've got no idea who we can get over there to pick up the pieces at such short notice. It's driving me crazy.'

'Have you met that Simon on the fifth floor? He is in the same line of work. Very bright and looks like he is going a long way. He was telling me that he and his wife had a great holiday in Goa a couple of years ago. He seems to like India. Could be worth a chat.'

'Hey thanks. I'll check him out.'

'No problem. They don't seem to be able to improve this coffee though, do they?'

(Harris and Brewster, 1999: 497)

It is suggested that the multinational's organisational processes are used to legitimise the decision that has already been taken informally at the coffee machine. There are however several disadvantages of this type of selection system. Not only are candidates not formally evaluated against agreed criteria, but also the pool of potential candidates is highly restricted and in general it reflects a reactive rather than strategic approach to the management of expatriation (Harzing, 2004).

While this work gives some important insights into the selection systems for international managers, it is important not to generalise as selection processes can be influenced by factors such as the maturity of the multinational, its stage in the internationalisation process and its size and industry sector (Dowling and Welch, 2004).

Table 4.2 Harris and Brewster's selection typology

Formal	*Informal*
Open	
● Clearly defined criteria	● Less defined criteria
● Clearly defined measures	● Less defined measures
● Training for selectors	● Limited training for selectors
● Open advertising of vacancy (internal/external)	● No panel discussions
● Panel discussions	● Open advertising of vacancy
	● Recommendations
Closed	● Selectors' individual preferences determine
● Clearly defined criteria	selection criteria
● Clearly defined measures	● No panel discussions
● Training for selectors	● Nominations only (networking/reputation)
● Panel discussions	
● Nominations only (networking/reputation)	

Source: Harris, H. and Brewster, C. (1999) 'The coffee-machine system: how international selection really works', *International Journal of Human Resource Management*, 10: 488–500, http://www.tandf.co.uk

Alternative resourcing approaches

Selection criteria for international managers are changing slowly to reflect changes in the purposes of international assignments. Technology transfer or the establishment of corporate control are still important reasons for international transfers but the growth of international networking forms of organisation means that international managers increasingly need to seek information, negotiate and seek cooperation far more than in a traditional assignment. Selection criteria are shifting slowly from ones based on technical and intelligence related criteria to a wider range of skills and personality and the ability to manage ambiguity is increasingly seen as a core competence for international managers.

Sparrow (1999b) argues that international role specifications now stress that managers must be:

● proactive
● willing to take risks
● action oriented
● constructive
● capable of multidimensional vision
● able to cope with information from many sources
● sensitive to the needs of others
● able to delegate and trust staff
● able to cope with ambiguity and uncertainty.

Are these competencies best developed or selected? Many HR managers doubt the feasibility of developing some of the more sophisticated higher-level international competencies which highlights the critical importance of selection in this context.

Sparrow (1999b) argues that there are tensions between not only the skills and competencies that organisations *think* they should be looking for when they recruit but also the skills and competencies that are *actually needed* to be successful in an international assignment. Three broad alternative resourcing approaches can be identified reflecting the different views about the feasibility of developing international management competencies:

- the traditional psychological approach
- behavioural competency approaches
- clinical risk assessment approach.

The traditional psychological approach

This approach suggests that there are identifiable competencies linked with effective performance in an international assignment and that these can be used to predict effective performers in international positions. Some studies conducted by consulting firms such as Saville and Holdsworth identified the key qualities needed for success in an international role, including the following:

- flexibility
- open-mindedness
- interpersonal sensitivity
- sociability
- strategic thinking and vision
- leadership based on consent
- energy and determination
- intellectual capability
- resilience.

Behavioural competency approaches

Some large consulting groups have researched and promoted their own set of international competencies and some have applied behavioural competency approaches to international recruitment and selection. Some consultancies introduced a focus on 'international mindset' and this competency requires managers to be able to adapt their own behavioural style, have tolerance for the views of others and not allow their own managerial style and values to override the approach of others. This approach reflected the company's wish to build a genuine 'global culture' and not one reflecting its parent country or the dominant Anglo-Saxon model (Sparrow, 1999b).

Clinical risk assessment approach

This approach suggests that the reasons for failure in international assignments are more complex than the cultural adaptability and adjustment of the manager and include factors such as dual career, adaptability of the spouse etc. (Mendenhall and Oddou, 1985). Also, shortages of international management talent often limit the selection context (Scullion, 2001) which is further influenced by recent developments such as the rapid growth of international joint ventures and alliances (Schuler *et al.*, 2004). In other words, the clinical risk approach reflects a critique of the competency approach and suggests that the use of competencies may be:

- too inflexible in the context of international recruitment and selection
- unable to actually predict success
- difficult to measure based on the quality of data available (Sparrow, 1999b).

This critique has led to growing use of cultural adaptability assessments. In this approach, while the role of some important individual attributes are recognised, the assessment of an individual against the relevant criteria is seen as only part of the equation and crucially, not predictive of performance. The management of risk is central to international selection under this approach.

Indeed growing pressures such as downsizing and restructuring on the one hand and growing resistance to international mobility on the other (Scullion and Starkey, 2000) often reduce the range and quality of potential candidates and selection choice becomes more limited. In these circumstances the option of designing the assignment around the individual manager is becoming increasingly attractive, as in the case of NCR whose European HR managers are increasingly moving toward designing the assignment to match the skills of the manager, rather than the reverse (Scullion and Collings, 2005).

Finally, a study of 30 leading UK multinationals (Scullion and Starkey, 2000) highlights the growing importance of using skills databases and tracking systems to manage senior and high potential talent across the organisation. The top 150 to 400 managers worldwide, depending on the size of the company, including all those classed as internationally mobile or potentially mobile, were tracked by the centre and the databases contained much qualitative information on issues such as willingness to move to a particular country, dual career status and information on other soft resourcing issues (Scullion and Starkey, 2000). Having discussed the broad selection strategies that international firms can pursue, the following section will consider the methods which organisations actually use to attract international managers.

Methods of attracting and sourcing international managers

Internal recruitment

The most effective and the most common form of expatriate recruitment seems to be internal recruitment, where the international firm identifies the potential expatriate from within their domestic or foreign operations. For example, Torbiörn (1982) found that 85 per cent of the Swedish companies in his survey had been recruited internally. In a similar vein Hogan and Goodson (1990) reported that all of the Japanese expatriates in their study were recruited internally. Internal recruitment offers a number of advantages to the international firm. These have been summarised by Finn and Morley (2002):

- selectors have personal knowledge of the candidate's personality, skills, and family situation
- the candidate is familiar with the culture and goals of the organisation
- accessing the internal labour market is cost-effective.

In addition, research evidence suggests that internally recruited expatriates adjust more quickly than those recruited externally. For example, Torbiörn (1982) showed that expatriates who are recruited internally normally require up to six months in order to adjust to the new work situation and the new culture, while the typical expatriate recruited externally requires over nine months to adjust. This is similar to the difficulties experienced by inpatriate managers, who not only have to adjust to a different external cultural environment, but also may be newcomers to the organisation and thus may also have to adjust to the organisational culture (Harvey *et al.*, 1999; see also Chapter 8 in this volume).

External recruitment

There are numerous external sources that a selector can recruit from: competitors, suppliers, distributors or customer employees in both the domestic and international market (Finn and Morley, 2002). In this section, we will focus on two activities which are becoming more significant in international recruitment and selection – headhunting and cross-national advertising.

Headhunting

Headhunting is concerned with the targeted recruitment of senior executives and specialists. Clients increasingly expect headhunter firms to offer an integrated global service with no barriers to cross-border business activity. In response to demands from clients to offer an increasingly global service some leading headhunting firms have recently undergone a period of considerable restructuring involving mergers and acquisitions and consolidation (Harris *et al.*, 2003).

A key trend in the headhunting and executive search industry has been the development of partnerships. The major benefit of these partnerships is to allow a much wider geographical sourcing of candidates. Interestingly the highest growth rates for executive search firms have been in the emerging markets such as China, Russia, India and Eastern Europe (Garrison-Jenn, 1998). Also, it has been suggested that up to 50 per cent of executive searches are now cross-border, highlighting the importance of cross-border capability and geographic spread of individual search firms (Harris *et al.*, 2003).

Cross-national advertising

Multinationals are increasingly looking beyond national borders to attract managers and professionals (Scullion and Brewster, 2001) despite the potential high cost of mistakes in global advertising campaigns. Many advertising agencies operate as part of an international network and while trends in advertising vary across sector, there has been a shift away from press advertising to more creative alternatives such as:

* targeted outdoor poster sites
* airport lounges
* journey to work routes
* airline magazines.

As more international managers come into the organisation from a variety of countries it becomes more important for the selection technology which is used to be globally fair and to be seen to be globally fair. International advertising agencies increasingly need to ensure that recruitment campaigns are culturally sensitive in the local markets and need to understand the softer cultural issues such as the wording of adverts and the design of brochures and marketing material (Harris *et al.*, 2003).

Sourcing international managers

In this section, attention will be paid to three of the most important sourcing routes for international managers, namely Internet recruitment, international graduate programmes and the recruitment of host country national managers.

Internet recruitment

Internet recruitment has become a significant source of recruitment for international managers since the mid-1990s (Harris *et al.*, 2003) and has proved most useful for:

* attracting highly qualified graduates
* specialised roles such as international marketing and information technology (IT)
* interim managers.

Advantages of using Internet recruitment include the following:

- broadens the sources of recruitment at low cost
- targets specific sources of graduates such as MBA career centres
- encourages applicants to use more personal search which can attract applicants with a more specialised skills match
- allows a more sophisticated approach by targeting particular lifestyle or culture-fit groups.

Disadvantages of using Internet recruitment include the following:

- a key problem is that some of the data used may be of questionable accuracy
- those who engage with Internet firms may get unwanted calls
- targeting particular populations is often problematic and applications may be received from unexpected sources
- the quality of applications is often more mixed than from traditional methods
- the company brand may not be as well known as assumed
- there will be considerable attention from people who fall outside the target group and are not serious candidates.

Despite these disadvantages the Internet has become one of the fastest growing methods of recruitment for filling senior international manager and technical positions and it is likely that it will become more popular in the future as the Internet spreads to more countries in the less developed world (Harris *et al.*, 2003).

International graduate programmes

The external recruitment of graduates into international roles is another form of international sourcing which has become much more significant since the mid-1990s. Many international firms have attempted to develop an international management career for graduates partly in response to shortages of international managers (Scullion, 2001). Some international companies such as Rolls-Royce and Tesco have attempted to attract graduates by not only using various types of marketing to highlight the international nature of their activities but also offering the prospect of early international experience to target graduates who are specifically seeking an international career (see Box 4.2).

A growing number of UK multinationals have broadened their sources of graduate recruitment to include some continental European countries (Scullion and Brewster, 2001). One example is Scottish and Newcastle International, a leading UK-based international brewing group, which in response to the growing internationalisation of the business is seeking to recruit high potential graduates from across Europe and seeks to integrate them into the core of the organisation. As an international cadre they are expected to develop a loyalty to the group as a whole rather than to any particular function. Initially this trend was stimulated by the growth in competition for high-potential graduates following the advent of the Single European Market. An example

Box 4.2 Recruiting high potential graduates in the textile industry

This type of approach can be illustrated by two leading UK textile companies who had a policy of sending young graduates on international assignments within three to six months of joining the firm. This policy was very effective in recruiting and retaining high potential graduates who were particularly interested in an international career. The corporate HR director of one of the textile companies commented:

Textiles is not a particularly fashionable industry. We are competing for the best graduates with companies that enjoy a more glamorous image. The fact that we can offer the opportunity of very early international experience is the main reason we can attract some high potential graduates when the big guns such as Shell, BP, and ICI are fishing in the same pool.

of this development is two computer firms which introduced Euro-graduate management development programmes, a feature of which was that graduates were recruited from several European countries for a two-year period of training and development in the United Kingdom. On completion of their training, graduates were transferred to a management position in a third country. The need to develop more flexible succession planning systems to support the development of Euro-graduates was identified as a key issue by firms operating this type of programme.

Problems associated with graduate recruitment   Research has identified a number of problems associated with international graduate programmes:

- the programmes are long term in nature and only slowly make an impact on the level and pace of internationalisation
- graduate retention rates may be lower than anticipated
- local subsidiaries may not have the know-how to manage the new recruits
- problems with visa issues
- compensation and benefits for graduates are becoming more complex
- international mobility for graduates is a growing problem.

Many organisations are finding that graduates are more reluctant to move and that quality of life issues and lifestyle issues can be more important than gaining international experience (Scullion, 1994; Sparrow, 1999a).

Recruitment of host country national managers

In general multinational companies staff their subsidiaries – below top management level – with local or host country nationals. Increasingly, the adoption of localisation strategies means that multinationals are seeking to recruit and develop HCN managers for senior management positions in the local subsidiaries. However, despite the considerable attractions of localisation strategy the implementation of this strategy is often difficult and may take many years (see Chapter 7).

Finding, developing and retaining local talent is a major concern for multinationals, particularly in emerging markets where there is often a scarcity of managerial talent (Sparrow *et al.*, 2004). Indeed the process of global leadership development increasingly begins with the selection of high potentials who senior management identify as having the potential to become future leaders of the company (Black *et al.*, 1999).

The recruitment of host country managers is difficult for a number of reasons:

- lack of image in the foreign market
- lack of knowledge of local labour markets
- ignorance of the local education system
- lack of knowledge of the status of qualifications
- language and cultural problems at interviews
- trying to transfer recruitment methods which work well in the home country to foreign countries
- trying to recruit to a formal set of criteria when flexibility is required.

(Scullion, 1994, 2001)

For example, Wrigley, the US-based confectionery group, learned that it had to relax its strict formal recruitment criteria when recruiting in the emerging markets of Russia and Eastern Europe. The managers at the European headquarters of Wrigley who were responsible for developing these markets soon realised that they had to largely abandon the strict recruitment criteria they operated with in Germany and the United Kingdom and operate much more flexibly in the emerging markets. Many international firms have tended to neglect the training and development needs of their host country managers and focus virtually all of their management development efforts on their PCN managers (Scullion, 1994). However, some research suggests that a good reputation for training and skill development can enhance recruitment, particularly in emerging markets. It is also suggested that when seeking to recruit high potential managers international firms should emphasise their localisation strategy and link their plans for localisation to the career prospects of local managers (Evans *et al.*, 2002). This was a strategy successfully employed by Scottish and Newcastle International, a UK-headquartered drinks group, when developing its international business activities in Eastern Europe and Russia.

Methods of selecting international managers

This section examines to what extent assessment centres and psychological testing – two of the most important selection techniques – can be adapted for use in the international context to take account of cross-cultural differences.

Psychological testing

Until recently psychological testing for selection was used rather infrequently by multinational companies (Brewster, 1991; Enderwick and Hodgson, 1993). More recently there has been a growth in their use for three reasons:

- the more rapid pace of internationalisation
- the internationalisation of education
- the increased mobility of international managers.

This increase in cross-cultural assessments conducted by multinationals, however, poses some difficult questions:

- Can organisations use psychological tests fairly in multicultural settings?
- Can psychological tests be developed which are 'culture-free' or 'culture-fair'?
- Can the psychometric properties of tests be adapted to different cultural groups?

(Sparrow, 1999b)

In practice the use of psychological tests has become an increasing problem in international selection for several reasons:

- in order to benchmark global manager candidates multinationals extend beyond their normal recruitment field
- many test publishers are global and sell tests to a large number of countries
- psychological tests may be seen as a way of avoiding the subjective bias of other options such as interviews
- the demand for tests in a wider range of countries has increased due to the greater international mobility of managers.

(Harris *et al.*, 2003)

Are psychological tests transferable across cultures?

As noted above a key question with regard to psychological testing is the transferability of tests across cultures. In this context, research suggests that only a minority of the tests available in most countries have been checked for suitability in cross-cultural assessment and that even the most sophisticated tests are not seen as totally culture free (Poortinga and Malpass, 1988). For example, Willis (1984) argues that most of the relevant tests have been devised in the United States and, therefore, may not be culture-free. Van de Vijver (1998) argues that the costs of cultural bias in psychology tests do not lie mainly in the reduced performance of the candidates. Rather the problem is one of fairness. For example, candidates whose poor English limits their test performance may find that they do not progress as well through the internal selection systems. More generally, the internationalisation of psychological testing has led to concerns about the ethicality and fairness of using psychological tests across cultures (Dowling and Welch, 2004).

Also, the different pattern of usage of psychological tests across countries should be highlighted. Marx (1996) found that under 5 per cent of the German companies in her survey used such tests compared with just over 15 per cent in UK firms. A major survey (Price Waterhouse, 1997) highlighted that only 12 per cent of firms used assessment centres and suggested that in practice traditional selection methods such as interviews were still the ones most commonly used. Gertsen (1989) argues that the use of personality traits to predict intercultural competence is further complicated by the fact that personality traits are not defined and evaluated in the same way in different cultures.

Assessment centres

Assessment centres are surprisingly rarely used in the selection of international managers (Mendenhall et al., 1987), but where they are used they can enable selectors to test the individual's suitability to become a successful international manager and they offer selectors a number of advantages. Role plays, orientation exercises, simulation exercises and discussions (traditionally part of assessment centres) can help selectors eliminate candidates who have poor communication or listening skills, or those who fail to show cultural empathy or flexibility (Finn and Morley, 2002). Organisations which utilise advanced recruitment methods such as assessment centres face significant problems similar to organisations using more traditional methods. For example, western managers will require training in cross-cultural awareness when conducting interviews in Asian countries. Bognanno and Sparrow's (1995) case study which examined the introduction of BP's corporate-wide competencies programme in the early 1990s highlighted that while management competencies were transferable in terms of expressed purpose and key outputs, the specific behavioural indicators used to evidence each competency needed adjustment to reflect cultural norms.

A key challenge for selectors is to adapt assessment centres to the local environment. There is a need for flexibility and adaptability as opposed to having too much structure and to customise the process in major subsidiary operations. For many organisations retention of graduates and high potential managers is a critical HR issue and growing attention is being paid to assessing whether graduates fit into the new culture or country of operation (Chao, 1997).

Conclusion

In this chapter we have discussed the debate around expatriate failure and adjustment which we argued was an important area in international recruitment and selection because the high costs of failure in international assignments in both economic and human terms highlighted the importance of effective recruitment and selection. We then discussed the core competencies required by the global manager and considered the three main research streams which have contributed to our knowledge in this area. We then examined three broad alternative approaches to resourcing, and further evaluated some important methods which international companies use to source and attract international managers, with a particular focus on the extent selection techniques could be adapted for use in the international context. An important concluding comment however is that for international recruitment and selection to be truly effective in MNCs, it must be supported by other congruent HR policies and practices which support the strategic objective of the assignment, such as appropriate appraisal and compensation polices (see the companion text by Milkovich in the *Global HRM Series*), the provision of cross-cultural training (see Chapter 6 of the current volume) and repatriation policies (see Chapter 10 of the current volume).

References

Abe, H. and Wiseman, R.L. (1983) 'A cross-cultural confirmation of the dimensions of intercultural effectiveness', *International Journal of International Relations*, 7: 53–67.

Anderson, B.A. (2005) 'Expatriate selection: good management or good luck?' *International Journal of Human Resource Management*, 16(4): 567–83.

Anderson, N. and Thomas, H.D.C. (1997) 'Work group socialisation', in M. West (ed.) *Handbook of Work Groups*, Chichester: Wiley.

Barham, K. and Wills, S. (1992) *Managing across Frontiers*, Ashridge: Ashridge Management Centre.

Baruch, Y. (2004) *Managing Careers: Theory and Practice*, Harrow: FT-Prentice Hall Pearson Education.

Björkman, I. and Gertsen, M. (1990) 'Corporate expatriation: an empirical study of Scandinavian firms,' in *Proceedings of the Third Symposium on Cross-cultural Consumer and Business Studies*, Honolulu, HI, December.

Black, J.S., Mendenhall, M. and Oddou, G. (1991) 'Toward a comprehensive model of international adjustment: an integration of multiple theoretical perspectives', *Academy of Management Review* 16(2): 291–317.

Black, J.S., Gregerson, H.B. and Mendenhall, M.E. (1992) Global Assignments: Successfully Expatriating and Repatriating International Managers, San Francisco, CA: Jossey-Bass.

Black, J.S., Gregerson, H.B., Mendenhall, M.E. and Stroh, L.K. (1999) *Globalizing People through International Assignments*, New York: Addison-Wesley-Longman.

Bognanno, M. and Sparrow, P.R. (1995) 'Integrating HRM strategy using culturally-defined competencies at British Petroleum: cross-cultural implementation issues', in J.M. Hiltrop and P.R. Sparrow (eds) *European Casebook on Human Resource and Change Management*, London: Prentice-Hall.

Brewster, C. (1991) *The Management of Expatriates*, London: Kogan Page.

Brewster, C. and Pickard, J. (1994) 'Evaluating expatriate training', *International Studies of Management and Organisation*, 24(3): 18–35.

Brewster, C. and Scullion, H. (1997) 'A review and an agenda for expatriate research', *Human Resource Management Journal*, 7(3): 32–41.

Briscoe, D. and Schuler, R. (2004) *International Human Resource Management*, London and New York: Routledge.

Chao, G.T. (1997) 'Complexities in international organisation socialisation', *International Journal of Selection and Assessment*, 5(1): 9–13.

Coyle, W. and Shortland, S. (1992) *International Relocation*, Oxford: Butterworth-Heinemann.

Dowling, P.J. and Welch, D. (1988) 'International human resource management: an Australian perspective', *Asia Pacific Journal of Management*, 6(1): 39–65.

Dowling, P.J. and Welch, D.E. (2004) *International Human Resource Management: Managing People in an Multinational Context*, London: Thomson Learning.

Dowling, P.J., Schuler, R.S. and Welch, D.E. (1994) *International Dimensions of Human Resource Management*, 2nd edn, Belmont, CA: Wadsworth.

Enderwick, P. and Hodgson, D. (1993) 'Expatriate management practices of New Zealand business', *International Journal of Human Resource Management*, 4(2): 407–25.

Evans, P., Pucik, V. and Barsoux, J.L. (2002) *The Global Challenge: Frameworks for International Human Resource Management*, Chicago: McGraw-Hill Irwin.

Feldman, D.C. (1994) 'Who's socialising whom? The impact of socialisation of newcomers on insiders, work groups and organisation', *Human Resource Management Review*, 4: 213–33.

Feldman, D.C. and Thomas, D.C. (1992) 'Career management issues facing expatriates', *Journal of International Business Studies*, 23: 271–93.

Feldman, D.C. and Tompson, H.B. (1992) 'Entry shock, culture shock: socialising the new breed of global managers', *Human Resource Management*, 31: 345–62.

Finn, G. and Morley, M. (2002) 'Expatriate selection: the case of an Irish MNC', in M. Linehan, M. Morley and J. Walsh (eds) *International Human Resource Management and Expatriate Transfers: Irish Experiences*, Dublin: Oak Tree Press.

Forster, N. (2000) 'The myth of the "international manager"', *International Journal of Human Resource Management*, 11(1): 126–42.

Furnham, A. (1990) 'Expatriate stress: the problems of living abroad', in S. Fisher and C. Cooper (eds) *On the Move: The Psychology of Change and Transition*, London: Wiley.

Garrison-Jenn, N. (1998) *The Global 200 Executive Recruiters*, San Francisco, CA: Jossey-Bass.

Gertsen, M. (1989) 'Expatriate selection and training', in R. Luostarinen (ed.) *Findings of the Fifteenth Annual Conference of the European International Business Association*, Helsinki, December.

GMAC Global Relocations Services (2003) *Global Relocation Trends: 2002 Survey Report*, Warren, NJ: GMAC.

Harris, H. and Brewster, C. (1999) 'The coffee-machine system: how international selection really works', *International Journal of Human Resource Management*, 10(3): 488–500.

Harris, H., Brewster, C. and Sparrow, P. (2003) *International Human Resource Management*, London: Chartered Institute of Personnel and Development.

Harris, P.R. and Moran, R.T. (1996) *Managing Cultural Differences*, 4th edn, Houston, TX: Gulf.

Harvey, M., Novicevic, M. and Speier, C. (1999) 'Inpatriate managers: how to increase the probability of success', *Human Resource Management Review*, 9: 51–82.

Harzing, A.W.K. (1995) 'The persistent myth of high expatriate failure rates', International Journal of Human Resource Management, 6(2): 457–75.

Harzing, A.W.K. (2002) 'Are our referencing errors undermining our scholarship and credibility? The case of expatriate failure rates', *Journal of Organizational Behaviour*, 23(1): 127–48.

Harzing, A.W.K. (2004) 'Composing an international staff', in A.W.K. Harzing and J. Van Ruysseveldt (eds) *International Human Resource Management*, London: Sage.

Hays, R.D. (1971) 'Ascribed behaviour determinants of success-failure among US expatriate managers', *Journal of International Business Studies*, 2: 40–6.

Hays, R. (1974) 'Expatriate selection: ensuring success and avoiding failure', *Journal of International Business Studies*, 5(1): 25–37.

Hogan, G. and Goodson, J. (1990) 'The key to expatriate success', *Training and Development Journal*, January: 50–2.

Jordan, J. and Cartwright, S. (1998) 'Selecting expatriate managers: key traits and competencies', *Leadership and Organization Development Journal*, 19(2): 89–96.

Marx, E. (1996) *International Human Resource Practices in Britain and Germany*, London: Anglo-German Foundation.

Mendenhall, M. and Oddou, G. (1985) 'The dimensions of expatriate acculturation: a review', *Academy of Management Review*, 10(1): 39–47.

Mendenhall, M.E. and Oddou, G. (1988) 'The overseas assignment: a practical look', *Business Horizons*, September–October: 78–84.

Mendenhall, M.E., Dunbar, E. and Oddou, G.R. (1987) 'Expatriate selection, training and career pathing: a review and critique', *Human Resource Management*, 26: 331–45.

Milkovich, G.T. (forthcoming) *Global Compensation*, London: Routledge.

Miller, E. (1972) 'The selection decision for an international assignment: a study of the decision-makers' behaviour', *Journal of International Business Studies*, 3: 49–65.

Organizational Resource Counselors (ORC) (2002) *Dual Careers and International Assignments Survey Report*, Washington, DC: ORC.

Pattison, J.E. (1990) *Acquiring the Future*, Homewood, IL: Dow Jones-Irwin.

Poortinga, Y.H. and Malpass, R.S. (1988) 'Making inferences from cross-cultural data', in W.J. Lonner and J.W. Berry (eds) *Field Methods in Cross-cultural Research*, Beverly Hills, CA: Sage.

Price Waterhouse (1997) *International Assignments: European Policy and Practice 1997/1998*. Price Waterhouse.

Schuler, R., Jackson, S. and Luo, Y. (2004) *Managing Human Resources in Cross-Border Alliances*, London and New York: Routledge.

Scullion, H. (1994) 'Staffing policies and strategic control in multinationals', *International Studies of Management and Organisation*, 3(4): 86–104.

Scullion, H. (2001) 'International human resource management', in J. Storey (ed.) *Human Resource Management*, London: International Thomson.

Scullion, H. and Brewster, C. (2001) 'The management of expatriates: messages from Europe', *Journal of World Business*, 36(4): 346–65.

Scullion, H. and Collings, D. (2005) 'The changing nature of international assignments', unpublished Working Paper, SIBU, Glasgow.

Scullion, H. and Starkey, K. (2000) 'In search of the changing role of the corporate human resource function in the international firm', *International Journal of Human Resource Management*, 11(6): 1061–81.

Shaffer, M.S., Harrison, D.A. and Gilley, K.M. (1999) 'Dimensions, determinants and differences in the expatriate adjustment process', *Journal of International Business Studies*, 30(3): 557–81.

Smith, M. (1989) 'Selection in high risk and stressful occupations', in P. Heriot (ed.) *Assessment and Selection in Organisations*, Chichester: Wiley.

Sparrow, P. (1999a) *The IPD Guide on International Recruitment, Selection and Assessment*, London: Institute of Personnel and Development.

Sparrow, P. (1999b) 'International recruitment, selection and assessment', in P. Joynt and B. Morton (eds) *The Global HR Manager: Creating the Seamless Organization*, London: Institute of Personnel and Development.

Sparrow, P. and Hiltrop, J-M. (1994) *European Human Resource Management in Transition*, London: Prentice Hall.

Sparrow, P., Brewster, C. and Harris, H. (2004) *Globalizing Human Resource Management*, London and New York: Routledge

Stahl, G. (1998) 'Development of an assessment center to select managers for international assignments', Twenty-fourth International Congress of Applied Psychology, San Francisco, CA, 9–14 August.

Torbiörn, I. (1982) *Living Abroad: Personal Adjustment and Personnel Policy in the Overseas Setting*, New York: Wiley.

Tung, R.L. (1981) 'Selection and training of personnel for overseas assignments', *Columbia Journal of World Business*, 16(1): 68–78.

Tung, R.L. (1982) 'Selection and training procedures of U.S., European and Japanese multinationals', *California Management Review*, 25(1): 57–71.

Tung, R.L. (1984) 'Human resource planning in Japanese multinationals: a model for US firms?' *Journal of International Business Studies*, 15(2): 139–49.

Van de Vijver, F.J.R. (1998) 'Cross-cultural assessment: value for money?' International Association of Applied Psychology, San Francisco, CA, August.

Willis, H.L. (1984) 'Selection for employment in developing countries', *Personnel Administrator* 29(7): 55.

5

International talent management

HUGH SCULLION AND DAVID G. COLLINGS

Introduction

Shortages of international managers are becoming an increasing problem for
multinational companies, and these shortages of international management talent are
increasingly constraining the implementation of international strategies. In recent years
a growing number of international firms have introduced talent management initiatives
which often include leadership development, short-term assignments, high potential
development, executive coaching and a range international opportunities. In this chapter
the following issues will be addressed:

- the reasons for the shortages of international management and the emergence
  of international talent management as a strategic response to this problem
- the key staffing issues which act as strategic constraints on the multinational
  company's ability to develop an adequate pool of global managers.
- the corporate HR role in managing and developing international management talent
  in different types of international firm
- the key challenges of developing transnational managers
- assessing the key competencies required of the HR function in the global firm and the
  competencies required of the international HR specialist in the future
- assessing the notion of the global-mindset.

As multinational companies have become increasingly important players in the global
economy and the effective management of human resources is increasingly being
recognised as a major determinant of success or failure in international business (Stroh
and Caligiuri, 1998), there has been a rapid growth of research on the strategies and
management practices of these firms. In particular the theoretical and empirical linkages
between HRM and strategy in the international context are increasingly being explored
by researchers. Some emerging literature (e.g. De Cieri and Dowling, 1999; Schuler
et al., 1993) not only recognises the MNC's need to balance the pressures for integration
with the pressures for local responsiveness (Doz and Prahalad, 1986) but also suggests
that, at the international level, the firm's strategic choices impose constraints or limits on
the range of international HRM options (Schuler *et al.*, 2002).

Leading strategy researchers have highlighted the neglect of implementation issues which are becoming increasingly problematic for many MNCs (Bartlett and Ghoshal 1998; Evans *et al.*, 2002). Indeed they suggested that many multinationals have less difficulty determining which strategies to pursue than how to implement them, and that the success of any global or transnational strategy has less to do with structural innovations than developing very different organisational cultures (Bartlett and Ghoshal, 1998). Research highlights the growing importance of staffing issues, particularly the problem of shortages of international managers on the effective implementation of international business strategies and it is argued that staffing issues will grow in significance as a result of the rapid growth of the emerging markets which has resulted in an increasing need for managers with distinctive competencies and a desire to manage in these culturally and economically distant countries (Collings and Scullion, 2005). The 'war for talent' means there is greater competition between MNCs for managers with the context-specific knowledge of how to do business successfully in such countries (Harvey *et al.*, 1999b).

Similarly research suggests that growing awareness of implementation problems in the rapidly increasing number of strategic alliances and cross-border mergers and acquisitions has further increased the strategic importance of staffing and talent management (Schuler *et al.*, 2004), particularly as the context of strategic alliances and global business is increasingly shifting from formal, developed and mature markets to informal, emerging and culturally distant markets (Doz and Hamel, 1998). There is a growing recognition that the success of international alliances depends most importantly on the quality of the management in the combined venture and learning, knowledge-acquisition and adaptation have been identified as important potential sources of competitive advantage (Björkman and Xiucheng, 2002; Schuler *et al.*, 2004). It has been argued that global organisational learning is driven by teamwork across borders and a willingness to tap into the potential of local managers (Pucik, 1992). In addition there is a growing recognition that, increasingly, the source of advantage for multinational firms is derived from the firm's ability to create, transfer and integrate knowledge across borders (Kogut and Zander, 1992; Mudambi, 2002). In the following section we seek to explain the reasons for the shortages of international managers and the key challenges faced by international firms who seek to develop a pool of global managers.

Constraints on the supply of international managers

This section will discuss some of the major challenges and constraints faced by international firms who seek to develop a pool of global managers. It will highlight the strategic importance of these constraints in relation to the implementation of global strategies. In this context, we consider issues regarding the international development of local managers, the low participation of women in international management, and constraints on the supply of international managers due to repatriation problems and barriers to international mobility. These issues are becoming more significant as shortages of 'international managers' are emerging as an increasing problem for many international firms and often constrain the implementation of global strategies (Gregerson *et al.*, 1998; Scullion, 1992, 1994). The McKinsey report (Chambers *et al.* 1998) – 'The War for Talent' – highlighted the significance of the issue of talent management and suggested that while the drive to attract and retain individual talent had emerged at the height of the economic boom it had now become a key strategic issue for senior management in many companies. In this section we identify and discuss some of the major constraints on the supply of international managers.

Limitations of the localisation process

Many MNCs have focused most of their management development efforts on their parent country national managers and have continued to neglect the development of their host country national managers (Dowling *et al.*, 1999). More recently researchers have suggested a number of important strategies for MNCs who are seeking to develop host country national managers (Scullion and Brewster, 2001) the most important of which is the need to utilise to a greater extent the practice of inpatriation (see Chapter 8 in this volume). It has been argued that this type of international transfer exposes host country nationals to the headquarters' corporate culture and facilitates both the development of a corporate perspective and global teams (Harvey *et al.*, 1999a). More generally, localisation, which can be taken to mean systematic investment in the recruitment, development and retention of local employees (Evans *et al.*, 2002), has become an important element in the globalisation strategy of many multinational companies. However, there is often a difference between the rhetoric and the reality of localisation and in practice progress is often slower than anticipated (Evans *et al.*, 2002). Research suggests there are a number of significant barriers to the implementation of the localisation strategy (see Chapter 7 of this volume for greater detail on localisation). First, finding and developing host country managers may be very difficult, particularly in emerging markets where there may be acute shortages of management talent (Harvey *et al.*, 1999b). Second, retaining local talent is increasingly becoming a major problem for multinationals as host country managers who receive training and development are very attractive to other multinationals and local organisations and there is often competition for their services (Black *et al.*, 1999). Third, many expatriates do not have the commitment to localisation nor possess the mentoring and coaching competences necessary to ensure effective implementation of the localisation process (Evans *et al.*, 2002).

The continued underrepresentation of women in international management

Despite the growing shortages of international managers (Scullion, 2001), the evidence suggests that the participation of women in international management remains relatively low (Adler, 2002). While there has been significant growth in female expatriates since the 1980s (e.g. 14 per cent of expatriates were female in the 2002 ORC survey compared to 5 per cent in 1992 ORC survey), women still remain significantly underrepresented in international management (Taylor *et al.*, 2002). Linehan's (2000) empirical research highlights that while organisations may be prepared to promote women through their domestic management hierarchy, far fewer women are given opportunities to expand their career horizons through access to international careers. The lack of willingness to recruit and develop women as international managers is of some concern as research conducted on the outcome of women's global assignments has indicated that female expatriates are generally successful in their global assignments (Napier and Taylor, 2002). As global competition intensifies, competition for global leaders to manage overseas operations will steadily intensify and MNCs must develop new ways to identify, attract and retain new pools of international executive talent (Black *et al.*, 2000; Mayrhofer and Scullion, 2002). Linehan and Scullion's (2002) research indicates that important formal and informal barriers remain to increasing women's participation in international management. An important informal barrier for women in international management is the lack of networking facilities. They argue that the exclusion of females from male networking groups perpetuates the more exclusively male customs, traditions and negative attitudes towards female international managers and they identify the detrimental effects of these covert barriers which include blocked promotion, blocked career development, occupational stress and lower salaries. They also suggest that corporate or organisational barriers are especially embedded in the managerial processes of traditional industries, with the newer, faster moving industries such as electronics, software and e-commerce affording women greater opportunity for career progression. Finally, recent research suggests that the dual career issue may prove to be a greater barrier for female mobility as males are more reluctant to accompany their spouse/partner (Linehan, 2005). (For a more detailed discussion of staffing issues related to women in international management see Chapter 9 of this volume.)

Ineffective repatriation policies and practices

The third area which impacts on the supply of international managers is the failure by many companies to systematically address repatriation problems. Repatriation has been identified as a major international HRM problem for multinational companies in Europe and North America (Black and Gregerson, 1999; Scullion, 1992; Stroh *et al.*, 1998). Further, it has been argued that the failure by many companies to address concerns over repatriation impacts adversely on the supply of international managers. There is growing recognition that where companies are seen to deal unsympathetically with the problems faced by expatriates on re-entry, especially concerns about losing out on opportunities at home, managers will be more reluctant to accept the offer of international assignments (Scullion, 2001). North American research indicates that 20 per cent of all managers who complete foreign assignments wish to leave their company on return (Adler, 1986). Yet while it is generally accepted that retention of expatriates is a growing problem and that the costs of expatriate turnover are considerable (Dowling and Welch, 2004), many international firms have failed to develop repatriation policies or programmes designed to assist the career progression of the expatriate (Black *et al.* 2000).

Since the early 1990s, the repatriation problem has become more acute for many European MNCs because internationalisation had often taken place at the same time as downsizing of the domestic business, which reduced opportunities for expatriate managers on re-entry (Scullion, 1994). Also, empirical research has indicated that managing repatriation was more problematic in the decentralised multinationals due to the weaker influence of the corporate HR function and the less well developed career and succession planning systems (Scullion and Starkey, 2000). Empirical studies confirm that many firms continue to adopt an ad-hoc approach to repatriation and that many expatriate managers continue to experience the repatriation process as falling far short of expectations, and suggest the need for MNCs to develop a more strategic approach to repatriation and international career management (Stroh *et al.*, 1998). For MNCs this approach is becoming increasingly necessary in order to retain valuable employees and to encourage the acceptance of international positions (Forster, 2000). (See Chapter 10 of this volume for greater detail on the issues surrounding repatriation.)

Barriers to international mobility

The demand for expatriates is increasing steadily while the availability of people who are willing to accept global assignments is not increasing at the same rate (Adler, 2002; Caligiuri and Cascio, 1998). For many MNCs finding the required numbers of people with the desired competencies for international assignments is a major challenge (Gupta and Govindarajan, 2002; Schuler *et al.*, 2004). Research suggests that growing barriers to international mobility are emerging as a major constraint on the ability of MNCs to implement their internationalisation strategies. For example, Scullion's (2001) review indicated that international mobility was becoming more problematic in many firms due to several factors, including, uncertainties associated with re-entry, the growing unwillingness to disrupt the education of children, the growing importance of quality of life considerations and finally, continued uncertainty regarding international terrorism and political unrest.

Dual-career and family issues

There is some evidence to suggest that families are less willing to accept the disruption of personal and social lives associated with international assignments than was the case in the past (Forster, 2000). In addition, dual career problems and disruption to children's education are seen as major barriers to future international mobility in many different countries and pose considerable restrictions on the career development plans of multinationals (Harvey, 1998; Mayrhofer and Scullion, 2002).

Research highlights that the increase in the numbers of dual-career couples is a worldwide trend which is posing a major dilemma for both multinationals and employees alike. Some of the key problems facing dual-career couples in international transfers have been highlighted by Harvey (1998):

- potential negative impact on the expatriate's career path
- the trailing spouse having to abandon his/her career
- the expatriate commuting between home and host countries in order to try to maintain both careers
- inability to maintain the trailing spouse's income during expatriation
- potential candidates for expatriation refusing to relocate due to dual-career family considerations.

This final point suggests that the growth of dual-career couples combined with the ageing population and other family-related factors combine to make more people less mobile. Employees nowadays are much less reluctant to cite family issues and concerns as the reason for the refusal of international assignments, reflecting the growing influence of non-work factors such as family and quality of life issues in relation to employment issues (Dowling and Welch, 2004).

Indeed, global surveys on international assignments have highlighted that dual-career/spousal issues were the most commonly cited reasons for rejecting international assignments reported by North American and European firms (ORC, 2002; GMAC, 2000). In contrast, concern for ageing parents and children were the major barrier to the acceptance of international assignments in Asian firms (ORC Worldwide). Dowling and Welch (2004) highlight a number of implications of this trend for MNCs:

- MNCs are increasingly required to select from a diminishing pool of candidates who may be less qualified.
- MNCs are being increasingly required to use more third country nationals.
- Staff availability emerges as a key factor in expatriate selection criteria.
- Career orientation not only affects the couple's willingness to move but also may negatively affect performance and retention in the foreign location.

Dowling and Welch (2004) argue that some MNCs are seeking to overcome the constraints on international mobility arising from dual-career and spousal issues through two distinctive approaches:

- developing alternative forms of international working (see Chapter 8)
- introducing dual-career or 'family friendly' assignment policies which are discussed below.

Employment search assistance

Through the payment of employment agency fees, the provision of career counselling and advice on the local labour market the multinational seeks to support the partner/spouse with employment search in the host country. Increasingly some MNCs offer a 'look-see' visit to the host location for the family as well as the expatriate (Brewster and Scullion, 1997). A recent global survey indicated that one-fifth of all responding firms offered employment search assistance for partners/spouses and that just over one-sixth of firms paid employment agency fees for spouses (GMAC, 2002).

Career development support

Many leading multinationals such as Unilever and Motorola have dual career policies which offer financial support to support career development activities to assist partners/spouses to find acceptable employment in the host country. While there is considerable variation in the range of activities which may be included by different companies, since the mid-1990s it has been increasingly common for large MNCs to make lump sum payment for education expenses (payment for particular courses) and in addition, to pay for seminar attendance, language training and professional fees.

Multinational company networking

Multinationals often seek to place the partner/spouse with another multinational operating in the same host location. For example, a UK multinational may develop informal arrangements with a French multinational operating in Bangalore, India which involves them in seeking to find employment for each other's respective partners. Also, companies such as Rolls-Royce, BT and Scottish and Newcastle International have developed arrangements with joint venture partners to employ partners/spouses.

Intra-company employment

This approach involves sending the dual-career couple to the same foreign subsidiary. This seems like a straightforward solution but can be problematic as both companies and dual-career couples often have considerable reservations about it. Dual-career arrangements which involve couples working in the same subsidiary where the partner reports directly to the spouse needs careful monitoring as this may create considerable tensions and HR problems.

A global survey indicated that education and career development assistance was provided by just over one-third of the responding firms (GMAC, 2002). The provision of other assistance to partners/spouses aims to:

- establish contacts and networks in the host market
- to compensate for the loss of income of the partner/spouse
- to maintain and develop skills so that the spouse may find work on re-entry into the home country.

Dowling and Welch (2004) argue that such proactive attempts by MNCs can assist them overcome this significant barrier to international mobility. And, while they are cautious about assessing the effectiveness of such schemes in overcoming the dual-career barrier, they point to the considerable growth in companies including provisions for expatriate spouses which increased from one-quarter in the GRS 1999 survey to 56 per cent in the 2002 GRS survey. They conclude that more multinationals are now more committed to addressing the dual career issue and to seeking creative solutions.

International talent management and the role of the corporate HR function

Scullion and Starkey (2000) have highlighted that relatively little attention has been paid to the role of the corporate HR function in the international firm and that considerable variation existed across Europe and the United States on the perceived role of the formation of HR in corporate strategy. Some have suggested that the HR function remains low in influence relative to other major functions (Kochan *et al.*, 1992), while others have argued that the status of HR has increased due to the perception that its contribution to business performance has increased (Schuler *et al.*, 2002). Few would disagree with the summary of Hunt and Boxall (1998: 770): 'While there is some divergence of opinion, the dominant view in the international literature is that HR specialists, senior or otherwise, are not typically key players in the development of corporate strategy.'

Similarly the earlier case study work on the role of the corporate HR function research suggested that the role was being reduced due to the trend towards decentralisation (Purcell, 1985), while other studies suggested that the tendency for corporate HR role be downgraded was far from universal (Sisson and Scullion, 1985). Further research argued that corporate HR managers were playing more of a monitoring and control function as a result of the shift to a decentralised approach (Purcell and Ahlstrand, 1994), and that the corporate HR function was itself being downsized as some functions such as recruitment were increasingly being outsourced (Paauwe, 1996). A major weakness of these studies was the failure to consider the impact of the internationalisation of business on corporate HR roles. Scullion and Starkey (2000), however, directly addressed this question through an empirical study of 30 UK MNCs focused on the role of the corporate HR function specifically in the context of the international firm.

Previous research had highlighted that the corporate centre has developed the ability to manage the process of integration in the international firm. Ghoshal and Gratton (2002) showed that this process has four key components:

- operational integration through standardised technology
- intellectual integration through the creation of a shared knowledge base
- social integration through the creation of collective bonds of performance
- emotional integration through a sense of shared identity and meaning.

Scullion and Starkey's (2000) research added another key integration role – the *strategic management of international management talent* (Harris *et al.*, 2003). Scullion and Starkey (2000) demonstrated that a key integration role for the corporate HR function in the international firm was the strategic management of talent on an international basis. Their work highlighted the importance of attracting, retaining, motivating and developing talent more systematically on a global basis and showed that the management of staff identified as strategic human resources was seen as vital to the future success of the international business. In summarising the talent management role of the corporate HR function in the international firm Scullion and Starkey (2000: 1065) concluded that:

> There is a growing recognition that the success of international business depends most importantly on the quality of top executive talent and how effectively these critical resources are managed and developed.

A further key conclusion from Scullion and Starkey's (2000) research was that international talent management was important in both centralised and decentralised companies, but that the approach varied in significant ways in different types of firm. They identified three distinctive groups of companies: centralised HR companies, decentralised HR companies and transition HR companies and the contrasting approaches to talent management in each are discussed below.

Centralised HR companies

The first group comprised ten companies which all operated in a large number of countries and were characterised by a high degree of coordination and integration of their foreign operations. The large corporate HR staffs exercised control over the careers and mobility of senior management positions and high potentials worldwide. Scullion and Starkey (2000) argue that in the global firms the greater degree of central support for international talent management reflected an increasingly strategic role for the corporate HR function. One indicator of the integration of the global talent management system was that international assignments were increasingly linked to the organisational and career development process and the management development function became increasingly important for developing high potential local talent. In particular, the practice of inpatriation, that is developing local talent through developmental transfers to corporate HQ (see Chapter 8 of this volume) was becoming increasingly important in the global firms (Harvey *et al.*, 1999a). This trend toward identifying potential from the local ranks through decentralising the responsibility for recruitment to the local subsidiaries (who seek to recruit not just for jobs but also for potential) reflects the emergence of a global staffing function in MNCs (Evans *et al.*, 2002). A corporate management development director of a global pharmaceutical company outlined the advantage of this approach:

> The co-ordination of the mobility of senior managers internationally and a monitoring role for the international transfer of high potential managers allows the centre to influence expatriate mobility in the long term strategic interests of the business as a whole.
>
> (cited in Scullion and Starkey, 2000: 1068)

The decentralised companies

This group of sixteen MNCs (comprising five service MNCs and eleven manufacturing) operated with a decentralised or highly decentralised approach. These companies tended to have a smaller number of corporate HR managers responsible for a more limited range of activities than their counterparts in the first group. The problem of shortages of international managers was more acute in the decentralised companies and some of these firms have experienced problems in graduate recruitment due to the lack of a strong corporate image. However, a key finding of the research in terms of the approach to talent management was that two-thirds of the decentralised companies reported an *increased* influence of central HR over the management of top management and senior expatriates in the previous five years. Why? The need for greater coordination and integration associated with globalisation led to a shift away from the highly decentralised approach of the early 1990s (Storey *et al.*, 1997). This was reflected in their approach to international talent management and resulted in significant efforts by the centre to establish and maintain control over the careers and mobility of expatriates. However, while the identification of high potential local talent was becoming a growing consideration for a number of decentralised companies who were globalising, attempts to coordinate and control the mobility and careers of high potential staff was more fragmented, at an earlier stage and more limited than in the global companies. Also, the coordination of international talent management initiatives and international transfers of managers in the highly decentralised businesses was more problematic due to greater tensions between the short term needs of the operating companies and the long term strategic management development needs of the business.

The HR director of a leading engineering multinational commented on these tensions:

> concerns over repatriation are particularly acute in the manufacturing companies because ongoing rationalization of domestic operations had reduced the number of positions available in the domestic organization. Also, due to the decentralized philosophy it is more difficult for the centre to persuade the operating companies to employ expatriate managers

at the end of their assignments for the greater good of the company [.] it is not impossible, however, and we are gradually seeing more influence exerted by the centre in this area.

(cited in Scullion and Starkey, 2000: 1071)

Scullion and Starkey (2000) highlight the increasing use of informal and subtle management processes by corporate HR to introduce a degree of corporate integration into the decentralised firm. In this context Bartlett and Ghoshal (1989) refer to the necessity of creating a matrix in the mindset of managers in order to deal effectively with all the diversity and complexity involved in managing a transnational organisation. Paauwe and Deuwe (1995: 68–9) address the question of how this can be achieved, and argue that the socialisation of managers in key positions (at headquarters and subsidiaries) is crucial. They argue that cultural transformation is needed in order to achieve socialisation and normative integration and suggest a number of methods to help achieve this including:

- job rotation
- developing informal networks
- forums to encourage cross-border transfer of knowledge and learning and
- encouraging other informal communication channels.

Transition HR companies

The final group comprised four highly internationalised companies who had grown mainly through acquisitions. They were transition HR companies in the sense that they were in the process of shifting away from the decentralised approach adopted in the mid-1990s. There was a greater degree of central control over management development and the management of expatriates than in the decentralised companies, and talent management and strategic staffing had emerged as important issues primarily due to the growing importance of international acquisitions. Retention emerged as a strategic talent management/staffing issue in international acquisitions and research highlights that retention of key employees is vital to achieving acquisition objectives. A key challenge for corporate HR was to achieve the required degree of central control of the talent management process without undermining the decentralised control system which suggests that central control over management of managers in the international firm has not been abandoned (Arkin, 1999).

Managing the talent pipeline in the international firm

Research indicates that talent management on a global basis also has some broader dimensions and shows that in practice talent markets still operate very much in the national contexts of the particular countries (Harris *et al.*, 2003). Leading multinationals increasingly seek to combine local recruitment strategies with a more global approach due to the need to manage the growing mobility of labour in a more coordinated manner.

This research also highlights that the competition for talent is becoming more generic – which involves international firms competing with each other as well as with leading local organisations (Patel, 2002).

Brewster *et al.* (2002) argue that the topics of employer branding and talent management are closely linked for most organisations who are very concerned with their 'talent-pipeline'. Sparrow *et al.* (2004: 121) highlight that talent management in the international context requires international HR managers to 'develop a much deeper level of understanding about the links between the business agenda and the capabilities of the most talented people in the organization, and also understand the potential for mobility around these people'. This attempted 'calibration' of talent on a global basis often requires multinational employers to think about talent on a more global basis and also to think about ' who they are' and ' what they stand for' (Sparrow *et al.*, 2004: 121).

Sparrow *et al.* (2004: 126) identify a number of factors to explain why organisations are coordinating their talent pipelines on a more global basis:

- Talent has become more mobile.
- Competition with other employers has become more generic and has shifted from the country level to the regional and global levels.
- The need for more nationality and gender diversity requires a shift away from a headquarters mindset.
- Economies of scale are important and global networks can transfer best practices across countries.

Box 5.1 Key indicators in talent management

The key indicators used to evaluate talent management include the following:

- added value per employee
- recruitment (what proportion of talented recruits to total recruits?)
- graduates (what proportion of graduates stay with the organisation for longer than three years?)
- development (how many hours of training per employee is provided?)
- internal appointments (what proportion of vacancies are filled internally?)
- retention (what proportion of vacancies are filled internally?)

Source: adapted from Sparrow *et al.* (2004: 125)

One of the key notions underlying much of the talent management/war for talent thinking was the notion of the employee value proposition (see Box 5.1). Sparrow and Cooper (2003) show the links with the concept to the psychological contract:

it is a human resource management policy influenced very much by marketing thinking that cuts across the whole of the employment experience and applies to all individuals in the organization. It is the application of a customer value proposition – why should you buy my product or service – to the individual – why would a highly talented person work in my organization? It differs from one organization to the other, has to be as distinctive as a fingerprint, and is tailored to the specific type of people the organization is trying to attract or retain.

(Sparrow and Cooper 2003: 160)

Brewster *et al.* (2002) identify a number of common responses to such challenges:

● researching into 'consumer insights' with current and potential employees and agencies
● managing the talent pipeline – a more proactive and strategic approach to recruitment
● increasing awareness in universities and other companies to get the people you want
● developing internal talent pools around the world
● creating skilled assessors across the globe
● managing recruitment suppliers on a global basis
● using e-technology to communicate messages about employer brand.

Sparrow *et al.* (2004) highlight that a major challenge facing organisations seeking to coordinate their talent pipelines on a more global basis at the operational level is the need to consider the cross-cultural relevance and fairness of the tools and techniques which are employed (see Chapter 6 for a discussion of this in the context of recruitment and selection). However, despite the hype about talent management since the mid-1990s there is little evidence to suggest that many organisations do it in a coordinated and efficient manner (Scullion and Starkey, 2000). One study reported that under 20 per cent of senior managers strongly agreed that their organisation brought in highly talented people, under 10 per cent thought that they retained all their high performers, while under 5 per cent thought that their organisation developed people quickly and effectively, or removed low performers (Michaels *et al.*, 2001). Also, many companies are frequently unaware of where their best talent is located (Evans *et al.*, 2002). In the McKinsey study cited above only 16 per cent of the executives surveyed believed that their employers knew who their high performers were. A key problem in the retention of key employees following an international acquisition is the difference in performance measures and standards (Scullion and Brewster, 2001).

Retaining talent has emerged as the key issue in talent management (Frank and Taylor, 2004). This is due to a number of factors such as demographic changes, the globalisation of the workforce and the growth of the Internet which has enabled employees to become more knowledgeable and sophisticated about employment and job searches (Hansen, 2001), thus making multinationals more vulnerable to employee turnover. Retention issues are particularly important in acquisitions and many acquired businesses lose key employees soon after the acquisition, and this is a major contributing factor to failure in acquisitions, particularly where the main assets are intangible and where intimate knowledge of the customer may be a key factor (Stahl *et al.*, 2004). Specifically retention of talent is particularly important where the value of the deal lies with the knowledge and skills of the people inside the acquired firm as in many of the acquisitions in the high technology sector (Chaudhuri and Tabrizi, 1999).

The failure to pay enough attention to retaining talent often leads to many of the most talented employees leaving as they will have the most choices and attract the most attention from headhunters (Stahl *et al.*, 2004). Research on US acquisitions shows that the probability of executives leaving increases significantly when the firm is acquired by a foreign multinational (Krug and Hegarty, 2001). While the link between talent retention and the success of the acquisition is widely recognised, Evans *et al.* (2002) show that this does not always lead to the introduction of the required HR measures. They cite a global survey of leading MNCs where three-quarters of respondents indicated that talent retention was the most critical element of the integration process, yet under 10 per cent of respondents cited HR as their top priority during integration (Watson Wyatt, 1999, cited in Evans *et al.*, 2002: 532). It is further argued that the lack of clear measures of talent retention is a key part of the problem, and that the lack of such retention data undermines the ability of companies to measure the success of their talent management initiatives (Evans *et al.*, 2002).

Effective and open communication has been identified as a key element for success in retaining talent with financial incentives, such as stock options or retention bonuses, also important. However, research identifies that senior management involvement is critical to the long-term retention of high potential staff. High potential staff expect senior managers to pay close attention to their development and career aspirations and generally will not accept distance as a reason for failure in this respect (Stahl *et al.*, 2004). For example, Scottish and Newcastle International, the Scottish-based international brewer introduced an event to network senior executives with high potential managers from across Europe following a number of acquisitions in several European countries. In this context a key challenge for the acquiring company is to integrate high potential employees into the leadership development of the new parent company (Krug and Hegarty, 2001).

In a critical article titled 'Fighting the war for talent is hazardous to your organization's health', Pfeffer (2001: 249) identifies a number of problems which can arise when companies adopt the 'war for talent' mindset:

- There is an emphasis on individual performance and rewarding individual stars which encourages destructive internal competition and diminishes teamwork.
- There is a tendency to downplay the talents of internal staff and exaggerate the talents of external staff.
- Those labelled as low ability become less able because less is expected of them.
- Less attention is paid to the real issues affecting performance as the focus is on solving problems by bringing in new people.
- The development of an elitist and arrogant attitude.

Pfeffer (2001: 257) concludes that it is very difficult to wage the war for talent and not fall into these problems. He points to the considerable evidence which suggests that teams can outperform groups of more talented individuals. Also, he suggests that the performance of staff can vary and will be influenced by the leadership they receive and the help they get from others in their immediate environment. Finally, he cautions that the focus on external talent as a solution to problems can demotivate a large portion of the workforce and produce an elite which is arrogant and unwilling to listen to their colleagues or customers.

Marriott's Human Capital Review

The lack of integration of the key elements of the talent management system is another common weakness of such approaches (Sparrow *et al.*, 2004; Conference Board 2004). One notable attempt to overcome this weakness is the Strategic Human Capital Review introduced by Marriott, a leading worldwide hospitality company, headquartered in Washington, DC and employing 130,000 employees in 70 countries. Marriott has developed a talent and succession system that provides line managers with the tools, skills and impetus to ensure continuous alignment of talent and organisational capabilities with business priorities (see Figure 5.1).

Step 1

As we can see in Figure 5.1, the first step of Marriott's Human Capital Review (HCR) expands business leaders' focus to include aligning both talent and organisational capability with business priorities.

Step 2

Step 2 involves enhancing talent assessment criteria through the introduction of Marriott's Leadership Talent Development Inventory (LTDI), which is a tool used to gather critical information to improve discussions about talent development, performance and organisational impact. Under the LTDI approach executives and high potential talent participate in a rigorous talent assessment which includes the following:

- in-depth accomplishments review
- detailed career history review
- multi-source assessment centres
- supervisor evaluation.

For each individual the LTDI provides the following:

- performance overview
- strength and development areas
- development action items
- identifies possible next assignment
- readiness for next assignment.

Marriott's Human Capital Review (HCR) expands business leaders' focus to include aligning both talent and organisational capability with business priorities

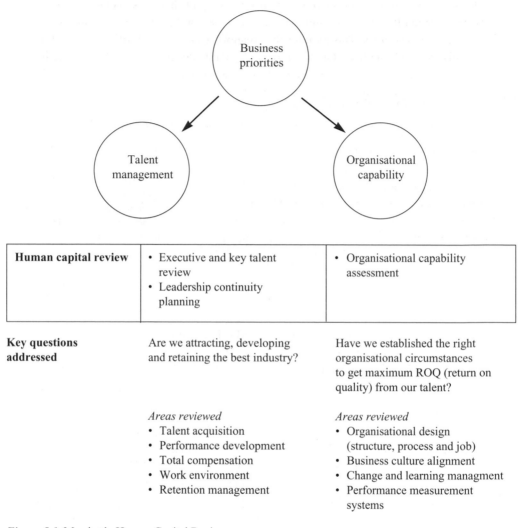

Human capital review	• Executive and key talent review • Leadership continuity planning	• Organisational capability assessment

Key questions addressed	Are we attracting, developing and retaining the best industry?	Have we established the right organisational circumstances to get maximum ROQ (return on quality) from our talent?
	Areas reviewed • Talent acquisition • Performance development • Total compensation • Work environment • Retention management	*Areas reviewed* • Organisational design (structure, process and job) • Business culture alignment • Change and learning managment • Performance measurement systems

Figure 5.1 Marriott's Human Capital Review
Source: Marriott International, Inc., Washington, DC.

Step 3

Marriot uses an Organisational Capability Review (OCR) tool to help business unit managers assess the degree to which their organisational environment is supporting business priorities and utilising talent. The OCR tool uses targeted questions to help focus managers' attentions on key OD and talent utilisation issues. In addition, other questions encourage managers to think locally about the overall talent environment.

Step 4

Marriott's Organisational Capability department supports business leaders in the Human Capital Review follow-up to better align their unit's talent and organisation with business priorities. This requires the creation of an HR centre of excellence for Organisational Capability – Organisational Capability department. And as we see in Figure 5.2, Marriott's expanded Human Capital Review has created a more dynamic role for HR in the talent management process.

Marriott's expanded Human Capital Review has created a more dynamic role for HR professionals

Traditional human resources talent process

- Concerned with talent supply
- Targets successors to key positions
- Slowly reacts to changes in business strategy
- Focused on annual process style
- Led by HR

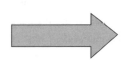

Marriott's Human Capital Review

- Considers both talent and organisational design
- Constantly considers job design in addition to type and supply of talent
- Drives business strategy with talent and organisational data
- Dynamic activity drives accountability for delivering results
- Line owned and led, with HR support

– and supports broader efforts to integrate HR into the company's business planning process

Previous HR role in business planning

- Limited opportunity and resources to play this role

- Inconsistent participation depending on the business issue

- HR participates in debate

- HR manages talent supply to meet chosen strategy

| Evaluation of business environment |
| Strategy development |
| Strategy selection |
| Strategy execution |

New HR role in business planning

- Anticipates future human capital requirements based on business and socio-economic trends

- Expected to contribute to business strategy formulation by providing an expert perspective on human capital issues

- Provides expert point of view on how to drive business strategies through talent and organisational actions

- Ensures that the 'right' talents are in the 'right' jobs and that the organisation is optimally designed to meet strategy and prepare for future priorities.

Figure 5.2 A new role for human resources

Having reviewed the role of the corporate HR function in the management of talent internationally, the next section will consider the competencies required for the HR function and the IHRM function.

The competencies required for the HR function and the IHRM function

The question of the key competencies required of the HR function has been researched for some time by Michigan Business School. Large data sets were gathered and analysed in the United States in 1988, 1992 and 1997 (Brockbank and Ulrich, 2002). In the first two rounds, three competency categories were uncovered: business knowledge, HR functional capability and change management. In 1997, two additional categories were added: culture management and personal credibility.

In 1992 the Michigan research team and its associated partners around the globe added more countries and continents in their Human Resource Competency Study (HRCS). They conducted research in North America, Latin America, Asia and Europe, covering 250 companies and more than 7000 respondents. The research clearly highlighted the following five factors as making a positive difference for both the performance of the firm and the personal performance of the HR manager: *strategic contribution, personal credibility, HR delivery, business knowledge and HR technology* (Brockbank and Ulrich 2002). These are examined in more detail below.

Strategic contribution

High-performing companies have senior HR managers involved in the business at a strategic level. These HR managers manage culture, facilitate fast change, are involved in the strategic decision making and create market driven connectivity. These four factors – culture management, fast change, strategic decision making and market driven connectivity – together comprise the HR competency domain of strategic contribution.

Personal credibility

Senior HR managers must be credible to both their HR counterparts and line managers. They need excellent networking skills and need to demonstrate a track record of achieving results. In addition, senior HR professionals must have effective communication skills. The three factors – effective relationships, gets results and personal communication – determine the domain of personal credibility.

HR delivery

HR activities are delivered to the business in four major categories:

- *Development* (individual development and organisation-wide development): designing challenging developmental programmes and experiences, facilitating internal communication processes, providing career planning advice and counselling.
- *Structure and HR measurement*: restructuring the organisation, measuring impact of HR practices and managing global implications of HR practices.
- *Staffing*: attracting, promoting, retaining and outsourcing.
- *Performance management*: designing integrated performance-based management systems and processes.

Business knowledge

Senior managers must demonstrate knowledge of the business and industry they operate in including a practical understanding of the integrated value chain (how the firm horizontally integrates) and the firm's value proposition (how the firm creates wealth). The final factor that constitutes the domain of business knowledge is the factor labour, representing institutional constraints such as labour legislation.

HR technology

Technology is increasingly becoming a key delivery vehicle for HR services. Increasingly, HR managers need to be able to leverage technology for HR practices and use e-HR/web-based channels to deliver value to their customers.

Following our review of the competencies required for the effective functioning of the HR function, we turn our attention to the competencies which will be required by the international HRM specialists of the future.

What are the competencies which will be required for the international HRM role in the future?

The problem of how to internationalise the HRM function itself has been identified as a major issue facing international firms, and it is recognised that the same HR policies will not produce the same effects in different country contexts (Scullion, 2005). A review of European and North American research which examined the major problems MNCs face when seeking to internationalise the HR function in many different markets concluded:

Paradoxically, then, the function in charge of implementing internationalization is rather parochial. This lack of international experience and understanding no doubt helps to explain why devising the appropriate human resource strategies remains problematic.

(Schneider and Barsoux, 2003: 175)

Brewster *et al.* (2002) have identified four key strategic pressures driving the internationalisation of the HR function:

- Maximising shareholder value – the driving force behind most global HR functions' recent restructuring efforts has been the need to deliver global business strategies in the most cost-efficient manner.
- Building global presence – many MNCs are required to be visible and gain a presence in many foreign markets.
- Developing strategic partnerships – to develop as global players the growth of international joint ventures and strategic alliances may bring the need to work in partnership with former competitors and collaborators.
- Creating core business processes – international HRM can play a key role in the reorientation of business strategy, particularly in the implementation of new international business strategies.

Black *et al.* (1999) found that in the late 1990s, in spite of the high priority that MNCs place on IHRM tasks such as global leadership development as a key to future competitiveness, the majority of firms they researched felt the international HRM function was not up to the task in their organisations. They also suggested that the recruitment and development of international HRM managers will become a key challenge for many MNCs. One study outlines the growing importance of the IHRM role and offers a basic framework to help us think about IHRM in the future. In particular, it explains how being aware of macro trends will become increasingly important for the IHRM specialist in the future (Taylor and Napier, 2005). Four key macro trends are discussed:

- the changing profile of MNCs
- the growing interdependencies of the links across economics, politics, social, technological and environmental factors influencing MNCs
- the increasing global fragmentation arising from the growing divisions in ethnic, religious and social spheres
- the growth of the psychic shock syndrome where individuals become unable to cope with the changes taking place in the environment both globally and locally.

It is argued that these trends will influence the future mandate of the IHRM area and a key message for those aspiring to be IHRM specialists of the future is the need to learn to look at the wider environment in order to understand the competencies which will be required to achieve successful performance of the IHRM role in the future. Indeed it is argued that IHRM professionals of the future will need to be knowledgeable about the world on many more levels than before in order to be an effective partner in the management of the MNC (Taylor and Napier, 2005).

The challenge of developing transnational managers

Bartlett and Ghoshal (1989, 1998) refer to the transnational as the ultimate organisational form for operating successfully in a rapidly changing international context which encourages most MNCs to develop multidimensional and heterogeneous strategies and structures. This development poses considerable challenges for the transnational managers who have to develop and implement these strategies. In this section we will discuss the roles and responsibilities of transnational managers. It has been argued that it is virtually impossible for one person to possess all the skills necessary to be an effective transnational manager.

The transnational manager is seen by Bartlett and Ghoshal (1992: 124) as 'a network of specialists, not a single individual' and they argue that roles and responsibilities of transnational managers will vary in different parts of the organisation. Based on Bartlett and Ghoshal (1992), we distinguish three different management forms:

- global business management
- worldwide functional management
- geographic subsidiary management.

In a final subsection we will also discuss the necessary capabilities for top-level corporate management.

Global business management

Effective global business management complies with the demands of global efficiency and competitiveness. Capturing scale and scope economies and coordinating and integrating activities across national and functional barriers are the fundamental tasks of the global business manager. In order to perform these tasks a global business manager has three core roles and responsibilities:

- *Worldwide business strategist*: in this role the global business manager tries to reconcile the different perspectives of geographic, functional and business management in order to provide an integrated competitive strategy for the business.
- *Architect of a worldwide asset and resource configuration*: in this role the global manager coordinates the distribution of key assets and resources to support the competitive strategy taking into account the company's administrative heritage of existing assets and resources.
- *Coordinator and controller*: the flow of materials, components and finished products has to be coordinated by global business managers in their role as cross-border coordinator, which in transnational companies is a very complex task.

Worldwide functional management

The development and diffusion of knowledge on a worldwide basis is a key challenge for worldwide functional management. Most worldwide functional managers play three basic roles:

- *Worldwide scanner of specialised information and knowledge*: as worldwide intelligence scanner the worldwide functional manager scans the whole world for opportunities and threats, which may be in the form of a technological breakthrough or an emerging consumer trend. Functional managers are linked through informal networks, so that information is transmitted rapidly. In a transnational company subsidiaries can be an important source of capabilities, expertise and innovations, which can be transferred to other parts of the organisation.
- *Cross-pollinator of 'best practices'*: it is the worldwide functional manager in his/her role as cross-pollinator of 'best practices' who identifies opportunities and transfers knowledge in a way that breaks down the 'not invented here' syndrome.
- *Champion of transnational innovation*: 'locally leveraged' transnational innovation follows from the 'best-practices' approach – local innovations that can be generally applied. A more sophisticated form of transnational innovation is termed 'globally linked' innovation. 'This type of innovation fully exploits the company's access to worldwide information and expertise by linking and leveraging intelligence sources with internal centres of excellence wherever they may be located' (Bartlett and Ghoshal, 1992: 785).

Geographic subsidiary management

The key requirement for effective geographic subsidiary management is local responsiveness, that is responding to the needs of national customers and satisfying the demands of host country governments. However, it also demands defending a company's position against global competitors and leveraging local resources and capabilities. The geographic subsidiary manager's complex task can be divided into three main roles:

- *Bicultural interpreter*: in this role the geographic subsidiary (or country) manager must not only understand the demands of the local customers, competitors and government, but also interpret this information and communicate it effectively to managers at headquarters who might not understand its importance. On the other hand, the country manager must also interpret the company's overall strategies, objectives and goals in such a way that can be understood by local employees while respecting local cultural norms.
- *National defender and advocate*: in this role the country manager should try to counterbalance excessive centralising pressures from global business managers and make sure that the interests of the local subsidiary are taken into consideration.
- *Frontline implementer of corporate strategy*: this is a very challenging role as the country manager faces pressures from local governments, unions and customers

on the one hand and is subject to constraints imposed by the global strategy that often offers little scope for manoeuvre on the other. This manager's actions 'must be sensitive enough to respect the limits of the diverse local constituencies, pragmatic enough to achieve the expected corporate outcome, and creative enough to balance the diverse internal and external demands and constraints' (Bartlett and Ghoshal, 1992: 788).

Top-level corporate management

Top-level corporate management has to take all the transnational challenges (efficiency, learning and responsiveness) into account which involves:

- creating different management groups and giving them specific roles and responsibilities
- seeking to maintain the 'organisational legitimacy' of each group: balancing and integrating diverse and often conflicting interests is the key challenge for top-level corporate management.

In doing so, there are three basic roles to fulfil:

- *Providing direction and purpose*: a common vision and a shared set of values are required to lead a multidimensional and heterogeneous company towards common goals. It is the task of top-level corporate management in its role as provider of direction and purpose to create this common vision which is a long-term strategy.
- *Leveraging corporate performance*: top management's role of leveraging corporate performance makes sure that the company survives in the short run. Top management needs to balance the different coordination devices (formalisation, centralisation and socialisation) to maximise corporate performance. Also, in practice there is a need to balance between a focus on the long-term mission and on short-term performance.
- *Ensuring continual renewal*: the third role of top management is to ensure continual renewal. Goals and values have to be adaptive; they are continually questioned and challenged to achieve the flexibility that is vital in a transnational environment.

Having reviewed the major roles and responsibilities of the transnational manager, our final section will examine the notion of the global mindset.

Global mindset

This section examines the concept of the global mindset. The ability to live and work across cultures is the essential competency of managers with a global mindset. Developing this mindset is both an emotional education as well as an intellectual one and the lessons are both professional and personal (McCall and Hollenbeck, 2002). It is argued that 'it is the complexity of the professional lessons and the transformational quality of the personal lessons that leads to the broader perspective of those with the global mind-set' (Briscoe and Schuler, 2004: 287). It is in fact this unique perspective that underlies this quality called a global mindset (Briscoe and Schuler, 2004). Rhinesmith (1993) argues that a global mindset requires the ability to scan the world from a broad perspective and is a 'way of being' rather than a set of skills. Evans *et al.* (2002) view the global mindset in terms of its psychological and its strategic perspectives.

The psychological perspective

This perspective of global mindset views it as *the ability to accept and work with cultural diversity*. Firms with a global mindset accept diversity and heterogeneity as a source of opportunity (Talbott, 1996). Rhinesmith (1993) shows how the global mindset compares with the traditional domestic mindset and this is illustrated in Table 5.1. Managers with global mindsets have broader perspectives and try to understand the context for decisions. They tend not to accept 'one best way solutions' and change is seen as an opportunity rather than a threat.

Table 5.1 Global mindset compared to traditional 'domestic' mindset

Traditional domestic mindset	Global mindset	Personal characteristics
Functional expertise	Broad and multiple perspectives	Knowledge
Prioritisation	Duality – balance between contradictions	Conceptual ability
Structure	Process	Flexibility
Individual responsibility	Teamwork and diversity	Sensitivity
Predictability	Change as opportunity	Judgement
Trained against surprises	Open to what is new	Learning

Source: adapted from S.H. Rhinesmith (1993) *A Manager's Guide to Globalization* (Burr Ridge, IL: Business One Irwin).

The strategic perspective

This focuses on a way of thinking that reflects conflicting strategic orientations. The ability to manage contradictions is a central challenge for senior managers in multinational companies and considerable attention has been paid to the cognitive orientations of senior managers and the need for balanced perspectives (Bennett and Bennett, 2003). Seibert *et al.* (1995) argue that in this context the task is not to build a sophisticated structure, but to create a matrix in the mind of managers. This notion yields some good insight into the idea of the global mindset and highlights that contradictions cannot be resolved by structure but need to be built into the way of thinking of senior managers in the multinational enterprise (Murtha *et al.*, 1998; Yan *et al.*, 2002).

The strategic perspective of global mindset refers 'to a set of attitudes that predispose individuals to balance competing business, country and functional priorities which emerge in international management processes rather than to advocate any of these dimensions at the expense of others' (Evans *et al.*, 2002: 386–7). This requires sharing information, knowledge and expertise across boundaries and flexibility in the way resources are transferred across sub-units.

Characteristics of a global mindset

While there is general agreement that learning a global mindset requires the development of a new set of competencies there is no consensus over exactly what are the characteristics of those who possess the global mindset. However, Briscoe and Schuler (2004) effectively synthesise the various efforts to describe these characteristics. They argue that those with a global mindset exhibit the ability to:

- manage global competitiveness
- work and communicate in multiple cultures
- manage global complexity, contradiction and conflict
- manage organisational adaptability
- manage multicultural teams
- manage uncertainty and chaos
- manage personal and organisational global learning.

This suggests that managers with a global mindset need to have broad business skills and an ability to show awareness of national differences, global trends and options as well as developing a sensitivity to different cultures and cultural values. The ability to manage the global corporate culture and to manage diverse groups of people are important (Barham and Wills, 1992). In particular, the ability to effectively manage cross-border and multicultural teams is increasingly important given the rapid growth of new forms of international working (see Chapter 8 of this volume).

Developing a global mindset

International assignments and transfers are the best way to develop the global mindset as this requires managers to live in another culture and experience and hopefully overcome culture shock (Briscoe and Schuler, 2004). Evans *et al.* (2002: 391) highlight that international transfers develop many different aspects of global mindset:

- They encourage the development of integrative leadership skills.
- They develop the portfolio of skills associated with the global mindset such as championing global strategy and handling diversity.

- They develop skills in handling cultural diversity.
- Managers will gain experience of international project groups.
- The development of informal personal global networks provide managers with access to information and resources to operate effectively in the transnational.
- The need to meet the performance requirement of the local subsidiary and the demands of headquarters staff provides an excellent training in global mindset.

The rapid growth of cross-border project teams is another increasingly important method for developing global mindset, and unlike traditional expatriate assignments these are not limited to the small minority identified with high potential (Scullion and Brewster, 2002). Evans *et al*. (2002) argue that cross-border projects involve working through local–global and related problems and are an excellent way of developing global mindset; in addition, they suggest this will be the most important mechanism for developing global mindset in the future.

> These cross-border projects enable managers to learn a set of skills that underlie global mindset – the ability to work with people who have very different perspectives and over whom one has no authority, setting goals on important but ambiguous tasks, working through conflict and the like.
>
> (Evans *et al*. 2002: 393)

Indeed they go on to argue that nobody should be sent on an international transfer without prior experience of international project work (Evans *et al*., 2002: 393)

Conclusion

Since the mid-1990s international talent management initiatives have been introduced by a growing number of MNCs in response to the growing problem of shortages of international managers which is increasingly seen as a major constraint on the implementation of international strategies. This chapter has examined the reasons for both the shortages of international managers and the emergence of international talent management initiatives. The chapter examines the key staffing issues which limit the MNC's ability to develop an adequate pool of international managers and assesses the key challenges of developing transnational managers. The corporate HR role in coordinating and developing international management talent in different types of firms is critically examined and some key problems and weaknesses of international talent management initiatives are discussed. The chapter assesses the key competencies required of the HR function in the global firm and identifies some of the competencies which will be required of the international HR function in the future. Finally some methods for developing a global mindset are examined.

References

Adler, N.J. (2002) 'Global managers: no longer men alone', *International Journal of Human Resource Management*, 13(5): 743–60.

Arkin, A. (1999) 'Return to centre', *People Management*, 6 May: 34–41.

Barham, K. and Wills, S. (1992) *Managing across Frontiers*, Ashridge: Ashridge Management Centre.

Bartlett, C.A. and Ghoshal, S. (1989) *Managing across Borders: The Transnational Solution*, London: Hutchinson.

Bartlett, C.A. and Ghoshal, S. (1990) 'The multinational organisation as an interorganisational network', *Academy of Management Review*, 16(2): 262–90.

Bartlett, C.A. and Ghoshal, S. (1992) *Transnational Management*, Homewood, IL: Irwin.

Bartlett, C.A. and Ghoshal, S. (1998) *Managing across Borders: The Transnational Solution*, 2nd edn, London: Random House.

Bennett, J.M. and Bennett, M.J. (2003) 'Developing intercultural sensitivity: an integrative approach to global and domestic diversity', in D. Landis, J.M. Bennett and M.J. Bennett (eds) *The Handbook of Intercultural Training*, Thousand Oaks, CA: Sage.

Björkman, I. and Xiucheng, F. (2002) 'Human resource management and the performance of Western firms in China', *International Journal of Human Resource Management*, 13(6): 853–64.

Black, J.S. and Gregerson, H.B. (1999) 'The right way to manage expats', *Harvard Business Review*, March–April: 52–63.

Black, J.S., Gregerson, H.B., Mendenhall, M.E. and Stroh, L.K. (1999) *Globalizing People through International Assignments*, Reading, MA: Addison-Wesley.

Black, J.S., Morrison, A.J. and Gregerson, H.B. (2000) *Global Explorers: The Next Generation of Leaders*, New York: Routledge.

Brewster, C. and Scullion, H. (1997) 'A review and an agenda for expatriate HRM', *Human Resource Management Journal*, 7(3): 32–41.

Brewster, C., Harris, H. and Sparrow, P.R. (2002) *Globalising HR: Executive Brief*, London: Chartered Institute of Personnel and Development.

Briscoe, D.R. and Schuler, R.S. (2004) *International Human Resource Management*, 2nd edn, London: Routledge.

Brockbank, W. and Ulrich, D. (2002) *The New HR Agenda: 2002 HRCS Executive Summary*, University of Michigan Business School.

Caligiuri, P.M. and Cascio, W. (1998) 'Can we send her there? Maximising the success of western women on global assignments', *Journal of World Business*, 33(4): 394–416.

Chambers, E.G., Foulon, M., Hanfield-Jones, H. and Michaels, E. (1998) 'The war for talent', *McKinsey Quarterly*.

Chaudhuri, S. and Tabrizi, B. (1999) 'Capturing the real value in high-tech acquisitions', *Harvard Business Review*, September–October: 123–30.

Collings, D. and Scullion, H. (2005) 'Global staffing', in G.K. Stahl and I. Bjorkman (eds) *Handbook of Research in International Human Resource Management*, Cheltenham: Edward Elgar.

Conference Board (2004) *Integrated and Integrative Talent Management: A Strategic HR Framework*, New York: Conference Board.

De Cieri, H. and Dowling, P.J. (1999) 'Strategic human resource management in multinational enterprises: theoretical and empirical developments', in P.M. Wright, L.D. Dyer, J.W. Boudreau and G.T. Milkovich (eds) *Research in Personnel and Human Resources Management: Strategic Human Resources Management in the Twenty-First Century*, Supplement 4, Stamford, CT: JAI Press.

Dowling, P.J. and Welch, D. (2004) *International Human Resource Management: Managing People in a Multinational Context*, London: Thomson Learning.

Dowling, P.J., Welch, D.E. and Schuler, R.S. (1999) *International Human Resource Management: Managing People in an International Context*, 3rd edn, Cincinnati, OH: South Western College Publishing, ITP.

Doz, Y.L. and Hamel, G. (1998) *Alliance Advantage: The Art of Creating Value through Partnering*, Boston, MA: Harvard Business School Press.

Doz, Y. and Prahalad, C.K. (1986) 'Controlled variety: a challenge for human resource management in the MNC', *Human Resource Management*, 25(1): 55–71.

Evans, P., Pucik, V. and Barsoux, J.L. (2002) *The Global Challenge: Frameworks for International Human Resource Management*, New York: McGraw-Hill-Irwin.

Forster, N. (2000) 'The myth of the "international manager"', *International Journal of Human Resource Management*, 11(1): 126–42.

Frank, F.D. and Taylor, C.R. (2004) 'Talent management: trends that will shape the future', *Human Resource Planning*, 1 March: 33–41.

Ghoshal, S. and Gratton, L. (2002) 'Integrating the enterprise', *Sloan Management Review*, 44(1): 31–8.

GMAC (2002) Global Relocation Services, US National Foreign Trade Council and SHRM Global Forum, Global Relocation Trends 2002 Survey Report, 'Dual Careers and International Assignments Survey', ORC Worldwide, Organization Resources Counselors.

Gregersen, H., Morrison, A. and Black, J.S. (1998) 'Developing leaders for the global frontiers', *Sloan Management Review*, 40(1): 21–32.

Gupta, A.K. and Govindarajan, V. (2002) 'Cultivating a global mindset', *Academy of Management Executive*, 16(1): 116–26.

Hansen, F. (2001) 'Currents in compensation and benefits', *Compensation and Benefits Review*, November–December: 6–9.

Harris, H., Brewster, C. and Sparrow, P.R. (2003) *International Human Resource Management*, London: Chartered Institute of Personnel and Development.

Harvey, M. (1998) 'Dual-career couples during international relocation: the trailing spouse', *International Journal of Human Resource Management*, 9(2): 309–331.

Harvey, M., Novicevic, M. and Speier, C. (1999a) 'Inpatriate managers: how to increase the probability of success', *Human Resource Management Review*, 9(1): 51–82.

Harvey, M., Speier, C. and Novicevic, M. (1999b) 'The impact of the emerging markets on staffing the global organisation', *Journal of International Management*, 5(3): 167–86.

Hunt, J. and Boxall, P. (1998) 'Are top human resource specialists strategic partners? Self perceptions of a corporate elite', *International Journal of Human Resource Management*, 9(5): 767–81.

Kochan, T., Batt, R. and Dyer, L. (1992) 'International human resource studies: a framework for future research', in D. Lewin, O.S. Mitchell and P.D. Schere (eds) *Research Frontiers in Industrial Relations and Human Resources*, Madison, WI: Industrial Relations Research Association.

Kogut, B. and Zander, V. (1992) 'Knowledge of the firm's combinative capabilities and the replication of technology', *Organization Science*, 3(3): 383–97.

Krug, J. and Hegarty, W.H. (2001) 'Predicting who stays and leaves after an acquisition: a study of top managers in multinational firms', *Strategic Management Journal*, 22: 186–92.

Linehan, M. (2000) *Senior Female International Managers: Why so Few?* Aldershot: Ashgate.

Linehan, M. (2002) 'Senior female international managers: empirical evidence from Western Europe', *International Journal of Human Resource Management*, 13(5): 802–14.

Linehan, M. (2005) 'Women in international management', in H. Scullion and M. Linehan (eds) *International Human Resource Management: A Critical Text*, London: Palgrave Macmillan.

Linehan, M. and Scullion, H. (2002) 'Repatriation of European female corporate executives: an empirical study', *International Journal of Human Resource Management*, 13(2): 254–67.

McCall, M.M. and Hollenbeck, G.P. (2002) *Developing Global Executives: The Lessons of International Experience*, Boston, MA: Harvard University Press.

Mayrhofer, W. and Scullion, H. (2002) 'Female expatriates in international business: empirical evidence from the German clothing industry', *International Journal of Human Resource Management*, 3(5): 815–36.

Mudambi, R. (2002) 'Knowledge management in multinational firms', *Journal of International Management*, 8: 1–9.

Murtha, T.P., Lenaway, S.A. and Bagozzi, R.P. (1998) 'Global mind-sets and cognitive shift in a complex multinational corporation', *Strategic Management Journal*, 19: 97–114.

Napier, N.K. and Taylor, S. (2002) 'Experiences of women professionals abroad: comparisons across Japan, China and Turkey', *International Journal of Human Resource Management*, 13(5): 837–51.

Organizational Resource Counselors (ORC) (2002) *Dual Careers and International Assignments Survey Report*, Washington, DC: ORC.

Paauwe, J. (1996) 'Key issues in strategic human resource management: lessons from the Netherlands', *Human Resource Management Journal*, 6(3): 76–93.

Paauwe, J. and Dewe, P. (1995) 'Organizational structure of multinational corporations: theories and models', in A.W.K. Harzing and J. van Ruysseveldt (eds) *International Human Resource Management*, Thousands Oaks, CA: Sage.

Patel, D. (2002) 'Managing talent', *HR Magazine*, March.

Pfeffer, J. (2001) 'Fighting the war for talent is hazardous to your organization's health', *Organizational Dynamics*, 29(4): 248–59.

Pucik, V. (1992) 'Globalization and human resource management', in V. Pucik, N. Tichy and C.K. Barnett (eds) *Globalizing Management*, New York: Wiley.

Purcell, J. (1985) 'Is anybody listening to the corporate personnel department?' *Personnel Management*, September.

Purcell, J. and Ahlstrand, B. (1994) *Human Resource Management in the Multi-Divisional Company*, Oxford: Oxford University Press.

Rhinesmith, S.H. (1993) *A Manager's Guide to Globalization: Six Keys to Success in a Changing World*, Homewood, IL: Business One Irwin, and Alexandria, VA: American Society for Training and Development.

Schneider, S. and Barsoux, J.L. (2003) *Managing across Cultures*, 2nd edn, London: Financial Times/Prentice Hall.

Schuler, R.S., Dowling, P.J. and De Cieri, H. (1993) 'An integrative framework of strategic international human resource management'. *International Journal of Human Resource Management*, 4(4): 717–64.

Schuler, R.S., Budhwar, P.S. and Florkowski, G.W. (2002) 'International human resource management: review and critique', *International Journal of Management Reviews*, 4(1): 41–70.

Schuler, R.S., Jackson, S.E. and Luo, Y. (2004) *Managing Human Resources in Cross-Border Alliances*, London: Routledge.

Scullion, H. (1992) 'Strategic recruitment and development of the international manager: some European considerations', *Human Resource Management Journal*, 3(1): 57–69.

Scullion, H. (1994) 'Staffing policies and strategic control in British multinationals', *International Studies of Management and Organization*, 4(3): 18–35.

Scullion, H. (2001) 'International human resource management', in J. Storey (ed.) *Human Resource Management*, London: International Thompson.

Scullion, H. (2002) 'The management of managers in international firms: strategic HR issues for the corporate HR function', in M. Linehan, M. Morley and J. Walsh (eds) *International Human Resource Management and Expatriate Transfers: Irish Experiences*, Dublin: Blackhall.

Scullion, H. (2005) 'International HRM: an introduction', in H. Scullion and M. Linehan (eds) *International Human Resource Management: A Critical Text*, London: Palgrave Macmillan.

Scullion, H. and Brewster, C. (2001) 'Managing expatriates: messages from Europe', *Journal of World Business*, 36(4): 346–65.

Scullion, H. and Paauwe, J. (2005) 'Strategic HRM in multinational companies', in H. Scullion and M. Linehan (eds) *International Human Resource Management: A Critical Text*, London: Palgrave Macmillan.

Scullion, H. and Starkey, K. (2000) 'The changing role of the corporate human resource function in the international firm', *International Journal of Human Resource Management*, 11(6): 1061–81.

Seibert, K.W., Hall, D.T. and Kram, K.E. (1995) 'Strengthening the weak link in strategic executive development: integrating individual development and global business strategy', *Human Resource Management*, 34: 549–67.

Sisson, K. and Scullion, H. (1985) 'Putting the corporate personnel department in its place', *Personnel Management*, December: 36–9.

Sparrow, P.R. and Cooper, C.L. (2003) *The Employment Relationship: Key Challenges for HR*, London: Butterworth-Heinemann.

Sparrow, P.R., Brewster, C. and Harris, H. (2004) *Globalizing Human Resource Management*, London: Routledge.

Stahl, G.K., Pucik, V., Evans, P. and Mendenhall, M.E. (2004) 'Human resource management in cross-border mergers and acquisitions', in A.W.K. Harzing and J. van Ruysseveldt (eds) *International Human Resource Management*, London: Sage.

Storey, J., Edwards, P. and Sisson, K. (1997) *Managers in the Making: Careers, Development and Control in Corporate Britain and Japan*, London: Sage.

Stroh, L. and Caligiuri, P.M. (1998) 'Strategic human resources: a new source for competitive advantage in the global arena', *International Journal of Human Resource Management*, 9(1): 1–17.

Stroh, L., Gregerson, H.B. and Black, J.S. (1998) 'Closing the gap: expectations versus reality among repatriates', *Journal of World Business*, 33(2): 111–24.

Talbott, S.P. (1996) 'Building a global work force starts with recruitment', *Recruitment Staffing Sourcebook, supplement to Personnel Journal*, March, reprinted in M.H. Albrecht (ed.) (2001) *International HRM: Managing Diversity in the Workplace*, Oxford and Malden, MA: Blackwell.

Taylor, S. and Napier, N. (2005) 'International HRM in the twenty-first century: crossing boundaries, building connections', in H. Scullion and M. Linehan (eds) *International Human Resource Management: A Critical Text*, London: Palgrave Macmillan.

Taylor, S., Napier, N.K. and Mayrhofer, W. (2002) 'Women in global business: an introduction', *International Journal of Human Resource Management*, 13(5): 739–42.

Watson Wyatt (1999) *Watson Wyatt Worldwide's 1998/99 Mergers and Acquisitions Survey*, Washington, DC: Watson Wyatt.

Yan, A., Zhu, G. and Hall, D.T. (2002) 'International assignments for career building: a model of agency relationships and psychological contracts', *Academy of Management Review*, 27(3): 373–91.

6 Cross-cultural training

EMMA PARKINSON AND MICHAEL J. MORLEY

Introduction

International assignees often emerge as a critical node in an organisation's international network. The organisation's capacity to harness, develop and effectively utilise the international assignee's intellectual capital and nurture the human resources required to implement an international strategy are of critical importance to MNCs (Dowling and Welch, 2004). The effective management of international assignees and the development of a competent global workforce is increasingly being recognised as a major determinant of success or failure in international business (Briscoe and Shuler, 2004) and cross-cultural training (CCT), designed to meet individual and organisational needs, is increasingly emerging as an important element of the landscape of international business (Caligiuri *et al.*, 2005). However, it is important to note at this juncture that CCT is significant as one component in an integrated suite of congruent HR policies.

The increased necessity to provide CCT has been influenced by the progressively more important roles that international assignees are assuming in securing the maintenance and development of the organisational philosophy in the host environment to ensure the success of the multinational organisation. Indeed, a fundamental criterion for a company's success is its employees' ability to understand, appreciate and adapt to other cultures and to develop a global mindset (Lewis, 2003; see also Chapter 5 of this volume). As such, the value of being culturally sensitive, adaptive and fundamentally culturally literate when operating internationally has been well documented. These competencies must be achieved both from an individual and organisational perspective if many of the problems associated with maladjustment are to be avoided (Hutchings, 2003). Researchers also suggest that it is essential to ensure that international assignees are adequately trained so as to maximise the benefits that are to be gained from the international career move both in terms of advancing one's own career and also in terms of adding value to the organisation (Downes and Thomas, 2000; Scullion and Donnelly, 1998). In this chapter, we

- define CCT and distinguish between pre-departure and post-arrival training, highlighting some cited advantages and disadvantages of each approach

- identify different forms of CCT, namely cognitive, experiential and integrated and associated techniques
- review several studies that have been conducted in the area in an attempt to assess the role and value of CCT in preparing assignees for international assignments.

Defining and classifying cross-cultural training

For the purpose of this chapter cross-cultural training is defined as any formalised intervention designed to increase the knowledge and skills of international assignees to live and work effectively in an unfamiliar environment.

Conceptually, academics have classified CCT along two broad dimensions, namely *pre-departure training* and *post-arrival training*. While a third category, on-arrival training, has been suggested, for the purposes of this chapter, the term post-arrival training refers to any training received after the commencement of the international assignment in the host location.

Pre-departure training

Early practitioners and researchers viewed the process of preparing people to undertake international assignments as that which would familiarise assignees with the differences in social interactions between the two cultures. However, contemporary researchers realise the need for training programmes to do more than merely orient assignees to live in a foreign environment. Bennett *et al.* (2000) highlight the importance of pre-departure CCT programmes, suggesting that:

> Pre-departure training allows the employee and family members to enter the assignment already equipped with realistic expectations; a basic understanding of the destination culture, country and city; practical information related to living in the area; work-related insights that can be applied on arrival; a grasp of the culture shock process and how to manage it; less anxiety about the 'unknown'; and generally greater confidence about their being successful.

> (Bennett *et al.*, 2000: 244)

Training in the cross-cultural setting, therefore, requires more than knowledge of differences; it also requires acceptance of differences (Bhagat and Prien, 1996: 223–4) and an appreciation of the host culture (Treven, 2003).

Despite the perceived advantages of pursuing effective CCT programmes, research indicates that the amount of CCT undertaken is modest in most multinational corporations (Black *et al.*, 1992; Selmer, 1995). High costs and the extensive and largely unproductive 'running-in' period are reasons that frequently act as a disincentive to companies to invest in pre-departure training (Aycan, 1997; Katz and Seifer, 1996). As Torbiörn (1994) indicates, training programmes are usually of too short a duration to have any significant or prolonged effect. Further, the return on the investment of CCT is generally difficult to quantify (see Chapter 5 in this volume for a general discussion on ROI). Selmer (2001) notes that while inadequate training can impede the international assignee's adjustment in the host culture, a more noteworthy problem relates to the issue of trying to relate the training to the international assignee's receptiveness. In the case of global staffing, pre-departure training takes place when the international assignee's concept of what is normal is still related to the home culture. This may prove particularly problematic if an individual is undertaking their first assignment.

Table 6.1 provides a brief comparison of pre-departure and post-arrival training along a number of dimensions, specifically time, frequency (referring to how often each dimension is employed) and the key advantages and disadvantages of each.

Table 6.1 Pre-departure and post-arrival training: some comparisons

Dimension	Pre-departure	Post-arrival
Time	Conducted before commencement of assignment	Conducted on arrival or after commencement of assignment
Frequency	Not used very often – usually due to costs associated with it	More frequently employed as it is felt it is more effective because assignees are more open to it
Advantages	Allows the assignee to have realistic expectations of the assignment and a basic understanding of the culture to which they are going	Potentially more effective as expatriates can relate more readily to the training as real-time issues emerge
Disadvantages	Sometimes seen as being of too short duration to have any long-term effect; also pre-departure stressors may be very different from the reality of the situation	Unless there is a real-time element to such an intervention, post-arrival training may be reactive

Post-arrival training

Several of the weaknesses associated with pre-departure training have strengthened the belief among many organisations that post-arrival training may be more worthwhile (Bennett *et al.*, 2000; Mendenhall and Stahl, 2000). Black and Gregersen (1999) promote the concept of post-arrival training as a means of addressing 'real-time' issues with which international assignees must contend. In reality, making an individual aware in advance that they will encounter different business and social customs is not sufficient, as simple awareness of such disparities does not translate into competence in the host culture. As we have alluded to in our discussion of pre-departure training, an international assignee's pre-departure evaluation of the stressors they will encounter may be unrealistic and significantly different from the subsequent reality that confronts them on the ground. Therefore, according to Mendenhall and Stahl (2000), it is erroneous for organisations to believe that pre-departure training alone is sufficient to equip expatriates with the requisite knowledge and skill required by international assignees. Since living in a foreign environment is a complex task, pre-departure training can provide the international assignee with sufficient knowledge to survive but not excel. This may be because cultural differences are best understood in post-arrival training sessions after they have been experienced by the expatriate (Sanchez *et al.*, 2000: 100). Apposite to this, while there is a real-time element to such training, a key issue here is that since by definition post-arrival instruction occurs after the assignee's arrival in the host location (and sometimes up to three months afterwards), it tends to be reactive resulting in an increased probability that the individual will have to experience practical difficulties in the host environments, before these emerging problems are engaged with.

A core issue underlying this perceived inadequacy of pre-departure training and consequent apparent supremacy of post-arrival training appears to rest more with the shortcomings of human capital and not so much with the training itself. CCT programmes will be effective only if they are based upon clearly defined theoretical frameworks. Nonetheless, the majority of such initiatives are undertaken in organisations without appropriate conceptualisation of the various essential theoretical issues or clearly defined course objectives (Landis and Bhagat, 1996). In general, 'training should be based on explicit models or theories designed to explain the interaction towards which the training is directed' (Graf, 2004: 199). Therefore, as Bird *et al.* (1999) suggest:

> perhaps it is not the pre-departure training *per se*, but rather the faulty, non-customized nature of past approaches to this training that recently has led to the conclusion that on-site, real time learning for expatriate managers is much more important and effective.
>
> (Bird *et al.*, 1999: 154)

The role of cross-cultural training in international staffing

Cross-cultural training has been reported to deal with many problems encountered in international staffing. Here we highlight the potential role that CCT plays in dealing with three particular dimensions of the international experience, namely culture shock and transitional adjustment, potential assignment failure and premature re-entry and broader family considerations, often particular to the international move. (See also Chapter 4 of this volume for a more detailed discussion of these issues.)

Culture shock and transitional adjustment

Early contributions and much subsequent writing on international adjustment focused primarily in terms of adjustment on degrees of distress or 'culture shock'. Oberg (1960: 177) originally defined culture shock as 'an occupational disease of people who have suddenly been transported abroad' and suggested it is 'precipitated by the anxiety that results from losing all our familiar signs and symbols of social intercourse'. The term essentially explains the international assignee's reaction to a new, unpredictable and consequently uncertain environment (Black and Mendenhall, 1990).

While a study conducted by Hawes and Kealey (1981) suggested that culture shock does not inevitably result in inefficiency, Guy and Patton (1996), by contrast, point to the fact that in the event that an expatriate suffers from culture shock, the job becomes the logical venue for failure. A study by Cushner and Landis (1996) adds further credence to this suggestion. Results indicated that trained subjects were better adjusted and responded more favourably to hypothetical interpersonal problem-solving situations in an intercultural setting. Therefore, instruction in how to cope with culture shock is critical, as maintaining morale is particularly challenging when the assignee experiences adjustment difficulties (Webb and Wright, 1996).

Although CCT cannot completely overcome the effects of culture shock, it can provide international assignees with some resources to recognise the symptoms of culture shock and deal with the effects of it when it arises. As such, CCT can help shorten the adjustment timeframe and alleviate some of the symptoms of culture shock. Black and Mendenhall (1990) suggest that such training enables the individual to acquire skills and cultural knowledge that minimise misunderstandings and provide the framework for effective behaviour. Furthermore, this enhanced cultural awareness improves interpersonal relationships with those who hold contrasting behavioural patterns and social values, i.e. host-country nationals (Ashamalla, 1998).

Black and Mendenhall (1990) suggest that in dealing with culture shock, a social-learning theory approach that combines cognitive and behavioural strategies is appropriate to help CCT effectiveness. Successful control of the culture shock experience depends, according to Winkelman (1994), on a conscious sensitivity of the situation, a mental orientation that facilitates adaptation, and the acquisition of behavioural skills that negate culture shock. Cross-cultural training plays a significant role in two ways. Firstly, when it is conducted prior to departure, it assesses an individual's aptitude to adaptation in an alien environment, and secondly, CCT prepares expatriates for problems by using resources that will promote coping mechanisms and adjustment, thereby limiting the experience of culture shock.

Assignment failure and pre-mature re-entry

For a protracted period, there has been much discussion about the persistent challenge of expatriate failures due to poorly prepared international assignees (Ashamalla, 1998; Black *et al.*, 1992; Harvey, 1996; Mendenhall and Oddou, 1985). Estimates regarding the extent of expatriate failures vary widely (Black *et al.*, 1991; Harvey *et al.*, 2001; Scullion and Brewster, 2001; Selmer and Leung, 2003; Tung, 1981). However, there is a lack of strong empirical evidence to support high estimations (Forster and Johnsen, 1996;

Harzing, 1995, 2002). Advocating this argument, Hofstede (1998) noted: 'Does anybody really think that multinationals would have continued expatriating managers or other personnel if they kept getting such dramatic failure rates?' (cited in Harzing 2002). Regardless of the true extent of expatriate failures, the existence of unsuccessful assignments is undeniable.

Arguably, CCT may play a role in addressing this issue in a number of ways. First, Tung (1981) contends that the following four factors determine the success or failure of cross-cultural assignments: technical competence, personal traits (or relational abilities), capacity to cope with environmental variables and the family situation. Therefore, by intervening to address these four variables, CCT programmes can potentially reduce the number of unsuccessful overseas assignments. A survey conducted by Tung (1987) indicated that the more rigorous the training intervention applied, the lower the failure rate. Similarly, an analysis of Japanese companies by Hogan and Goodson (1990) attributed the low expatriate failure rates to the custom of selecting candidates a year in advance and conducting intensive training to prepare them before departure.

From the point of view of the international assignee, CCT also plays a role in ensuring assignees' expectations are met or positively exceeded. Through the use of briefings or other targeted interventions, intercultural training furnishes the expatriate with accurate and realistic job and location previews. Iverson and Deery (1997) identify role clarity, role discretion and organisational support to be significant determinants of job satisfaction. In relation to expatriates, job satisfaction will be greater when the assignee has clearly assigned performance goals and support from the organisation. Black *et al.* (1991) and Shaffer and Harrison (2001) have found these dimensions to be important antecedents of expatriate adjustment. Since successful adjustment reduces the likelihood of expatriate failures, it is in the organisation's interest to provide the requisite support. Garonzik *et al.* (2000) suggested that utilising CCT indicates commitment to the assignment and targets the organisation towards achieving a specific objective value in the form of maximising the assignee's performance. This increases employee satisfaction and minimises the tendency for the assignee to consider terminating the assignment prematurely. While the provision of CCT may not be able to ensure that the assignee subsequently defines their expectations accurately, it may play a significant role in assisting adjustment on arrival in the host country and reducing the prospect of failed assignments through the support mechanism it creates.

Family considerations during the international move

Much of the literature points to the need to provide CCT for the accompanying spouse/partner (cf. Black *et al.*, 1992; Eschbach *et al.*, 2001; O'Sullivan, 2002; Selmer and Leung, 2003). An international assignment undertaken as a family unit usually requires the spouse/partner to forfeit the accustomed structure and continuity of his/her life, which can be highly problematic for the expatriate couple (Linehan and Scullion, 2001). In contrast to the defined role that awaits the assignee, a set of responsibilities inherent in the job and a structured support system, the spouse/partner and family often face an unstructured arrival into the host location. Furthermore, as the spouse/partner and family are generally more directly involved in the local environment and for the most part have vastly different responsibilities to what they were accustomed to in the home environment, they potentially face a greater risk of failure to adjust (Shaffer and Harrison, 2001). It is plausible to argue, therefore, that spouses/partners and families who opt to travel with the assignee encounter more real challenges than the international assignee themselves. The need to speak the foreign language, to cope with culture shock, to understand different laws and customs, and to interact with local nationals may form a more integral part of the trailing spouse's daily life in the international base. This may lead to feelings of isolation that may be heightened if the accompanying individuals are not adequately informed in advance of the assignment.

First, the provision of language skills as a fundamental tenet of the CCT intervention is deemed essential. A study conducted by Shaffer and Harrison (2001) indicated that trailing spouses, who mastered the language, at least to a rudimentary level, were more likely to have had a positive experience while on assignment. This study reflects Mael's (1991) findings, which suggested that insufficient personal resources in the form of language acquisition might undermine one's self-belief and confidence. Through the acquisition of linguistic competence, the spouse and family increases the possibility of building networks with host nationals and creating a new social identity in his/her new environment (Bauer and Taylor, 2001). This can help create a smoother adjustment for the spouse.

Of critical importance, however, is that the training intervention is targeted at the specific needs of the spouse and family as these are often at variance with those of the expatriate. While many organisations assume responsibility for organising housing and the like on behalf of the international assignee, this is inadequate preparation for the trailing spouse. In order to engage with the needs of the accompanying family the provision of specific information in relation to the new location, the logistics of the transfer or indeed allowing for a look-see visit with the international assignee and their family have been emphasised (cf. McDonald, 1993). Relevant, timely information in this regard may diminish apprehension prior to the family's departure. By enabling the spouse to assess their potential to acculturate prior to departure, the prospect of expatriate failures due to the spouse's inability to adjust may be greatly moderated and capacity to engage with the new environment is greatly enhanced. Moreover, this form of preparation increases general self-efficacy, which is reflected in the individual's ability or confidence in dealing with the new situation.

Finally in relation to this discussion on family considerations for the international assignment, Pierce *et al.* (1991) maintain that the impression that one could count on family and friends facilitates psychiatric well-being. Similarly, the perception that the organisation is actively assisting and supporting the expatriate and family and preparing them for life overseas can alleviate many of the stressors that accompany withdrawal from familiar surroundings. This is likely to be particularly significant as the assignee's accompanying spouse will not have regular immediate contact with family, friends and work-related support resources. Therefore, the inclusion of the family in CCT interventions displays corporate commitment to the assignment and not solely to the adjustment of the expatriate but rather to the family as a whole.

Forms of cross-cultural training: experiential, cognitive and integrated approaches

Having defined cross-cultural training and summarily outlined its potential role in addressing some of the likely problems that arise in moving internationally, we now turn our attention to the different forms of cross-cultural training that may be employed by those engaged in global staffing.

Various contributors advance rather disparate techniques by which to classify CCT (Black and Mendenhall, 1990; Gudykunst *et al.*, 1977; Mendenhall and Oddou, 1985). These models have undoubtedly been influential in the field. However, subsequent contributions have incorporated these different elements into two generic dimensions, experiential training and cognitive training (Kealey and Protheroe, 1996; Zakaira, 2000). In the following subsection we will discuss some of the most prevalent approaches within these generic categories.

Experiential training

The experiential approach is underpinned by the belief that people, especially adults learn better by doing (Harris and Kumra, 2000). Kolb *et al.*'s (1991) work on the learning cycle proffers that action theories arise from experiences, which then are subject to continual transformation to improve their effectiveness. The efficacy of this approach is dependent upon the learner's perception that the procedures and strategies inherent in this method are beneficial and the belief that they can subsequently utilise them. Essentially, this means that the learner must sense that their response to the procedures and strategies and consequent behaviour will produce a positive outcome for themselves and for others.

This form of training 'should trigger affective and behavioural responses, which are the basis of intercultural effectiveness skills and thus enhance psychological adjustment' (Zakaira, 2000: 1). In essence, therefore, experiential training is beneficial to the extent that it reinforces the assimilated information through experience. It focuses on individual characteristics as opposed to situational characteristics. Such approaches to training include interactional learning, role-plays and behaviour modelling among others.

Cognitive training

By contrast the cognitive approach rests on the assumption that cognitive understanding and engagement is an important prerequisite to successful interaction with individuals from another culture. Thus such training facilitates socio-cultural adjustment through encouraging intellectual responses, particularly cultural awareness and interpersonal skills. According to Fowler (1994), the cognitive dimension addresses the expatriate's need for both information and behavioural skills. However, an organisation's ultimate goal is to impart information that will enable them to maintain the benefits of the training after completion of the programme. In this regard, Bennett *et al.* (2000) suggest that a learning to learn approach will produce more sustainable outcomes as it instructs trainees on how to pursue their learning and apply the new knowledge far beyond the boundaries of the programme itself.

Cognitive approaches, primarily in the form of area studies, or didactic approaches have dominated the field of CCT as the way to secure relevant information. Frequently considered among these intellectual approaches are lectures, audio-visual, environmental briefings, and cultural orientation programmes that are designed to provide assignees with factual information about a particular country. As such, these programmes mirror a conviction that providing information that facilitates an individual to understand the destination and its people equips them with the relevant tools to aid intercultural competence (Blake *et al.*, 1996).

Cross-cultural training: an integrated approach

Grove and Torbiörn (1985) proposed that CCT should endeavour to bring about changes in the international assignee in three ways, namely, applicability of behaviour, clarity of mental frame of reference, and level of mere adequacy.

> This would result in the newcomer maintaining their sense of personal identity while adjusting certain assumptions, values, attitudes, opinions, ideas, styles of reasoning and patterns of behaviour to bring them into line with those prevailing in the new environment.
>
> (Eschbach *et al.*, 2001: 273)

New skills must be developed and to ensure their effective transmission, such skills should be continued at least intermittently after the expatriate's arrival in the host location. Eschbach *et al.* (2001: 273) further note that this would 'allow a gradual process of adaptation in which the intellect gains in awareness and understanding while the emotions are prevented from reaching the point where the newcomer loses self-control'. While some empirical research suggests that short-term sensitivity training may be effective in increasing cultural awareness and potentially modifying beliefs and attitudes (Hammer and Martin, 1992; Pruegger and Rogers, 1994), it neglects to consider that cross-cultural training is a complex and long-term process. 'Our biases, prejudices, and stereotypes run deep and die hard!' (Sue, 1991: 104). Consequently, it is imperative that in order to bring about the necessary change and not merely an appreciation, intercultural training needs to extend beyond merely the pre-assignment phase. Furthermore, the use of both cognitive and experiential training methods reinforces the information assimilated by the participants and can effectively integrate culture-general and culture-specific skill.

The type of training initiative employed will be directly related to the purpose of the assignment. In this regard Caligiuri *et al.* (2005) have suggested classifying global assignments according to four disparate categories:

- technical
- developmental/high potential
- strategic/executive
- functional/tactical.

These classifications affect the training policies pursued in so far as the cross-cultural competencies required for each type will be varied, for example, somebody sent on a technical assignment may only require knowledge of the basics of living in the respective country. By contrast, an individual who is assigned to a developmental/high potential role will require training in interacting with host nationals in addition to language acquisition training. Table 6.2 illustrates a suite of approaches, derived largely from major contributions to the field, that may be employed in conducting CCT. Each technique is categorised according to the relevant form i.e. cognitive or experiential, and also arranged in terms of its respective delivery time i.e. pre-departure or post-arrival or both. Furthermore, Table 6.2 appraises each approach in respect of its potential advantages and limitations.

While a number of similarities may be identified among these approaches, the advantages of each technique seem to have different concentrations. Specifically, the literature appears to offer some consensus in relation to the possibility of providing international assignees with insights and giving them relevant information that ultimately may facilitate adjustment (Ashamalla, 1998; Blake *et al.*, 1996; Eschbach *et al.*, 2001; Fiedler *et al.*, 1971). However, these methods differ according to how they are applied, i.e. is it presented in a group context or an individual basis, for example, the use of role-plays, although conducted in a group context, focuses exclusively on the individual's personal response. This is in contrast to lectures and briefings which, according to Blake *et al.* (1996), provide information focused on the global assignee's requirements, and not his/her response. Similarly, culture assimilator training (Fiedler *et al.*, 1971) seems to suggest a targeted approach to training. It assesses an individual's knowledge of cultural variances and relates this to subsequent behaviour.

When we examine the limitations highlighted in the framework, the literature seems to agree that the key weakness of cognitive approaches is that they may fail to provide adequate information, which could increase apprehension or hostility towards the host destination (Blake *et al.*, 1996; Fiedler *et al.*, 1971; Hutchings, 2003; Linehan and Scullion, 2001).

Table 6.2 Cross-cultural training techniques

Form	Techniques	Benefits	Limitations	Classification
Cognitive	Lectures/briefings	• Focuses on cognitive domain through acquisition of learning • Information transmitted through a live source • Information may be tailored to the needs of the audience • Possible for IA to seek clarification on material presented • Structured setting, so ensures certain minimum amount of relevant information is imparted	• Informal nature may mean information necessary for cultural appreciation is omitted	Pre-departure
Cognitive	Language	• Allows assignee to function in the host environment • Fosters cognitive flexibility and creativity • Gives sense of efficacy, confidence and being in control • Allows greater insight into culture which may aid adjustment	• Conducted solely in a pre-departure context is not sufficient and only provides the most rudimentary of skills	Pre-departure and post-arrival
Cognitive	Culture assimilator training	• Assesses an individual's knowledge of cultural differences and the effects of this cultural distance in relation to their own functioning in that environment • Allows individuals to confront their fears in a relaxed atmosphere	• As it's a written set of instructions it may not be fully applicable to every location and may omit important issues	Pre-departure

continued

Table 6.2 (continued)

Form	Techniques	Benefits	Limitations	Classification
Experiential	Interactional learning	• Appropriate tool to the extent that interactions involve guided learning and practising appropriate conduct • Expatriate's motivation levels are at their peak at this point	• Sole reliance on this approach may increase the potential for cultural faux pas as it is based on interactions and learning from mistakes and does not use pre-departure cultural information as a base. • In a business context, it is unlikely that such cultural faux pas will be excused; therefore, the business may suffer as the individual may be viewed as unprofessional and ethnocentric.	Post-arrival
Experiential/ Cognitive	On-site training	• Provides opportunity for international assignee to analyse and discuss various stressors after they have come in contact with them • Can receive technical training specific to the job	• It involves highlighting the disparity between cultures and this may destroy the harmony between the expatriates and host nationals	Post-arrival
Cognitive	Mentoring/informal briefing with other international assignees	• May counteract the out-of-sight, out-of-mind syndrome and facilitate adjustment • Information provided is based on fact and actual difficulties encountered	• Value of this approach may depend on the relationship between the expatriate and his/her mentor • As people relate to experiences differently, the problems experienced by one person may be at variance with how other IAs would view the situation and so the value of the information they provide may be limited. • There are no checks and balances to ensure that accurate and valuable information is given	Pre-departure and post-arrival

Experiential	Simulations/role plays	• Can sensitise the individual to important concepts, • May provide valuable insights into situations that occur at a future date • By artificially creating uncertain situations, trainees can learn to recognise pervasive ambiguity and can think more clearly about lowering their expectations of clarity while on assignment	• May have positive or negative ramifications in dealing with such unforeseen events	Pre-departure
Experiential	Look–see visit	• Reflects organisation's commitment to expatriate success • Provides comprehensive introduction to host culture • Enables assignee to condition their expectations to what is real • May be ultimately more cost effective than formal CCT	• It can be an expensive process	Pre-departure
Experiential	Behaviour modelling	• Allows trainee to acquire social skills necessary to function in the other culture • Demonstrates and reinforces appropriate behaviour while allowing the individual to apply his/her unique interpretation.	• Advised as a method effective in preparing IAs for a supervisory position abroad. May therefore not be as effective for other positions.	Pre-departure
Experiential	Immersion programmes	• Allows trainees to develop a deep understanding of a culture without the simultaneous pressures of work • Involves repatriation feedback • Enables trainees to establish if they would be able to function in the environment thus reducing the possibility of failed assignments	• Short duration (2–3 months) may not allow for full experience of culture shock • Organisation is not gaining financial benefits from these workers while they are on this programme	Pre-departure

Sources: adapted from: Ashamalla (1998); Bhawuk and Brislin (2000); Blake et al. (1996); DeCenzo and Robbins (1996); Eschbach et al., (2001); Fiedler et al. (1971); Grove and Torbiörn (1985); Gupta and Govindarajan (2002); Hutchings (2003); Linehan and Scullion (2001); Webb and Wright (1996).

From an experiential point of view, Table 6.2 illustrates similarities between the various approaches. Arguably, there is agreement among academics that experiential techniques help to sensitise the assignee to the prospective location, thereby helping the expatriate to formulate realistic expectations (Bhawuk and Brislin, 2000; DeCenzo and Robbins, 1996; Webb and Wright, 1996). Based on Table 6.2, it is also plausible to argue that the core limitations associated with experiential techniques revolve around adjustment difficulties. For instance, Grove and Torbiörn (1985) suggest that without relevant pre-departure information, interactional learning may increase the potential for cultural faux pas. Indeed Blake *et al.*'s. (1996) discussion of simulation suggests that expatriates may encounter difficulties if events arise that are different from those for which they have rehearsed responses.

Irrespective of the technique employed, research indicates that the determining factor in the success of a CCT programme is its rigour. Training rigour is defined by Black *et al.* (1999: 92) as 'the degree of mental involvement and effort that the trainer and the trainee must expend for the trainee to learn the required concepts'. However, the expulsion of time and energy will be futile if the cross-cultural training programme fails to address key facets of effective performance in the host destination. Therefore, CCT as an investment, is most valuable when the rigour of the training is congruent with the nature and the specific requirements of the assignment (Black *et al.*, 1999). Figure 6.1 highlights the degree of training rigour against the degree of participant involvement. As the involvement of the trainee increases, we notice a corresponding intensification in the training rigour.

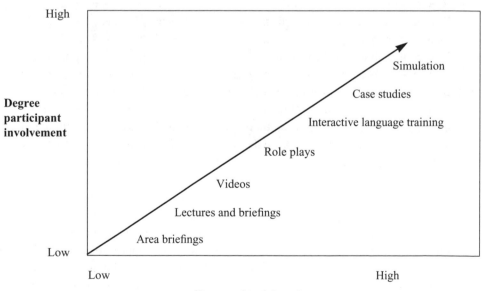

Figure 6.1 Degrees of training rigour

Source: Black *et al.* (1999: 93). Reprinted with permission.

The efficacy of cross-cultural training

A critical issue involved in the provision of CCT from an organisational point of view is whether and to what extent such training makes a discernible difference to the success of the international assignment (Kealey and Protheroe, 1996). Unless firms can see the financial benefits of such an outlay in terms of the successful completion of the global assignment, it is unlikely that those responsible for global staffing will embrace CCT. Several studies have sought to address this issue and determine the value of investment in such programmes. We now turn our attention to reviewing the key themes emerging from empirical work in this regard in order to illustrate the potential value of cross-cultural training interventions in the context of international staffing.

Much of the earlier empirical work in the area of cross-cultural training focused on methods employed by MNCs in this regard. For example, Tung (1981), Earley (1987) and Bird et al. (1993) concentrated their research on the contribution of area studies to expatriate success. Harrison (1992) extended his analysis to incorporate two different types of CCT, namely cognitive-based assimilators and behaviour modelling. While the results of these studies primarily advocated the utilisation of cross-cultural training techniques, Tung (1981) expressed reservations about the value of area studies as an appropriate technique to engage with the problems that arise in the course of the international experience. Her study concluded that purely informational briefings were insufficient to substantially alter participants' attitudes or enhance empathy, which it was posited would significantly impact interpersonal and professional effectiveness overseas. In a similar vein, Bird et al. (1993) suggested that area studies alone are insufficient to prepare individuals for global assignments. However, the researchers maintain that pre-departure training programmes are valuable, but that area studies should be used in conjunction with other methods. Their results suggest such programmes may be an advantageous mechanism for establishing cultural awareness. However, 'the impact of this knowledge on other factors believed to be associated with cross-cultural adaptation appears limited' (Bird et al., 1993: 432–3). Apposite to this, Harrison concluded that 'combining the cultural assimilatory and behaviour modelling has a significantly greater effect on behaviour criteria . . . than no training . . . [or] either of the individual methods alone' (Harrison, 1992: 959). Earley's (1987) study also highlights the increased effectiveness of combining cognitive and affective training. Those assignees who received a combination of documentary and interpersonal training received the most impressive evaluations from their supervisors in terms of work performance and cross-cultural adjustment than those who received no training or only one type of preparation. In summary, these studies would appear to advocate the adoption of a variety of techniques to maximise the potential of cross-cultural training to successfully enhance the international experience and ensure value-added for the organisation.

The ultimate test regarding the effectiveness of CCT interventions is the extent to which it can enable the organisation to successfully utilise and nurture the international assignee to implement an international strategy to ensure the success of the international assignment. One of the most significant reviews of empirical literature was conducted by Black and Mendenhall (1990) who reviewed twenty-nine empirical studies on the effectiveness of CCT programmes in relation to three desired outcomes: cross-cultural skills development, personal and family adjustment and performance in the host country. While their analysis has been the subject of some criticism, primarily by Kealey and Protheroe (1996), in terms of the kind of studies included in their review. Black and Mendenhall (1990) concluded with a modest acknowledgement that the empirical studies give guarded support to their proposition of the effectiveness of CCT. However, they do acknowledge that 'more longitudinal studies are needed that include rigorous research designs before definitive conclusions about the impact of training over time can be made' (1990: 119). Despite this, Kealey and Protheroe (1996) posit that Black and Mendenhall's conclusion is overly optimistic given the above-mentioned limitations. Caligiuri *et al.* (2001) and Eschbach *et al.* (2001) in their respective studies both supported the utilisation of CCT. The former study concluded that relevant intercultural training is valuable to the extent that it manages expatriates' expectations. Specifically Caligiuri *et al.* (2001: 366) noted that 'highly relevant cross-cultural training created either accurate expectations or expectations of difficulty prior to the assignment'. Similarly, Eschbach *et al.* (2001) who examined the extent to which rigorous intercultural training administered prior to departure aids the adjustment process found that 'The general pattern [of the results] demonstrated that those with integrated cross-cultural training had a better level of adjustment and higher levels of skill development' (Eschbach *et al.*, 2001: 285). However, by contrast, Selmer (2001) conducted a cross-national study to empirically examine pre-knowledge (an expatriate's knowledge of a foreign culture prior to undertaking the training) and socialisation tactics used by Swedish expatriates and their immediate Hong Kong subordinates in learning to interact with each other. He concluded that pre-departure training was unhelpful for the expatriates. In addition, Selmer (2001) maintains that training the subordinates was superfluous due to their failure to implement what little pre-departure knowledge they had. Overall, therefore, while there is an empirical literature questioning the value of CCT and its effectiveness in facilitating intercultural transitional adjustment, some work does point to its value in composing an international staff.

Table 6.3 summarises these studies and provides details of the purpose of the study, the method used to conduct it and the overall findings in each case.

Conclusion

In this chapter we have examined the relevance and role of cross-cultural training as a mechanism to prepare global staff to undertake international assignments in a manner that will advance corporate objectives and add value to the organisation. Irrespective of whether a cognitive, experiential or integrated approach is utilised, the ultimate aim should be to enhance the cross-cultural competence of the assignee. In this chapter, we

Table 6.3 Key empirical studies which examined the value of CCT

Author	Year	Purpose of study	Methodology	Implication for value of CCT
Tung	1981	To examine whether and to what extent area studies assist expatriate success	Questionnaires administered to 300 MNCs	No clear evidence of value of CCT; purely information briefings are insufficient to alter participants' attitudes or enhance empathy
Earley	1987	To examine documentary and interpersonal training methods of preparing managers to work overseas	Use of crossed-factorial design with 20 randomly assigned participants in each condition; self-assessment and assessment from supervisor post the expatriate experience	Positive value established for CCT but this study highlights the increased effectiveness of combining cognitive and experiential training i.e. area studies and experimental based interpersonal skills training
Black and Mendenhall	1990	To review 29 empirical studies with the view to developing a framework for developing the field	Review of extant literature and studies conducted	CCT is seen as valuable to a certain extent but only guarded support is offered by researchers; caveat included
Harrison	1992	To assess the impact of pursing two different CCT methods	Analysed experimental and control group	Harrison (1992) supports the view that CCT is valuable but the results indicate that a combination of methods was better than any one method alone or no training
Bird et al.	1993	To identify more precisely the effects of informational training	Quasi-experimental treatment group given a one-week series of seminars	Value and benefit in using area studies for overseas adaptation and performance but alone they are insufficient to have any real impact

continued

Table 6.3 (continued)

Author	Year	Purpose of study	Methodology	Implication for value of CCT
Caligiuri *et al.*	2001	To assess if relevance of pre-departure training impacts expatriates' expectations	Questionnaires	CCT valuable to extent that it provides accurate expectations among expatriates and therefore creates greater possibility for their expectations to be met or surpassed
Eschbach *et al.*	2001	To examine the extent to which rigorous intercultural training administered prior to departure aids the adjustment process	Survey of 79 repatriates	The authors unequivocally espouse the value of CCT; they found that those who received rigorous CCT exhibited cultural proficiency earlier than the other participants and performed more effectively at two months and at nine months
Selmer	2001	To empirically investigate the pre-knowledge socialisation tactics employed and their Hong Kong subordinates	Two information sets (one for Hong Kong and one for Western European countries). Both sets of responses were collected in person	Not perceived as valuable for Hong Kong subordinates as they didn't use what they learned from it – transfer of knowledge was poor; in this case the pre-departure knowledge had little impact

introduced several of the techniques that are used in training international assignees. These included role-plays, mentoring and language training, among others. The method for training international assignees is likely to alter in the future with the advent of electronic cross-cultural training. This approach has several advantages; it is an approach that targets individual needs. Furthermore, it is easy to administer and is useful in terms of effective time management as the individual can focus on their specific needs (Caligiuri *et al.*, 2005). While the studies cited provide mixed support for the provision of CCT, several do advocate the use and necessity of CCT. However, ultimately CCT is key as part of an integrated suite of congruent HR policies. As such its efficacy is closely aligned with the other HR policies. For instance, effective training is dependent on the recruitment of a suitable cadre of recruits. Therefore, the recruitment and selection process of international assignees is an important prerequisite. This is an issue that is explored in Chapters 4 and 5 of this volume. Finally, while much literature has focused on CCT for the traditional long-term international assignments, its importance must not be overlooked into the future for the emerging non-traditional forms of international assignments e.g. frequent flyers, global leadership programmes, rotational assignments (see Chapter 8 of this volume for greater detail).

References

Ashamalla, M. (1998) 'International human resource management practices: the challenge of expatriation', *Competitiveness Review*, 8(2): 54–65.

Aycan, Z. (1997) 'Expatriate adjustment as a multifaceted phenomenon: individual and organisational level predictors', *International Journal of Human Resource Management*, 8(4): 434–56.

Bauer, T.N. and Taylor, S. (2001) 'When managing expatriate adjustment, don't forget the spouse', *Academy of Management Executive*, 15: 135–8.

Bennett, R., Aston, A. and Colquhoun, T. (2000) 'CCT: a critical step in ensuring the success of international assignments', *Human Resource Management*, 39(2–3): 239 50.

Bhagat, R.S. and Prien, K.O. (1996) 'Cross-cultural training in organizational contexts', in D. Landis and R.S. Bhagat (eds) *Handbook of Intercultural Training*, London: Sage.

Bhawuk, D.P.S. and Brislin, R.W. (2000), 'Cross-cultural training: a review', *Applied Psychology: An International Review*, 49(1): 162–91.

Bird, A., Heinbuch, S., Dunbar, R. and McNulty, M. (1993) 'A conceptual model of the effects of area studies training programs and a preliminary investigation of the model's hypothesised relationships', *International Journal of Intercultural Relations*, 17: 415–36.

Bird, A., Osland, J.S., Mendenhall, M. and Schneider, S.C. (1999) 'Adapting and adjusting to other cultures: what we know but don't always tell', *Journal of Management Inquiry*, 8: 152–65.

Black, J.S. and Gregersen, H. B. (1999) 'The right way to manage expats', *Harvard Business Review*, 77(2): 52–63.

Black, J.S. and Mendenhall, M. (1990) 'Cross-cultural training effectiveness: a review and a theoretical framework for future research', *Academy of Management Review*, 15(1): 113–36.

Black, J.S., Mendenhall, M.E. and Oddou, G. (1991) 'Toward a comprehensive model of international adjustment: an integration of multiple theoretical perspectives', *Academy of Management Review*, 16(2): 291–317.

Black, J.S., Mendenhall, M.E., and Gregersen, H. (1992) Global assignments. San Francisco: Jossey-Bass.

Black, J.S., Gregersen, H.B., Mendenhall, M.E. and Stroh, L.K. (1999) *Globalizing People through International Assignments*, Reading, MA: Addison-Wesley.

Blake, B.F., Heslin, R. and Curtis, S.C. (1996) 'Measuring impacts of cross-cultural training', in D. Landis and R.S. Bhagat (eds) *Handbook of Intercultural Training*, London: Sage.

Briscoe, D.R. and Schuler, R.S. (2004) *International Human Resource Management*, London: Routledge.

Caligiuri, P., Lazarova, M. and Tarique, I. (2005) 'Training, learning and development in multinational organisations', in H. Scullion and M. Linehan (eds) *International Human Resource Management: A Critical Text*, Basingstoke: Palgrave Macmillan.

Caligiuri, P.M., Phillips, H., Lazarova, M., Tarique, I. and Burgi, P. (2001) 'The theory of met expectations applied to expatriate adjustment: the role of cross-cultural training', *International Journal of Human Resource Management*, 12(3): 357–73.

Cushner, K. and Landis, D. (1996) 'The intercultural sensitizer', in D. Landis and R.S. Bhagat (eds) *Handbook of Intercultural Training*, London: Sage.

DeCenzo, D. and Robbins, S.P. (1996) *Human Resource Management, 7th International Edition*, New York: Wiley.

Dowling, P. and Welch, D. (2004) *International Human Resource Management: Managing People in a Multinational Context*, 4th edn, London: Thomson Learning.

Downes, M. and Thomas, A.S. (2000) 'Knowledge transfer through expatriation: the U-curve approach to oversee staffing', *Journal of Managerial Issues*, 12(2): 131–52.

Earley, C.P. (1987) 'International training for managers: a comparison of documentary and interpersonal methods', *Academy of Management Journal*, 30(41): 685–98.

Eschbach, D.M., Parker, G.E. and Stoeberl, P.A. (2001) 'American repatriate employees' retrospective assessments of the effects of cross-cultural training on their adaptation to international assignments', *International Journal of Human Resource Management*, 12(2): 270–87.

Fiedler, F.E., Mitchell, T. and Triandis, H.C. (1971) 'The culture assimilator: an approach to cross-cultural training', *Journal of Applied Psychology*, 55: 95–102.

Forster, N. and Johnsen, M. (1996) 'Expatriate management policies in UK companies new to the international scene', *International Journal of Human Resource Management*, 7(1): 177–205.

Fowler, S.M. (1994) 'Two decades of using simulation games for cross-cultural training', *Simulation and Gaming*, 25(4): 464–77.

Garonzik, R., Brockner, J. and Siegel, P.A. (2000) 'Identifying international assignees at risk for premier departure: the interactive effect of outcome, favour ability, procedural fairness', *Journal of Applied Psychology*, 85(1): 13–29.

Graf, A. (2004) 'Assessing intercultural training designs', *Journal of European Industrial Training*, 28(2–4): 199–214.

Grove, C.L. and Torbiörn, I. (1985) 'A new conceptualization of intercultural adjustment and goals of training', *International Journal of Intercultural Relations*, 9: 205–33.

Gudykunst, W., Hammer, M. and Wiseman, R. (1977) 'An analysis of an integrated approach to cross-cultural training', *International Journal of Intercultural Relations*, 1: 99–110.

Gupta, A.K. and Govindarajan, V. (2002) 'Cultivating a global mindset', *Academy of Management Executive*, 16(1): 116–26.

Guy, B.S. and Patton, W.E. (1996) 'Managing the effects of culture shock and sojourner adjustment on the expatriate sales force', *Industrial Marketing Management*, 25(4): 385–93.

Hammer, M.R. and Martin, J.N. (1992), 'The effects of cross-cultural training on American managers in a Japanese-American joint venture', *Journal of Applied Communication Research*, 20: 161–82.

Harris, H. and Kumra, S. (2000) 'International manager development cross-cultural training in highly diverse environments', *Journal of Management Development*, 19(7): 602–14.

Harrison, J.K. (1992) 'Individual and combined effects of behavior modeling and the cultural assimilator in cross-cultural management training', *Journal of Applied Psychology*, 77(6): 952–62.

Harvey, M. (1996) 'The selection of managers for foreign assignments: a planning perspective', *Columbia Journal of World Business*, 31(4): 102–19.

Harvey, M., Speier, C. and Novecevic, M. (2001) 'A theory-based framework for strategic global human resource staffing policies and practices', *International Journal of Human Resource Management*, 12(6): 898–915.

Harzing, A.W.K. (1995) 'The persistent myth of high expatriate failure rates', *International Journal of Human Resource Management*, 6(2): 457–74.

Harzing, A.W.K. (2002) 'Are our referencing errors undermining our scholarship and credibility? The case of expatriate failure rates', *Journal of Organizational Behavior*, 23(1): 127–48.

Hawes, F. and Kealey, D.J. (1981) 'Canadians in development: an empirical study of Canadian technical assistance', *International Journal of Intercultural Relations*, 5: 239–58.

Hofstede, G. (1998) 'The internationalisation of SIETAR international', *The SIETAR International Journal*, Fall: 47–57.

Hogan, G.W. and Goodson, J.R. (1990) 'The key to expatriate success', *Training and Development Journal*, 44(1): 50–2.

Hutchings, K. (2003) 'Cross-cultural preparation of Australian expatriates in organisations in China: the need for greater attention to training', *Asia Pacific Journal of Management*, 20(3): 375–96.

Iverson, R.D. and Deery, M. (1997) 'Turnover culture in the hospitality industry', *Human Resource Management Journal*, 7(4): 71–82.

Katz, J. and Seifer, D. (1996) 'It's a different world out there', *Human Resource Planning*, 19(2): 32–48.

Kealey, D.J. and Protheroe, D.R. (1996) 'The effectiveness of cross-cultural training for expatriates: an assessment of the literature on the issue', *International Journal of Intercultural Relations*, 20(2): 141–65.

Kolb, D.A., Rubin, I.M. and Osland, J.M. (eds) (1991) *Organizational Behavior: An Experiential Approach*, Englewood Cliffs, NJ: Prentice-Hall.

Landis, D. and Bhagat, R.S. (eds) (1996) *Handbook of Intercultural Training*, 2nd edn, Thousand Oaks, CA: Sage.

Lewis, M.M. (2003) 'The drama of international business: why cross-cultural training simulations work', proceeds from the Seventh International Human Resource Management Conference Exploring the Mosaic, Developing the Discipline, University of Limerick, 4–6 June.

Linehan, M. and Scullion, H. (2001) 'European female expatriate careers: critical success factors', *Journal of European Industrial Training*, 25(8): 392–418.

McDonald, G. (1993) 'ET go home? The successful management of expatriate transfers', *Journal of Managerial Psychology*, 8(2): 18–29.

Mael, F.A. (1991) 'A conceptual rationale for the domain and attributes of bio-data items', *Personnel Psychology*, 44: 763–92.

Mendenhall, M. and Oddou, G. (1985) 'The dimensions of expatriate acculturation', *Academy of Management Review*, 10(1): 39–47.

Mendenhall, M. and Stahl, G. (2000) 'Expatriate training and development: where do we go from here?' *Human Resource Management*, 39(2–3): 251–65.

Oberg, K. (1960) 'Culture shock – adjustment to new cultural environments', *Practical Anthropology*, 7: 117–82.

O'Sullivan, S.L. (2002) 'The protean approach to managing repatriation transitions', *International Journal of Manpower*, 23(7): 597–616.

Pierce, G.R., Sarason, I.G. and Sarason, B.R. (1991) 'General and relationship based perceptions of social support: are two constructs better than one?', *Journal of Personality and Social Psychology*, 61: 1028–39.

Pruegger, V.J. and Rogers, T.B. (1994) 'Cross-cultural sensitivity training: methods and assessment', *International Journal of Intercultural Relations*, 9: 247–69.

Sanchez, J.I., Spector, P.E. and Cooper, C.L. (2000) 'Adapting to a boundary less world: a developmental expatriate model', *Academy of Management Executive*, 14(2): 96–106.

Scullion, H. and Brewster, C. (2001) 'Managing expatriates: messages from Europe', *Journal of World Business*, 36(4): 346–65.

Scullion, H. and Donnelly, N. (1998) 'International human resource management: recent developments in Irish multinationals', in W.K. Roche, K. Monks and J. Walsh (eds) *Human Resource Strategies*, Dublin: Oak Tree Press.

Selmer, J. (1995) 'Expatriate executives' perceptions of their HCN subordinates' work values in South East Asia', in S.B. Prasad (ed.) *Advances in International Comparative Management: A Research Annual*, Greenwich, CT: JAI Press.

Selmer, J. (2001) 'Antecedents of expatriates/local relationships: pre-knowledge vs. socialisation tactics', *International Journal of Human Resource Management*, 12(6): 916–25.

Selmer, J. and Leung, A.S.M. (2003) 'Provision and adequacy of corporate support to male expatriate spouses: an exploratory study', *Personnel Review*, 32(1): 9–21.

Shaffer, M.A. and Harrison, D.A. (2001) 'Forgotten partners of international assignments: development and test of a model of spouse adjustment', *Journal of Applied Psychology*, 86(2): 238–54.

Sue, D.W. (1991) 'A model for cultural diversity training', *Journal of Counselling and Development*, 70: 99–105.

Torbiörn, I. (1994) 'Dynamics of cross-cultural adaptation', in G. Althen (ed.) *Learning across Cultures*, Washington, DC: NAFSA.

Treven, S. (2003) 'International training: the training of managers for assignment abroad', *Education and Training*, 45(8–9): 550–7.

Tung, R. (1981) 'Selecting and training of personal for overseas assignments', *Columbia Journal of World Business*, 16(1): 68–78.

Tung, R. (1987) 'Expatriate assignments: enhancing success and minimising failure', *Academy of Management Review*, 1(2): 117–25.

Webb, A. and Wright, P. (1996) 'The expatriate experience: implications for career success', *Career Development International*, 1(5): 38–44.

Winkelman, M. (1994) 'Culture shock and adaptation', *Journal of Counseling and Development*, 73(2): 121–6.

Zakaira, N. (2000) 'The effects of cross-cultural training on the acculturation process of the global workforce', International Journal of Manpower, 21(6): 492–510.

7 Localisation: societies, organisations and employees

WES HARRY AND DAVID G. COLLINGS

Introduction

Localisation has emerged as a key issue in the management of multinational corporations. The concept is however often used in generic terms without specific definition. In this regard Hideo Sugiura, the former vice-chairman of Honda, distinguished between four types of localisation: localisation of products, profit, production and people (cited in Evans *et al.*, 2002). Although the primary focus of this chapter will be on people, we will also touch on some of the other concepts in setting the context for our later discussions. In this regard a key debate centres on the extent to which MNCs' 'foreign affiliates (or subsidiaries) act and behave as local firms versus the extent to which their practices resemble those of the parent corporation or some other global standard' (Rosenzweig and Nohria, 1994: 229). Indeed based on their work on patterns of strategic control in multinationals, Doz and Prahalad (1986) have argued that responding to a variety of national demands while maintaining a coherent strategy is a key strategic challenge facing MNCs. In a similar vein Bartlett and Ghoshal (1998) call for organisations to maintain a 'dynamic balance' between globalisation (implementing globally standard practices) and localisation (adapting practices to account for the host environment) if they are to become truly transnational. The staffing orientations pursued by MNCs in their foreign affiliates are generally a key indicator of the firm's orientation in this regard (see Chapter 2 of this volume). Specifically firms which pursue an ethnocentric orientation are likely to fill key positions in subsidiary operations with parent country nationals or employees from the home country of the MNC. In contrast MNCs which pursue a polycentric approach are significantly more likely to fill key positions at subsidiary level with host country nationals or employees from the country in which the subsidiary is located. (The implications of pursuing these strategies are explored in detail in Chapter 2.)

Localisation of labour (sometimes called labour nationalisation, host country national development or indigenisation) is defined as: 'the extent to which jobs originally filled by expatriates are filled by local employees who are competent to perform the job' (Selmer,

2004: 1094) and it is often considered one of the crucial drivers of the employment policies of many nation-states. It also influences the state's relationships with foreign organisations seeking to operate within their national boundaries. Evans *et al.* (2002) see localisation as systematic investment in the recruitment, development and retention of local employees, which is an important element in the globalisation strategy of multinationals. However, they also point to the differences between the rhetoric and the reality of many localisation strategies and the barriers to the implementation of localisation strategies will be considered below.

Demographics and cost concerns are often key drivers of localisation, particularly in the Gulf Cooperation Council countries (Bahrain, Kuwait, Oman, Qatar, Saudi Arabia and United Arab Emirates) and failure to solve the problems of ineffective localisation may have wide-ranging and long-term consequences (Yamani 2000). Debates around localisation are not restricted to managerial employees however, and also concern the employment of HCNs at lower levels in the organisational hierarchy. In this regard it might seem easy to create jobs for locals but in practice the creation of worthwhile productive jobs depends on an appropriate education system, suitable work ethic within the host population and willingness on the part of employers to make a sustained and genuine effort to support and transfer skills, attitudes and behaviours. As should be apparent from the proceeding introduction the localisation of human resources at managerial and staff levels is important not only in the context of developing the human resources of the host economy but also in building mutually beneficial, long-term relationships between the employing organisation and the host society. Further, lower profit margins in developing countries and a growing unwillingness among governments in poorer countries to allow key positions in foreign MNCs to be occupied indefinitely by expatriates are forcing more and more organisations to examine alternatives to traditional expatriate staffing methods (Sparrow *et al.*, 2004; see also Chapter 8 this volume).

In this chapter we will first outline the key forces driving local responsiveness in international business. We then consider the business advantages and disadvantages of local responsiveness. Our discussion then focuses more specifically on the localisation of human resources and again the advantages and disadvantages of this will be outlined. After exploring the nature of localisation in practice, finally we consider the role of expatriates in the localisation process.

The changing meaning of local responsiveness in international business

At one time organisations from developed countries could virtually afford to ignore local needs and wishes in servicing foreign markets, particularly those in developing countries. They generally had a monopoly, or near monopoly, of goods and services and so could impose on local markets whatever they wanted to sell. Some imposed, or tried to impose, their business practices and cultures in foreign operations (cf. Hertz, 2001). Some international organisations could even impose their will on sovereign states. The power of the companies was generally applied and monitored by expatriates, usually nationals of the parent country of their employer.

The imposition of products, services and people was resented, particularly for the colonialist attitudes which came with the imposition. Further, citizens from developing countries continue to resent expatriates holding high paid jobs which they considered could be done by HCNs, and they often commented on the lack of commitment of expatriates to the local operations (Brewster, 1991). Since the 1960s, the desire to build nation-states and national economies has led to a strong move for nationalisation, local partnerships or at least significant investment within the host country (Sparrow *et al.*, 2004). In the following section we consider the business advantages and disadvantages of localisation.

The business advantages and disadvantages of localisation

There are many sound economic and ethical reasons for MNCs to develop a localisation strategy. Such developments are not without some difficulties and disadvantages however and these are discussed below.

Advantages

There are four main advantages in developing localisation policies. First, localisation of human resources may improve relations between foreign investors and host country governments. Selmer (2004) has argued that this is the case in the Chinese context as the government favours the development of local employees. Indeed Lasserre and Ching (1997) have shown that central and provincial authorities there may view localisation to be an indication of foreign firms' commitment to the country. Thus from the MNC's point of view a localisation strategy may help to ensure foreign operations operate with minimum levels of conflict with the host authorities. Further it may assist the firm in gaining lucrative contracts or tenders with public sector organisations.

Second, localisation of human resources may improve communication, and, ultimately business performance in the host country. This is because communication local to local is usually more effective than foreigner to local. Human nature tends to favour the familiar rather than the strange. In this regard customers generally want to be served by those who understand their needs and it is most often fellow nationals and long-term residents who understand what these needs are. Successful organisations recognise that a shared language, with the local nuances, helps in communications and understanding. Further, HCNs may provide a valuable resource in developing local contacts in the host environment. While expatriate managers may have greater access to higher level institutional contacts, local employees will generally be in a better position to develop business relationships with lower levels of organisational and government hierarchies (Lasserre and Ching, 1997; Selmer, 2004). This is particularly important in some societies such as China where guanxi is vital for developing business contacts and opportunities.

Third, host country labour is generally a more reliable resource than temporary workers, who even if they work in the country for a long time, have divided loyalty (Black and Gregerson 1992) and certainly see their ultimate destination as a different location. The loyalty of the foreign labour is purchased at a price which, with few exceptions, is more expensive than local labour. Harry and Banai (2005) have described the motivation of many senior expatriates and the costs of employing them – at rates much higher than most host country nationals. In a similar vein, it has been shown that expatriates operating in a Chinese context can be paid five times more than HCN comparators in total compensation (Economist Intelligence Unit, 1997; Selmer, 2004). Ruhs and Godfrey (2002) have shown that even for 'cheap' foreign labour, the costs, over the long term, are greater than most societies would willingly bear.

Finally, from an economic perspective, by responding to local needs, especially through investing capital and employing local labour, the organisation increases the wealth of the local population and so increases their ability to buy products and services sold by local businesses. Even if the market is small and poor, there can be good potential for growth and long-term profit (Prahalad, 2004). MNCs can create the capacity to consume by paying reasonable wages, training and developing staff and treating them well should be able to reap advantages from increased markets in the host country. Those organisations which develop local markets may gain a dominant market position which latecomers will find hard to overturn.

Disadvantages

There are four main disadvantages in developing localisation policies. First, understanding local markets takes time and effort. Sometimes local management can make costly mistakes or events can occur outside their direct control which will cost the parent company heavily in financial terms as companies such as Union Carbide in Bhopal India or Shell in Nigeria have found. The cost of educating customers who might not be familiar with a product or service, even those intended to meet apparent local needs, can be very high. So too can be the cost of adjusting the product or service to meet these local needs, for example smaller packets for those customers who cannot afford to buy enough to hold a stock of an item (Das, 1993) or different coloured materials to meet local preferences. On the basis of a cost-benefit analysis organisations may feel that the costs associated with the adaptation of products to account for the local context may outweigh the benefits associated with such an action (Shenkar and Luo, 2004). Further, organisations may on the basis of a user/need analysis of consumer needs even decide not to introduce a popular product or service into a particular market (Shenkar and Luo, 2004: 419–20).

Second, there are disadvantages in having to make changes in the ways of working to meet local conditions. For example the work patterns might be different from those expected or preferred such as split shifts giving a long break at midday, or twelve hour, six day working with long vacations. Indeed it has been argued (Nash, 2004) that the traditional Spanish siesta is coming under threat from globalisation as a growing number of MNCs are increasingly persuading executives that they cannot be absent from their desks for hours during the middle of the day. This indicates that these MNCs consider the siesta to be impractical in the modern globalised business environment. Thus they are not prepared to sacrifice their traditional working time arrangements for what they consider to be an impractical and unworkable tradition which is at odds with their ideology for how the business enterprise should be run.

Third, managing without expatriates involves looser coordination from an HQ perspective and potentially greater problems in communicating with HQ from a subsidiary perspective. Indeed empirical research has shown that the staffing decisions with regard to key executive appointments (with expatriates or locals) significantly impacted on the parent company's operational control of the host operations (Child and Yan, 1999). While more indirect methods of control have been effectively used to monitor subsidiary performance, a direct link with the subsidiary through a parent country national may aid in ensuring that communication lines between the HQ and the subsidiary are open and efficient. Without this link, the HQ may not have an accurate picture of how the subsidiary is performing. Specifically while more indirect control methods such as financial reporting can provide HQ with a quantitative overview of subsidiary performance, some of the nuances of the subsidiary operation may be lost in the figures. For example, in some situations profit levels in the local market may not meet international levels or expectations but nonetheless they can still make a steady and potentially increasing contribution to the organisation's portfolio. Likewise inefficiencies or financial problems could potentially be hidden in financial statements or other reporting procedures.

Fourth, a major concern of senior HQ managers with respect to localisation strategy is the fear of losing intellectual property rights, particularly in the emerging markets where the perception is that everything can be copied. Selmer (2004) describes this as an 'agency problem' and argues that expatriate presence may help to guard against local managers pursuing their personal self-interest in managing the subsidiary or making decisions which are incongruent with the organisation's global strategy. In this vein Boisot and Child (1999) have noted that due to concerns over embezzlement in the Chinese context, many foreign firms have reserved the option of appointing their chief financial officers from within the organisation.

Having examined the advantages and disadvantages of local responsiveness in international management in a broader sense, we will now focus specifically on the localisation of human resources.

Localisation of human resources

In this section we will consider the localisation of non-managerial staff in foreign subsidiaries. This is significant as the number of non-managerial staff employed in subsidiaries is generally far in excess of those in managerial roles. This cohort of employees are generally neglected in the extant literature however.

While globalisation appears to offer many advantages to international organisations it does have the potential disadvantage that these organisations are judged not just as economic entities but as social creations which are expected, not least by customers and domestic pressure groups, to behave in a responsible and ethical manner – wherever they operate. Thus localisation is not as straightforward a proposition as it may immediately appear. Hence in this context a key ethical decision for international HR managers to consider is what to do when an employment practice that is illegal or even viewed as morally suspect in the home country is legal and acceptable in the host country (Briscoe and Schuler, 2004)? Major international companies such as Shell, Union Carbine and Nike have found that their 'local' practices are judged by 'home' country ethical standards with the potential harm that does to reputation and sales (Litvin 2003). Take for example the criticism Nike has received in recent years due to the conditions prevailing in its outsourced productions facilities in lower wage cost countries (cf. Morris and Lawrence, 2003). In this regard there are sound ethical reasons for developing local human resources (Hailey, 1999). These reasons include human rights in terms of employment and training opportunities not being linked to race and nationality but to capability and with meeting the reasonable requirements of the whole stakeholder community and contributing to the greater human development.

It might seem straightforward to develop the skills required to localise many of the tasks required in large-scale industrialised operations and complex administrative services, but in the context of developing countries, it is important to note that the skills, attitudes, behaviours and methods of learning necessary in rural and small-scale industrial activities are not easily transferable to the large-scale and complex activities which characterise multinational investment. As most employees (and customers) will have little exposure to the requirements of industrialised and complex operations it will take time, much training and expenditure to develop the workers to meet the organisation's needs.

We will now examine the benefits and barriers of localising human resources.

The benefits of localising human resources

There are many benefits which arise from utilising local people rather than expatriates to fill key positions within foreign operations. Often these benefits are underestimated, particularly for senior positions, for reasons which are often based on racial or national stereotypes (Banai, 1992).

We have discussed above the advantages of provider and customer sharing a common language as well as common cultural communications and expectations. The impact of this sharing cannot be underestimated. As noted above HCNs may provide a valuable resource in developing local contacts in the host environment. Specifically we pointed to the fact that while expatriate managers may have greater access to higher level institutional contacts, local employees will, generally, be in a better position to develop business relationships with lower levels of organisational and government hierarchies (Lasserre and Ching, 1997; Selmer, 2004).

The cost of local employees is generally lower than that of expatriates. Expatriates' costs are usually a multiple of the national employee and expatriates are among the most expensive employees even in home country terms (e.g. Brewster, 1991; Harry and Banai, 2005; Scullion and Brewster, 2001). Even the cost of administering the expatriate employees conditions of service can be high, compared with that of the administration of host country nationals, with HR staff engaged in carrying out cost of living comparison studies, developing tax equalisation formulae and managing international careers (Dowling and Welch, 2004).

The lower costs of the host country staff and their longer-term employment means that the return on investment in recruiting and training these staff may be higher than for expatriates (see Chapter 3 in this volume for a general discussion on return on investment). Organisations which encourage the development and promotion of local staff are likely to see improved morale and greater retention rates of their best staff (see Chapter 2 in this volume). These staff will stay for longer ensuring that valuable knowledge and capability are retained within the organisation and thus making a potentially more valuable return from the investment in their recruitment and development than investing in expatriate staff. The long-term relationship between the local operation and the host population often means that the company is no longer seen as foreign but local. For example Ford of Dagenham is now generally considered British and not American and the Wellcome stores are generally considered a Hong Kong 'belonger' there.

As discussed earlier the localisation of human resources may also have a positive political impact. Host country governments may view the localisation process as an indication of attachment or commitment to the host country and thus may aid or, at least, not greatly hinder the operation of the MNC in the host country. Even if there are no short-term political benefits there are certainly long-term benefits, as Hailey (1999) and Litvin (2003) have shown, for taking an ethical stance not to exploit foreigners. In this regard Sparrow et al. (2004: 133) posit: 'regulators and governments look at the behaviour of a company against local legal, socio-cultural and environmental norms'. Thus ethical decisions in this regard are particularly complex as not only must MNCs be cognisant of host norms in this regard, but also they are constrained by home norms and beliefs as discussed above. A final advantage of using local managers to run the foreign subsidiary is that this staffing approach allows the MNC to adopt a lower profile in sensitive political conditions than would be the case with expatriates in charge (Scullion, 1992).

The barriers to localising human resources

While it might seem to make economic, financial and ethical sense to localise human resources there are many barriers which may mean that the continued use of expatriates is more practical and sometimes preferable. In this section we will outline some of the key challenges in this regard.

Most resistance to localising human resources is from the private sector organisations (national and international) where short-term costs are emphasised to the detriment of long-term benefits. In this section we will outline the key challenges to the localisation of human resources with a particular focus on non-managerial employees. Specifically we focus on: education and the workplace; jobs on offer that do not appeal; inappropriate selection methods; training; and costs.

Education and the workplace

Intelligence and potential are evenly spread in the human population and no race or nationality lacks the ability to develop necessary skills, attitudes or behaviours required by modern organisations. However, whereas most developed countries have built up their skilled workforces and managerial systems, along with the educational support systems over many decades, in developing countries such as the Gulf Cooperation Council, China and Eastern Europe the pace of development has been very rapid. The pace has been so rapid that insufficient members of the host population have been educated to develop the capability needed by employers. For example, Warner (1985) noted that two in three Chinese managers had no qualifications beyond middle school in the mid-1980s. Further their knowledge and skills in areas such as auditing, cost accounting, marketing and personnel were relatively weak. In a similar vein, Micklethwait (1996) posited that China was producing only 300 MBA graduates annually in 1995, when foreign joint ventures alone could have absorbed 240,000 of them.

The education systems in most developing countries are different from those in industrialised countries of the West. For most countries education has focused on basic literacy (if that) and learning from an older generation how to undertake agricultural, small-scale repair or retail tasks. Even in Eastern Europe and states of the former Soviet Union, where the standards of education were high in terms of technical knowledge, there were considerable differences in terms of attitudes towards work and behaviour at work. Indeed Kiriazov *et al.* (2000) posit that management training in Eastern European countries has traditionally focused on rote learning as opposed to action learning, thus limiting the potential contribution of these management graduates. Recently organisations such as the Open University have begun to operate in these countries and Bennett (1996) reports some 7000 annual enrolments in their courses in Russia alone. In many countries little money has been spent on education in general and in education for the workplace in particular (examples of this neglect are discussed

later in this chapter). In commenting on this issue in less developed international economies, a senior banking official commented:

> In countries like Vietnam and China, people are very keen to work for foreign multinational companies. The problem isn't getting people to come to work, the difficulty is with the government relations, *the language skills and standards of education*. You've got to support the employees with a lot of training.
>
> (quoted in Solomon, 1995: 64, emphasis added)

In these countries significant resources have gone into educating the elite in tertiary education establishments at home or abroad and little spent on basic education for the mass of the population. For example, within Saudi Arabia the dropout rate after primary schooling is 30 per cent. In this regard Yamani (2000) has demonstrated the wide gap between the expectations of the generation entering the workforce in Saudi Arabia and the reality of the workplace. Fewer than half of the 100,000 Saudis entering the employment market each year find a job (Economist 2002).

In the GCC, and many other countries, the emphasis in education is often on cultural or nation building rather than on ensuring employability in the workplace. In most countries, including in the developed world, technical subjects are shunned in favour of social sciences and other fields which might be useful in developing 'thinking skills' but are not immediately applicable in most work situations.

Jobs on offer do not appeal

In some countries, such as those of the GCC, even when young people are well educated, and qualified they may be reluctant to work in the type of jobs which are available. The socio-political elites who have access to the best education institutions are more likely to want to work in government or be entrepreneurs than to work for someone else. This is especially the case if the potential employer is a foreign organisation, although the prestige of a period in a well-known international organisation may be attractive at the beginning of a career.

Jobs which are not attractive to most HCNs, when they are wealthy enough to have a choice, include heavy manual work, domestic service and, in some parts of the Middle East, cash handling jobs including bank teller and jobs which involve providing direct service to a customer. Even poorly educated people will try to avoid such jobs. Thus employers have a choice of bringing foreigners from poorer countries or of harnessing technology to change the nature of the manual work or make changes in task design to make the job more attractive to HCNs. This is illustrated in many studies of the fast food sector where organisations such as McDonald's and Burger King regularly rely on cheap imported labour to fill jobs which are generally unattractive to large cohorts of the host population (see the various contributions in Royle and Towers, 2002).

Likewise Kiriazov *et al.* (2000) argue that in Eastern European countries the move from the command economy towards capitalism poses serious challenges to many employees.

Many of these employees were attached to the characteristics of the old command economy such as job security, guaranteed pay and highly structured jobs, as well as traditions such as nepotism and elements of the black economy which characterised the command economy (Kiriazov *et al.*, 2000). For these reasons, combined with the fact that these employees would have witnessed a high number of business failures among inward investing MNCs, local employees may not want to work for these MNCS and they may exhibit low levels of motivation if they are employed (ibid.).

In countries such as the People's Republic of China, sometimes it is not the job but the supervision which makes locals reluctant to accept the work. The potential recruit may prefer not to work for a foreign supervisor, especially if from a country which is not well regarded by the hosts, or if there is a female supervisor of a male, or a younger supervisor of an older worker or a supervisor from a different tribe or region. In this regard Gamble *et al.* (2003) provide some useful illustrations of reluctance to work under the supervision of Japanese expatriates in the retail sector.

Inappropriate selection methods

Even where there is a pool of available candidates seeking employment, MNCs may use inappropriate selection methods to select appropriate employee (Briscoe and Schuler, 2004; Sparrow, 1999). Selection methods utilised by the MNC may have been chosen based on their suitability in other cultures or are based upon the methods used for expatriates or other parent country nationals. Further, schools and other educational establishments generally fail to adequately prepare students for the methods used in selection and recruitment. Indeed the concept of being interviewed is a challenge in many cultures. Paper and pencil tests might also be unfamiliar to many candidates. It is considered, in some societies, immodest to outline achievements and shameful to ask for a job. In the past it is likely that a father or uncle would provide the employment and no application or selection was necessary.

This reliance on others to help find a job continues to be widely practised. The 'old school tie' may no longer work in the West but the network built up in business school, golf club or other gathering still helps executives find jobs. Weir and Hutchings (2006) have demonstrated in the Chinese context the significance of 'Guanxi' (the word 'Wasta' is used in a similar context in the Arab world) as the more usual methods used by local people to get jobs for themselves, their relations and friends. Capability is of much less importance than are connections. For a person with a role in selection it is fully expected, in many places, that power to appoint will be used to give jobs to 'their' people rather than to 'other' people. So tribal or political affiliation, shared nationality (particularly among expatriates), connections with customers or suppliers are all seen as crucial criteria when deciding who should be offered a job. While this nepotism may seem inappropriate in the global business context, it is important to note that empirical evidence in the European context has highlighted the importance of informal contexts in the selection of individuals for international assignments (see for example Harris and Brewster 1999 and Chapter 4 in this volume).

Training

A lack of appropriate training of HCNs is one of the crucial barriers in promoting successful localisation. As we have mentioned above, there are often gaps in the education system which mean that employers have to make greater efforts in training than are necessary in societies where the education system and employment needs have been more closely aligned.

In many countries the major task is not the issue of skills but rather attitudes and behaviours. The education system of the former Soviet Union, for example, produced people with good technical and professional skills but poor work attitudes, symbolised by the phrase 'Employers pretend to pay the staff and the staff pretend to work' (Harry 2006). Likewise Kiriazov *et al.* (2000) posit that the focus in training is on theory rather than application in Eastern European firms, resulting in poor quality levels and high scrap rates. Other examples are found in the GCC, where culturally students do not expect to work hard, and hence often resort to bullying of teachers and invigilators to pass and graduate (cf. Kapiszewski 2001; Yamani 2000). Students with these attitudes are poor at attending and concentrating on work and bringing with them, to employment, this undisciplined approach to work so are unable to work at the standards required by most employers. Expatriates often use the lack of self-discipline on the part of the HCNs as a reason or excuse to resist localisation.

Costs

It is not only with regard to training costs that HCNs can be expensive in the short term particularly for lower level jobs. Where the number of capable local staff is lower than the labour market requires, local candidates will often be more expensive to employ than expatriates. Thus in a country, such as many of those in the GCC, which is resource and capital rich but labour poor, the HCN will be more expensive than the expatriates employed in similar jobs. This higher cost is driven by low remuneration rates expected by third country nationals (in this context expatriates from poor countries) or those from countries with high income taxes and by host government providing social payments or alternative undemanding work which makes working for a foreign employer unattractive unless for very high pay. In time it can be expected that the high costs of locals in relation to expatriates in these, atypical situations, will decline as governments place more restrictions on the employment of expatriates and have less ability to offer high social security payments or undemanding jobs. Within the GCC, countries such as Bahrain, Oman and Saudi Arabia will soon reach a stage where local labour will be cheaper than that of the expatriates legally employed within the country.

The case study in Box 7.1 illustrates some of these points.

Box 7.1 Case study: Oman

Oman is one of the poorest of the Gulf Cooperation Council (GCC) States but has been host to many foreign workers, especially from South Asia. Prior to the 1970s Omanis had mainly been engaged in agriculture and fishing with some trading. Omanis also worked as expatriates in other GCC States especially in the military. During the 1980s the government took a fairly casual attitude to localisation believing that the employers of expatriate workers were committed to creating work for the growing numbers of Omanis 44% of whom were under 15 years of age (Economist 2002).

By the mid-1990s the government had lost patience with the promise of localisation 'tomorrow'. The attempt at partnership between government and employers had not worked as the employers had focused on short-term gains and preferred to use cheap and compliant foreign workers rather than the potentially more expensive, and probably less easily bullied local population for a wide range of jobs. So the government used the legislation and regulation to force employers to create employment for Omanis as a requirement of operating within the country.

The banking sector had to rapidly replace expatriates with Omanis so that by 2000 95% of clerical jobs and 75% of senior and middle level positions had to be occupied by Omanis, job categories such as human resource managers, bus drivers and delivery staff were to be reserved for Omanis and not only would no work permits be issued for these jobs but severe penalties would be imposed on those employers who did not comply.

Despite warnings from expatriates and employers' businesses, the picture was not of business failure. The banking sector did not collapse and although they have been forced to invest more in staff and in training the long-term benefits to the country and to businesses have been considerable.

Localisation in practice

While the implementation of a localisation strategy may seem relatively straightforward, research highlights the complexity of the process in practice.[1] Writing in this context Gamble's (2000) posits based on his empirical study:

1 The majority of this literature emanates from a Chinese context and thus this discussion is primarily based in this context. The potential for study on localisation in different economies is ample. In particular research on localisation in MNCs in more developed countries would be welcome.

localization is likely to proceed at a much slower pace than its main advocates may wish or anticipate, and that there are practical, cultural, and strategic factors which may, and perhaps should inhibit rapid localization.

(Gamble 2000: 883)

Thus in this section we briefly outline some of the key stages an organisation should follow in designing a strategy for the localisation of human resources. In this regard it is clear that the first step in implementing a successful localisation programme is the design of an appropriate strategy. At this stage it is important to first weigh up the costs and benefits of implementing a localisation strategy. If localisation is seen as appropriate then the MNC should formalise and codify clear localisation objectives (Law *et al.*, 2004; Wong and Law, 1999). In this context it is important to be cognisant of a number of key points.

First, Selmer (2004) posits that implementing a process of localisation for purely cost-cutting reasons may be inadvisable. MNCs would be better to pursue localisation when such programmes fit with the strategic goals of the organisation. Thus localisation should be driven by the search for strategic advantage as opposed to a forced compromise between home and host regimes (Taylor, 1999). Hence it is important in completing the cost-benefit analysis of the merits of localisation that the MNC ensures that a localisation strategy is congruent with the company's strategic objectives. Empirical research, while highlighting the importance of supportive HR policies, suggests that the development of objectives and planning for localisation is the key stage in ensuring the success of localisation efforts in MNCs (Law *et al.*, 2004).

The second key step in implementing a localisation programme is the *localising stage* (Wong and Law, 1999). During this stage, specific HR policies which support the localisation process should be adopted. However, while developing localisation policies is relatively easy, implementing them is not as simple and indeed localisation driven from above is not sufficient because implementation of these policies must account for host conditions and requires the buy-in of both host and expatriate managers (Fryxell *et al.*, 2004). Hence in designing localisation policies MNCs must provide opportunities and incentivise host managers, to promote their development so that they can assume the roles held by expatriates (Law *et al.*, 2004). In this regard training of HCNs emerges as key. Indeed Braun and Warner (2002) have demonstrated the significance of in-house training, assignments abroad and mentoring programmes in developing locals in the Chinese context. Significantly however Fryxell *et al.* (2004: 279) note that managers 'cannot expect simple recipes for successful localization', rather they must develop a programme based on a congruent package of policies and practices. Indeed they argue that successful localisation efforts are driven by an appropriate combination of elements rather that a linear relationship between separate elements of the programme. A further key element of this stage is the development of incentives for managers to implement the localisation programme and this will be considered in greater detail below.

The final stage in the localisation process is the *consolidation stage* which occurs when HCNs have the necessary skills and competence to assume roles traditionally held by expatriates (Wong and Law, 1999). During this stage the repatriation of expatriate managers emerges as a key factor. Specifically if the MNC fails to adequately manage the repatriation process and offer incumbent expatriate attractive packages on repatriation, the whole localisation effort may be jeopardised (Law *et al.*, 2004). This is because the self-interest of expatriates may dictate that they do not engage with the localisation process and perhaps even attempt to thwart efforts at localisation in an attempt to prevent repatriation and the associated career and personal issues associated with the process (see Chapter 10 in this volume for a discussion on repatriation and below for a further discussion on expatriates in this context).

Thus it should be apparent from the above discussion that localisation is in practice a relatively complex proposition. Nonetheless empirical research in the Chinese context appears to support the view that MNCs which are truly committed to the localisation process are likely to plan for localisation and support the programme with appropriate human resource management policies and practices. Further, it is unlikely the localisation programmes will have much success without top management commitment, planning and goal setting and the implementation of appropriate HR policies and practices (Fryxell *et al.*, 2004; Law *et al.*, 2004). In the final section we outline the role of expatriates in the localisation process.

The role of expatriates in the localisation of human resources

It has been argued that 'effective localization commences with the incumbent expatriates' (Selmer, 2004: 1094). Expatriates, perhaps because they can earn more abroad than at home, can also be serious obstacle to effective localisation. Expatriates' willingness and competence in developing competent HCNs as their own replacements is hugely significant in determining the success of the localisation process (Keeley, 1999; Law *et al.*, 2004; Rogers, 1999; Selmer, 2004).

The many roles of expatriate assignments include filling skills gaps where skills are not available among host employees (see Chapter 2 in this volume). In this regard if localisation programmes are to be successful then expatriate assignees must assume the roles of mentors and coach to host employees (Evans *et al.*, 2002; Law *et al.*, 2004). It is imperative that HCNs benefit from the knowledge and skills of the expatriate manager if they are to grow and develop and ultimately assume the responsibilities once held by the expatriate. This may be problematic for a number of reasons. First, expatriates may consider themselves unable to contribute to the localisation process (Selmer, 2004). Not all expatriates will be born mentors nor will they necessarily have the skills required for developing their HCN managers (Lynton, 1999; Melvin and Sylvester, 1997). In addition, many expatriates may fail to promote localisation due to the short-term nature of their foreign assignment brief which may promote the achievement of quantitative performance results such as return on investment or quality levels (Selmer, 2004). Further, there is growing evidence that the expatriate's individual self-interest may also potentially restrain localisation initiatives (Fuller, 2005).

Expatriates may give excuses about the locals not being hard working, not being interested nor capable, not trustworthy or too expensive to train and to employ. Empirical research (Selmer, 2004) however indicates that unwillingness rather than inability tends to impede localisation. In addition, Furst (1999) found that some expatriates neglect their responsibilities for local staff development as soon as they are faced with the uncertainties associated with the repatriation process (Law *et al.*, 2004; see also Chapter 10 of this volume).

Thus the challenge for MNCs deploying expatriates and host country employers of international itinerants (Banai and Harry, 2004) in selecting, training and assigning expatriates which the aim of promoting localisation is to articulate the importance of HCN development, to provide training in mentoring skills to the employees and to design reward packages which recognise and promote the localisation of human resources. For those who are motivated by extrinsic rewards, incentive schemes offering a bonus for handing over to a host country national within a specific period can be effective. The role of intrinsic motivators should also be recognised. Many individuals get satisfaction from passing on skills to others, enjoy learning new skills themselves (such as how to improve capability of others in foreign lands) or have the self-satisfaction of a job well done (Banai and Harry, 2004). Thus the challenge for the international HR manager is to develop a compensation system which accommodates these various motivators and encourages appropriate behaviours in expatriate employees. Further as noted above the significance of appropriate repatriation policies should be considered.

The expatriate's support is crucial to the success of the localisation process. Not only can expatriates transfer skills and knowledge but also they can set an example and pass on attitudes, behaviours and standards which the local will emulate. If the expatriate is resistant, cynical or incapable then effective localisation will fail or be postponed. In contrast if the expatriate is supportive the localisation is much more likely to succeed (Selmer, 2004) particularly where there is a climate of trust between expatriate and HCNs (Fryxell *et al.*, 2004).

Expatriates may fulfil an important role as conduits in disseminating corporate structure and culture to subsidiary, host country employees (Gamble, 2000). They can be a very effective means of passing on knowledge and can greatly assist the process of localisation – or retard the process. Those expatriates linked to a parent organisation can act as champions for the host country nationals being developed. Independent expatriates find that their career path is boosted by the ability to train, to advise and to be consultants helping with localisation (cf. Banai and Harry, 2004). The most effective expatriates will realise that they are no longer employed as 'doers' but as supporters of those who have taken over as producers.

Conclusion

In this chapter we have outlined the key forces driving local responsiveness in international business. We then considered the business advantages and disadvantages of local responsiveness. Our discussion then focused more specifically on the localisation of human resources and again the advantages and disadvantages of this were outlined. After exploring the nature of localisation in practice, we considered the role of expatriates in the localisation process. It should be apparent that localisation is not always the appropriate strategy for MNCs and should not be considered a panacea for problems in subsidiary operations. Nonetheless what should be apparent from our discussions is that localisation is a complex process and that successful localisation begins with appropriate planning and the development of an appropriate strategy. The implementation of this strategy requires top management support and the development of congruent HR policies which fit with the strategy and the host context. If these conditions are met then localisation can represent an important element of an MNC's internationalisation strategy.

References

Banai, M. (1992) 'The ethnocentric staffing policy in multinational corporations: a self-fulfilling prophecy', *International Journal of Human Resource Management*, 3(3): 451–72.

Banai, M. and Harry, W.E. (2004) 'Boundaryless global careers: the international itinerants', *International Studies of Management and Organization*, 34(3): 96–120.

Bartlett, C.A. and Ghoshal, S. (1998) *Managing across Borders: The Transnational Solution*, 2nd edn, Boston, MA: Harvard Business School Press.

Bennett, D.R. (1996) 'The stalled revolution: business education in Eastern Europe', *Business Horizons*, 39(1): 23–9.

Black, J.S. and Gregerson, H.B. (1992) 'Serving two masters: managing the dual allegiance of expatriate employees', *Sloan Management Review*, 33(4): 61–71.

Boisot, M. and Child, J. (1999) 'Organizations as adaptive systems in complex environments: the case of China', *Organization Science*, 10: 237–52.

Braun, W.H. and Warner, M. (2002) 'Strategic human resource management in western multinationals in China: The differentiation of practices across different ownership forms', *Personnel Review*, 31: 533–79.

Brewster, C. (1991) *The Management of Expatriates*, London: Kogan Page.

Briscoe, D.R. and Schuler, R.S. (2004) *International Human Resource Management*, 2nd edn, London: Routledge.

Child, J. and Yan, Y. (2001) 'Investment and control in international joint ventures: the case of China', *Journal of World Business*, 34: 3–15.

Das, G. (1993) 'Local memoirs of a global manager', *Harvard Business Review*, 71(2): 38–47.

Dowling, P.J. and Welch, D.E. (2004) *International Human Resource Management: Managing People in a Multinational Context*, 4th edn, London: Thomson Learning.

Doz, Y. and Prahalad, C.K. (1986) 'Controlled variety: a challenge for human resource management in the MNC', *Human Resource Management*, 25(1): 55–71.

Economist (2002) 'People pressure', *The Economist*, 21 March, www.economist.com [accessed 23 March 2002]

Economist Intelligence Unit (1997) 'Local Heroes', *Business China*, 9: 1–3.

Evans, P., Pucik, V. and Barsouxm, J.L. (2002) *The Global Challenge: Frameworks for International Human Resource Management*, Boston, MA: McGraw-Hill.

Fryxell, G.E., Butler, J. and Choi, A. (2004) 'Successful localization in China: an important element in strategy implementation', *Journal of World Business*, 39: 268–82.

Fuller, T. (2005) 'Skilled help hard to find in China', *International Herald Tribune*, Beirut edition, 16 March.

Furst, B. (1999) 'Performance management for localization', in J. Lee (ed.) *Localization in China: Best Practice*, Hong Kong: Euromoney.

Gamble, J. (2000) 'Localizing management in foreign-invested enterprises in China: practical, cultural and strategic perspectives', *International Journal of Human Resource Management*, 11(5): 883–1004.

Gamble, J., Morris, J. and Wilkinson, B. (2003) 'Japanese and Korean multinationals: the replication and integration of their national business systems in China', *Asian Business and Management*, 2(3): 347–69.

Hailey, J. (1999) 'Localization as an ethical response to internationalization', in C. Brewster and H. Harris (eds) *International HRM*, London: Routledge.

Harris, H. and Brewster, C. (1999) 'The coffee-machine system: how international selection really works' *International Journal of Human Resource Management* 10(2): 488–500.

Harry, W.E. (2006) 'History and HRM in Central Asia', *Thunderbird International Business Review*, 48(1).

Harry, W.E. and Banai, M. (2005) 'International itinerants', in M. Michael, N. Heraty and D. Collings (eds) *International HRM and International Assignments*, Basingstoke: Palgrave Macmillan.

Hertz, N. (2001) *The Silent Takeover: Global Capitalism and the Death of Democracy*, London: Arrow.

Kapiszewski, A. (2001) *Nationals and Expatriates*, Reading: Ithaca Press.

Keeley, S. (1999) 'The theory and practice of localization', in J. Lee (ed.) *Localization in China: Best Practice*, Hong Kong: Euromoney.

Kiriazov, D., Sullivan, S.E. and Tu, H.S. (2000) 'Business success in Eastern Europe: understanding and customising HRM', *Business Horizons*, 43(1): 39–43.

Lasserre, P. and Ching, P-S. (1997) 'Human resources management in China and the localization challenge', *Journal of Asian Business*, 13(4): 85–100.

Law, K.S., Wong, C.S. and Wang, K.D. (2004) 'An empirical test of the model on managing the localisation of human resources in the People's Republic of China', *International Journal of Human Resource Management*, 15: 635–48.

Litvin, D. (2003) *Empires of Profit: Commerce, Conquest and Corporate Responsibility*, New York: Texere.

Lynton, N. (1999) 'Building a unified corporate culture', in J. Lee (ed.) *Localization in China: Best Practice*, Hong Kong: Euromoney.

Melvin, S. and Sylvester, K. (1997) 'Shipping out', *China Business Review*, May–June: 30–4.

Micklethwait, J. (1996) 'The search for the Asian manager', *The Economist*, 338(7956): S3–S5.

Morris, R.J. and Lawrence, A.T. (2003) 'Nike's dispute with the University of Oregon', in D.C. Thomas (ed.) *Readings and Cases in International Management: A Cross-cultural Perspective*, London: Sage.

Nash, E. (2004) 'Spanish suffer lack of sleep as globalisation ends siesta', *The Independent*, 20 December.

Prahalad, C.K. (2004) *The Fortune at the Bottom of the Pyramid: Eradicating Poverty Through Profits*, London: Wharton School Publishing/Pearson.

Rogers, B. (1999) 'The expatriates in China: a dying species?', in J. Lee (ed.) *Localization in China: Best Practice*, Hong Kong: Euromoney.

Rosenzweig, P.M. and Nohria, N. (1994) 'Influences in human resource management practices in multinational corporations', *Journal of International Business Studies*, 25(2): 229–42.

Royle, T. and Towers, B. (eds) (2002) *Labour Relations in the Global Fast-Food Industry*, London: Routledge.

Ruhs, M. and Godfrey, M. (2002) 'Cheaper labour on tap: wage and productivity trends in Kuwait', unpublished paper developed from ILO Migrant project.

Scullion, H. (1992) 'Strategic recruitment and development of the international manager: some European considerations', *Human Resource Management Journal*, 3(1): 57–69.

Scullion, H. and Brewster, C. (2001) 'Managing expatriates: messages from Europe', *Journal of World Business*, 36(4): 346–65.

Selmer, J. (2004) 'Expatriates' hesitation and the localization of Western business operations in China', *International Journal of Human Resource Management*, 15(6): 1094–107.

Shenkar, O. and Luo, Y. (2004) *International Business*, Hoboken, NJ: Wiley.

Solomon, C.M. (1995) 'Learning to manage host-country nationals', *Personnel Journal*, March: 60–7.

Sparrow, P. (1999) 'International recruitment, selection and Assessment,' in P. Joynt and B. Morton (eds) *The Global HR Manager: Creating the Seamless Organization*, London: Institute of Personnel and Development.

Sparrow, P., Brewster, C. and Harris, H. (2004) *Globalizing Human Resource Management*, London: Routledge.

Taylor, B. (1999) 'Patterns of control within Japanese manufacturing plants in China: doubts about Japanization in Asia', *Journal of Management Studies*, 36(6): 853–74.

Warner, M. (1985) 'Training China's managers', *Journal of General Management*, 11(2): 12–26.

Weir, D. and Hutchings, K. (2006) 'Guanxi and Wasta: a review of the traditional ways of networking in China and the Arab world and their implications for international business', *Thunderbird International Business Review*, 48(1).

Wong, C.S. and Law, K.S. (1999) 'Managing localization of human resources in the PRC: a practical model', *Journal of World Business*, 34: 26–40.

Yamani, M. (2000) *Changed Identities*, London: Royal Institute of International Affairs.

Part 3

Global staffing: emerging themes

8 Alternative forms of international assignments

HUGH SCULLION AND DAVID G. COLLINGS

Introduction

Since the mid-1980s the main focus of research on international assignments has been on the traditional long-term expatriate assignment which usually involves the relocation of the expatriate and their family to a different environment (Scullion and Brewster, 2001). In this regard the international HRM literature has generally focused on the issues associated with selection, training, appraisal and development in the context of traditional expatriate assignments (Mayerhofer *et al.*, 2004). However, the focus of this chapter is on the growing importance of alternative types of international assignment which have become increasingly important features of the pattern of global staffing (Fenwick, 2004). The following issues will be addressed:

- the different forms of international assignment
- the reasons for the growth of more flexible forms of global staffing
- the challenges of managing the new 'flexpatriate assignments'
- the HR challenges of managing international business travellers
- the growth of global virtual teams and associated management challenges
- inpatriation as an emerging source of international management talent.

Although long-term expatriate assignments remain the most frequently utilised type of international assignment, it has been argued that they may become a less dominant aspect of international work in the future (Harris, 1999; Petrovic, 2000). Research suggests that organisations are now using a range of assignment options that were previously only considered within a limited geographical or national context. This means that more employees are 'international' in the sense that they travel widely to other countries on behalf of their organisations on a variety of schedules ranging from 'brief' visits to longer-term assignments (Harris *et al.*, 2001; Mayerhofer *et al.*, 2004). Researchers have highlighted the absence of empirical data about the utilisation of short-term assignments (Schuler *et al.*, 2002). However, Mayrhofer and Scullion (2002) differentiate between permanent expatriates and 'intermittent' expatriates, who return home regularly for briefing and do not move permanently. They cite the example of

German quality engineers with managerial and technical responsibilities in the clothing industry who travelled frequently in several countries in Eastern Europe, returning regularly for briefings, and probably to spend weekends with their families. Other researchers claim that the geographic situation in Europe means Eurocommuting and frequent visiting is a possible alternative to expatriate transfers (Mayrhofer and Brewster, 1997). It is suggested that these staff may be more truly 'global' managers in their orientation than expatriates whose focus is on one country only (Mayerhofer *et al.*, 2004).

These alternative forms of international assignment can be classified according to the length or duration of the assignment which is usually determined by the purpose of the transfer and the nature of the task to be performed (see Table 8.1).

Table 8.1 Forms of international assignment

Short-term assignments: between three months and one year	These are often temporary troubleshooting or project assignments and the aim is to fill a gap until a more permanent solution can be found.
Traditional expatriate assignments or long-term assignments	The duration of the assignment may vary between one and four or five years and the expatriate has a clear role in the foreign subsidiary operation.
Rotational assignments	Staff commute from the parent country to a workplace in another country for a short period followed by a break in the home country; for example, this type of arrangement is very common in the oil rigs.
International commuter assignments	This involves staff commuting from the home country to a workplace in another country, usually on a weekly or bi-weekly basis, while the family remains at home.
Frequent flyer assignments	Staff undertake frequent international business trips but do not relocate.
Contractual assignments	These are common where staff with specific skills which are essential for completing international projects are assigned for a limited period of 6–12 months. Mendez (2003) shows how the coordination of globalised research and development activities can be achieved through project teams.
Virtual assignments	Under these arrangements staff do not relocate to a host location but have a responsibility to manage international staff from the home base.

Sources: adapted from Dowling and Welch (2004); Harris (1999); Petrovic (2000).

However, within these broad types of international assignment there has been considerable growth of non-standard or alternative international assignments (Mayerhofer *et al.*, 2004).

Reasons for the development of more flexible forms of global staffing

Harvey *et al.* (2003) suggest that global firms need to go beyond expatriation to develop global networks. It has been argued that changing world business circumstances mean that more flexible forms of global staffing are increasingly being used as alternatives to expatriate assignments (Mayerhofer *et al.*, 2004). Four major circumstances are identified:

- Changing business relationships that include more joint ventures, licensing and contracting rather than the growth of wholly owned subsidiaries and the growth of international SME high technology and service organisations. Much of the research on expatriate staffing has focused on larger MNCs and has neglected newer forms of international organisation.
- Improved technology in communications and air transport have broadened the options for organisations which do not wish to invest in a long-term placement of their own staff.
- There are growing concerns regarding the balance between work and personal life.
- Access to a more globally competent workforce. Adler and Bartholomew (1992) differentiate between expatriates who may have experience in one or two cultures and global managers who adapt and operate across many cultures on a daily basis.

Some researchers have explored the experiences of those engaged in alternative forms of international working – a group who have largely been ignored in the IHRM literature. This research has identified similarities and differences between the operation and management of alternative forms and traditional expatriate assignments (Harris, 1999; Petrovic, 2000). Mayerhofer *et al.* (2004) (who call alternative forms of international working – flexpatriate assignments) addressed a specific research issue in their study: how do flexpatriate assignments differ from traditional expatriate assignments?

The major findings of their study of alternative forms of expatriation based on case study data are summarised below.

- The study provides further evidence that alternative forms of international working are a growing and important aspect of global staffing. An increasing number of global staffing transfers are not traditional expatriates – but those who undertake global assignments frequently and with flexibility.
- It suggests that alternative forms of international working provide flexibility to the organisation in terms of global staffing in contrast to the more inflexible contractual arrangements associated with traditional expatriate assignments.

- The research suggests that operational managers (who usually control alternative international assignments) tend to be a more accurate source of information about these assignments than HR managers.
- While alternative forms of international working involve more staff, the role of traditional expatriate assignments was still seen as critical to the MNC in providing a visible and long-term presence in a particular location.

While international HRM research literature has emphasised the importance of support for expatriate assignments (Tung, 2000) some research has highlighted the lack of HR support for alternative international assignees and suggested that the burden of managing these assignments is largely left with employees and their families (Mayerhofer *et al.*, 2004). It has also suggested that more of the personal cost of this type of assignment is managed by the employees and their families than in the case of traditional expatriate assignments and that assignments would be more successful for the organisation and for individuals if HRM policies and practices focused more on family friendly staffing policies (Mayerhofer *et al.*, 2004).

Overall, there is little evidence of a decline in the use of long-term assignments in favour of alternative forms of international working as suggested by McComb (1999). Rather what is happening is the emergence of a portfolio of international assignments within MNCs (Roberts *et al.*, 1998). Indeed some research suggests that we need refinements to the way in which international transfers are defined. Increasingly staff at all levels in the multinational organisation utilise information technology to develop alternative methods of global coordination and communication which may facilitate alternative forms of international working (Fenwick, 2004; Harris 1999; Mayerhofer *et al.*, 2004; Petrovic 2000).

Mayerhofer and colleagues suggest that staff involved in alternative international assignments play a proactive role in their own adjustment and use their networks and internet sources to meet the challenges they face (Mayerhofer *et al.*, 2004). Mayrhofer and Scullion (2002) also highlight the use of personal initiative and networks by expatriate staff working in Eastern Europe for German clothing manufacturers. However, in this case many of the German staff who were working in Eastern Europe returned home regularly and the family did not relocate.

Mayerhofer *et al.* (2004: 1385) argued that the success of managers on 'flexpatriate' assignments in their study depended on:

- individual initiative in work and cultural issues and on family support systems
- a sensible approach to the work–life balance equation
- the adaptation and support of the partner or family in relation to the professional life of the expatriate.

These findings support the conclusions of Feldman and Thomas (1992) who highlighted the importance of self-initiated activities for expatriates. The main advantages and disadvantage of flexpatriate assignments are summarised below.

Advantages

- Individual managers experience less disruption to their careers because they are not required to change jobs or promotion paths.
- Managers are not subject to the considerable difficulties associated with the repatriation process.

Disadvantages

- Flexpatriates may have regular travel commitments to many different countries and this puts further pressure on family and work commitments at home.
- Flexpatriates are also required to develop networks and personal relationships in a wide range of countries which adds to the stress of the job.

International business travellers

The role of the international business traveller has been relatively ignored in the IHRM literature which is surprising given that recent surveys show that business travellers across the world expect to maintain or increase their current business travel over the previous year (American Express, 2002, cited in Dowling and Welch, 2004: 72). This suggests that face-to-face meetings remain important in international business. Welch and Worm (2005) show that international business travellers (IBTs) are a diverse group of employees including expatriates and support visits to virtual teams. Their exploratory study of international business travellers identified a number of perceived negative and positive factors associated with international business travel and the responses of the IBTs to these challenges. These are summarised in Tables 8.2 and 8.3.

Research suggests that individual responses to the stresses and strains of international travel may be moderated by personal factors such as age, experience and family situation. For example, how individuals cope with the demands of international travel has an important consequence in terms of job satisfaction and staff turnover (Welch and Worm, 2005). Turnover of IBTs has the potential for valuable loss of information and knowledge and the loss of important networks with key contacts in the foreign market, particularly where IBTs take this knowledge to a competitor (Michailova and Worm, 2003). The level of organisational support provided to the IBT is also an influencing factor on the IBTs performance and job satisfaction. However, surprisingly, the evidence suggests that HR departments have had limited involvement in the management of IBT's (Brewster *et al.*, 2001). IBTs are frequently seen as non-expatriates and therefore outside the responsibility area of the HR function. For example, in a study of six Danish MNCs the HR directors regarded non-expatriate staff as the responsibility of the line management team (Welch, 2003).

Table 8.2 Perceived negative factors of international business travel

Family separation	The effect on family relationships of IBTs was a key negative factor. Missed birthdays and family events and missing out on quality time with the children can cause tension and frustration (De Frank *et al.*, 2000). Welch and Worm (2005) suggest that many short trips that followed one upon the other created more family problems than more infrequent yet longer absences.
Travel stress	Travelling can be very stressful and the stress is exacerbated by tight airline connections, delayed flights and long flights, hectic schedules of business meetings and problems with hotels. De Frank *et al.* (2000) highlight the ability to sleep as being important in order to cope with the wide range of challenges facing IBTs. A further problem was the expectation that the IBT would not require time off work in order to recover from travel stress when back in the domestic situation.
Health issues	In addition to the risk of contracting infectious diseases, the evidence suggests that constant travelling has negative consequences including poor diet, lack of physical exercise and weight gain.
Safety concerns	Physical safety has become an increasing concern for IBTs. Concerns about terrorist activity, kidnapping and harassment were growing in a number of countries and regions.
Incessant work demands	Modern technology can increase the pressure of work by bringing home office issues to the attention of the manager working in the foreign market and can also erode private time. Also, often insufficient time is allowed for the IBT to catch up with a backlog of work when they return home and this may negatively impact on the time available to spend with the family.

Source: adapted from Welch and Worm (2005).

Table 8.3 Perceived positive factors of international business travel

Variety/novelty of the job	IBTs often enjoyed the variety of tasks and destinations and enjoyed meeting people from many countries
Thrill of the deal	Many IBTs enjoyed 'the buzz' of performing well in challenging circumstances.
Lifestyle	IBTs felt there was an element of glamour linked to being a frequent traveller (such as staying in top hotels and flying business class) and some IBTs felt that international travel can become a lifestyle which is addictive.
Personal development	A number of self development opportunities were provided by the nature of the IBT jobs: • working with people from other cultures • coping with stressful situations • handling problems that would not normally be encountered.

Source: adapted from Welch and Worm (2005).

In exploring various methods of global communication and coordination we will now examine the growth of multicultural virtual teams, which have emerged as one of the most important methods of international team working.

Global virtual teams

As a result of increasing decentralisation and globalisation of work processes, many organisations have responded to their dynamic environments by introducing virtual teams, in which members are geographically dispersed and coordinate their work predominantly with electronic information and communication technologies e.g. video-conferencing and email (Hertel *et al.*, 2005). This trend has accelerated since the late 1990s due to the growth of the internet and other new communication technologies and many large businesses today employ virtual teams (Duarte and Snyder, 1999; Gibson and Cohen, 2003), which can be found in various fields, such as research and development, problem solving task forces, or customer services (Finholt *et al.*, 1990).

Maznevski *et al.* (2005) define virtual teams as groups of people who:

- work together using communications technology more often than face to face
- are distributed across space
- are responsible for a joint outcome
- usually work on strategic or technically advanced tasks
- are multifunctional and/or multicultural.

Hertel *et al.* (2005: 71) demonstrate that the various forms of 'virtual' work can be differentiated depending on the number of persons involved and the degree of interaction between them. Four types of virtual work are identified:

- *Telework (telecommuting)*: this is done partially or completely outside of the main company workplace using information and telecommunication services.
- *Virtual groups*: these exist when several teleworkers are combined and each member reports to the same manager.
- *Virtual teams*: these exist when the members of a virtual group interact with each other in order to accomplish common goals.
- *Virtual communities*: these are larger entities of distributed work in which members participate via the Internet guided by common purposes, roles and goals.

Hertel *et al.* (2005) argue that in contrast to virtual teams, virtual communities are not implemented within an organisational structure but are usually initiated by some of their members.

A global survey of more than eighty multinationals in thirteen countries showed that 28 per cent of the surveyed firms were expecting an increased use of virtual assignments, compared with 17 per cent two years previously (PriceWaterhouseCoopers, 2000). Almost two-thirds of firms who use virtual teams reported an increase in the number of virtual assignments used by their company and the same proportion indicated an expected increase in the next two years (cited in Dowling and Welch, 2004: 67). The two main reasons given by the firms in the survey for the growth of virtual assignments were the shortage of staff prepared to accept longer-term assignments and cost reduction pressures. While there has been a rapid growth in virtual teams since the mid-1990s, little is known about the management of virtual teams and in particular the management of human resources within these teams (Axtell *et al.*, 2004; Kirkman *et al.*, 2004). Creating effective virtual teams has in practice proved to be more difficult than expected (Duarte and Snyder, 2001). Research suggests that creating high performance virtual teams is problematic and requires careful structuring, support and detailed attention to processes and people for virtual teams to achieve their potential (Maznevski and Athanassiou, 2003).

Research has highlighted some disadvantages of virtual working such as role conflict, dual allegiance and identity issues. In addition, some aspects of interpersonal relations and work relationships become difficult given the potential for cultural misunderstanding and the lack of opportunities for normal group interaction in the virtual operation (Welch *et al.*, 2003). In this context the consequences of implementing high virtuality in teams can be evaluated at the individual, organisational and societal level (Hertel *et al.*, 2005). The advantages and challenges of high virtuality at each of these levels are summarised in Table 8.4.

Key challenges facing virtual teams

Communication

Maznevski *et al.* (2005) show that the challenges that virtual team members face with regard to communications come from two main sources:

- Technology has lower richness and social presence than face-to-face communication, team members lose much of the information they are used to rely on. This can result in misinterpretations and misunderstandings (cf. DiStefano, 2003).
- Most communications over technology take place in a staggered way – with a time lag between one message being sent and another received which reduces the immediacy and efficacy of feedback.

Research shows that reliance on virtual forms of communications technology makes it more difficult not only to reach consensus but also to pay full attention to social norms in their communication compared with those working face to face. In addition, verbal communication patterns are highly dependent on social contexts which are much less rich in virtual forms of communication (Lee, 1994; Von Glinow *et al.*, 2004). Similarly research shows that communicating effectively over technology is more difficult than in a face-to-face context. Face-to-face teams have better overall communication effectiveness than virtual teams which leads to higher levels of cohesion, satisfaction with the decision making process and outcomes (Maznevski *et al.*, 2005; Warkentin *et al.*, 1997).

Table 8.4 Advantages and challenges of high virtuality

Individual level of high virtuality

Advantages	• higher flexibility • greater control over time • higher responsibilities • higher work motivation • empowerment of the team members
Potential challenges	• feelings of isolation • decreased interpersonal contact • increased chances of misunderstanding and conflict escalation • increased risk of role ambiguity and goal conflicts due to commitments to different work-units

Organisational level

Advantages	• teams can be staffed based on members' expertise rather than their local availability • teams can work round the clock by having team members in different time zones • speed and flexibility in response to market changes can be increased • reduced expenses for travel and office space
Potential challenges	• problems in supervising the activities of team members • problems in preventing unproductive developments in time • additional costs for technology • problems of data security • additional training programmes

Societal level

Advantages	• helps to develop regions with high unemployment • helps to integrate persons with low mobility due to handicaps or family care duties • helps to decrease environmental strains by reducing commuting traffic and air pollution
Disadvantage	• increased isolation between people due to a technical work environment

Source: adapted from Hertel *et al.* (2005).

While some researchers suggest that virtual teams should be used only for non-routine tasks (Van der Smagt, 2000), other studies (Kiesler *et al.*, 1984) have identified a number of advantages of virtual teams including:

● more even participation
● broader decision shifts
● more uninhibited verbal behaviour

- personal opinions were expressed more freely online
- member participation was more equal.

One study showed, however, that some effective teams favoured resolving difficult conflicts by avoiding face-to-face situations preferring email and telephone. It was argued that the loss of emotional information was helpful in preventing conflicts from escalating beyond the task to the personal level (Maznevski and Chudoba, 2000). The following section deals with some of the key issues relating to building relationships in global virtual teams.

Building relationships

High quality relationships (characterised by trust and respect, cooperation and commitment) are even more important for virtual teams than for face-to-face ones: teams with good relationships can more easily work apart without concern for the process or the outcome (Canney Davison and Ekelund, 2004). Shared identity and trust are more difficult to achieve in virtual teams (DiStefano and Maznevski, 2000) as members of virtual teams tend to share context and identity much less than face-to-face teams and this can lead to higher levels of conflict (Shapiro *et al.*, 2002). Trust may be even more difficult to develop than shared identity and in virtual teams the absence of direct supervision may make trust even more important than in non virtual teams (Canney Davison and Ekelund, 2004).

Studies on virtual teams have highlighted that trust which was critical to the team's ability to manage decision processes could be built quickly (Jarvenpaa *et al.*, 1998). There was a basic willingness to trust each other by team members who were keen to progress their work objectives. Joint problem solving in the early phase of team development contributed to the early creation of a basis of trust or 'swift trust' (Meyerson *et al.*, 1996). However, this type of trust was very fragile and was completely broken after some minor infraction. This is consistent with research which suggests that virtual teams pay much more attention to relationship building than do their face-to-face teams, since it is more difficult to build identity, trust or cooperation in the former (Maznevski *et al.*, 2005).

Managing conflict

Virtual team members report that they experience more conflict due to communication problems and diverse composition (Baan, 2004). Further, virtual team conflicts often stay unresolved for longer periods of time due to dispersed locations and because virtual team members often have several other tasks and functions. Some studies suggest that the best way of solving conflicts in virtual teams are highly dependent on trust and culture (Paul *et al.*, 2004). It has also been demonstrated that virtual teams often develop implicit or even explicit norms and rules of communication (Montoya-Weiss *et al.*, 2001) that are enforced by means ranging from peer pressure to explicit sanctions and punishment. There is little empirical research on managing conflicts in virtual teams, but recent studies suggest that developing a better understanding of the complexities of conflict processes in virtual teams is vital (Maznevski *et al.*, 2005). Maznesvski *et al.* (2005: 12) show that the cultural element of conflict is far more ambiguous due to the diverse background of team members in global virtual teams:

- the issues leading to conflict differs between countries
- what is perceived/interpreted as conflict differs
- modes for resolving conflict differ.

The development of a fair and motivating reward system is a key issue for the effective working of global virtual teams (De Matteo *et al.*, 1998). Reward systems need to be adapted to specific aspects of the team, such as goals, task interdependence, autonomy, diversity and degree of virtuality and rewards should be linked to strategy (Lawler, 2003). It is suggested that rewards systems in virtual teams should use skill-based rather than job-based systems in order to encourage individuals to learn the necessary new skills that focus more on collective rather than individual performance and to encourage and support cooperative behaviours (Lawler, 2003).

Leadership

Leadership is a central challenge in virtual teams because direct control strategies are problematic when team managers are not at the same location as the team members (Bell and Kozlowski, 2002; Hertel *et al.*, 2005). Virtual teams are usually managed more effectively by empowerment and delegating managerial functions to the members (Duarte and Snyder, 1999). Research suggests that three aspects of team leadership are particularly important:

- structuring the process
- facilitating strong relationships
- maintaining and implementing the vision.

In virtual teams processes must be carefully managed and coordinated. This involves clearly defining roles, a clear task strategy and agreed operating norms (Kayworth and Leidner, 2001). Unlike in face-to-face teams where these processes can be implicitly negotiated by team members, virtual teams which do not manage these processes carefully are likely to fail (Maznevski *et al.*, 2005). Providing continuous feedback and building on the team's successes are key roles of the virtual team leader (Furst *et al.*, 2004). Facilitating relationships is a second key role of the virtual team leader, who is also required to manage relationships between the team and external stakeholders (Druskat and Wolff, 2001).

Developing and articulating a clear vision of the goals of the team is also a key aspect of leadership for several reasons:

- Team members are motivated to work toward the vision when they trust the leader and understand and are committed to the vision.
- A strong vision encourages more autonomy among team members as team members are more willing to trust each other to act in the interests of the team.
- In virtual teams a clear vision is an important coordination mechanism as the team leader cannot supervise all the team members.

In summary, Maznevski *et al.* (2005) describe six practices which effective virtual teams share:

- Communicate Thoughtfully.
- Manage Differences.
- Build a Rhythm of Regular Meetings.
- Empower the Team.
- Manage Dynamically and Fluidly.
- Use HR to support High Performance.

However, Maznevski *et al.* (2005) also recognise that every virtual team is different and that there is no simple best practice prescription for resolving difficulties and they raise some fundamental questions which need to be explored in order to provide guidance to organisations to help them prepare for the future. These are outlined below:

- How will people identify with their organisations when they are working more with people they never see than with people they see all the time?
- What kind of interpersonal skills do we need to develop given that the nature of interpersonal interaction is inherently unpredictable?
- Will poor countries catch up with rich countries in technology use, and how will that change the flow of communication and ideas?

Having discussed some critical issues in the management of virtual teams, the next section will examine the rapidly growing role of inpatriation as an emerging source of global staffing.

Inpatriates: an emerging source of international management talent

As we have demonstrated above, the majority of the extant literature focuses on staffing multinational subsidiaries as opposed to headquarter operations. Indeed there is a paucity of research on the role of HCNs and TCNs in corporate top management teams. This is a significant gap in the literature, as changes occurring within the globalisation process have rendered traditional bureaucratic and unidirectional models of management staffing in MNCs less suitable for organisations operating in the global sphere (Harvey *et al.*, 2000). This lack of global orientation also represents a constraint on the success of MNCs in the global business environment. The strategic employment of host and third country nationals can significantly aid in the development of management strategy in the global environment (Harvey *et al.*, 1999b; Reynolds, 1997).

In this regard there is a growing body of literature on the concept of inpatriate managers. Inpatriate managers have been defined as:

> host or third country managers who are transferred into the home organisation on a semi-permanent to permanent basis to enhance globalisation of business activities.
>
> (Harvey *et al.*, 2000: 154)

Arguably the impact of these inpatriate managers is more significant than the impact of the well-researched area of expatriate managers. This is because the majority of MNCs retain a large percentage of their personnel, production operation and research and develop capability in their home country (UNCTAD, 2004).

There are several key drivers of the recruitment of inpatriate managers including:

- a desire to create a global core competency, a diversity of strategic perspective, or a multicultural frame of reference among the top management team (Harvey and Buckley, 1997; Harvey *et al.*, 1999b)
- the emergence of developing markets, which are increasingly being recognised as difficult assignments for expatriate managers in terms of quality of life and cultural adjustment and thus less likely to be accepted by traditional expatriate pools (Harvey *et al.*, 2001)
- a desire to increase the capability of organisations to 'think global and act local', which can be aided through including inpatriate managers in the decision making process at HQ level (Harvey *et al.*, 1999b);
- providing career opportunities for high potential employees in host countries.

Thus inpatriate managers not only provide a subsidiary perspective on decision making within the organisation but also assist in a number of other strategic issues within the MNC. Indeed Harvey and Novicevic (2006) identify three factors which should be taken into consideration in determining when and how to utilise inpatriate managers most effectively:

- *Organisational level of globalisation*: as with other aspects of global staffing (see Chapter 3 in this volume) the strategic requirements of the organisation will change as it passes through various stages of internationalisation.
- *Existing heterogeneity of global operations*: obviously organisations with culturally homogenous top management teams are likely to face greater challenges as the significance of the organisation's international operations increase.
- *Future strategic trust of the organisation*: the firm's future intentions with regards to changes in present level and course of international operations.

Having outlined the factors which are driving the increasing use of inpatriate assignments we will now outline some of the opportunities and challenges associated with the inpatriation process.

Inpatriate management: opportunities and challenges

Opportunities arising from inpatriate assignments

Inpatriate managers offer many advantages to MNCs. First, inpatriate managers diffuse knowledge of different host environments throughout the MNC and aid in developing a multicultural perspective within the global management team. Further they can act as a 'linking pin' between HQ and foreign subsidiaries whereby as part of a global network they act as boundary spanners and thus valuable cogs in the MNC's effort to compete globally (Harvey *et al.*, 1999a). In an era where the global mindset is an increasingly valuable competency for international managers the significance of this role becomes more apparent. Further, as organisations are increasingly faced with shortages of international management talent they must look beyond traditional expatriate pools in fulfilling their requirements of international management talent. In this regard the potential of utilising host country nationals and third country nationals emerges as a more attractive strategic option. While traditionally IHRM efforts were limited to sourcing and selecting these employees, inpatriation offers this possibility of embedding these HCNs and TCNs into the organisation and providing them with defined career paths, while facilitating the learning of organisational culture, values and decision processes (Harvey *et al.*, 2001). This may further assist in ensuring that inpatriate's loyalty is primarily focused on the global organisation or the HQ rather than solely on the subsidiary operation. Also, the inpatriation of HCNs and their subsequent return to the host country operation facilitates the implementation of the localisation process (Evans *et al.*, 2002) which is a strategic objective of a growing number of MNCs. This is because not only are human resources localised through the promotion of HCNs to the higher echelons of the local management team but also these managers have an innate knowledge of the local business and institutional environment (see Chapter 7 of this volume). As noted above inpatriates also provide a cadre of employees who may be willing to accept assignments where traditional cohorts of expatriates may be unwilling. They may also provide an alternative when a certain location has proven to be particularly challenging for expatriate employees (Harvey *et al.*, 1999c). This is because the inpatriate managers may be citizens of the particular location or be from a country which is more culturally proximate than the parent country.

Having examined some of the main opportunities arising from inpatriate assignments, we will now examine some of the key challenges associated with the inpatriation process.

Challenges associated with the inpatriate assignment

Inpatriate assignment are not without their challenges and their successful integration into the HQ team presents a number of significant challenges for the MNC. Although it has been argued that the challenges associated with selecting and managing inpatriate managers are the same as those associated with expatriates except in reverse (Briscoe and Schuler, 2004), a review of the literature would suggest that, while some of the issues are similar, the process is more complex.

At an individual level, inpatriates not only have to adjust to a different external cultural environment, but also may be newcomers to the organisation and thus may also have to adjust to the organisational culture (Harvey *et al.*, 1999a). Further while PCNs assigned to subsidiaries also benefit from their status as HQ employees in gaining acceptance in foreign operations, inpatriates may find they are not as well received in the HQ operation (ibid.) There is also a possibility that HQ employees may fear a loss of authority or power to successful inpatriates and thus there may be a lack of cooperation on their part, which may also retard the effective integration of inpatriate employees (Harvey *et al.*, 1999b).

A number of challenges also emerge at the level of the organisation. Specifically, Harvey and Miceli (1999) point to the significance of sensitivity of HQ staff and trainers to culturally based differences among inpatriates in facilitating the integration and acceptance of inpatriates into the HQ operation. Thus, trainers need to be cognisant of inpatriates' frames of references in designing and delivering training sessions. In addressing these challenges Harvey and Miceli (1999) posit that training inpatriates requires the modification of the fundamental components of training programmes due to the diversity of inpatriate cultures (see also Harvey, 1997). Specifically they suggest that these training programmes require HR managers to be cognisant of the diverse cultures from which inpatriate managers originate and are likely to be recruited from in the future. Apposite to this appropriate management of group composition and learning venues relative to the learning styles of the various inpatriate managers must be taken into account. Thus it is important to note that the training need of a company's inpatriate population is significantly different to that of its expatriate employees.

Conclusion

For many years the main focus of research on international assignments has been on the traditional long-term assignment which usually involved the relocation of the expatriate and their family to a different country. In this chapter we have reviewed the different forms of international assignments, paying particular attention to the growing importance of alternative or non-traditional forms of international assignment, which may not involve moving the expatriate's family to another location. The reasons for the growth of more flexible forms of global staffing were examined and the major HR challenges of managing these 'flexpatriate' assignments were highlighted. In addition, the HR challenges of managing international business travellers were identified and discussed. The chapter also considered the key people management challenges associated with the rapid growth of virtual global teams and the international management challenges associated with the growth of inpatriation, which is becoming an increasingly important source of international management talent.

References

Adler, N.J. and Bartholomew, S. (1992) 'Managing globally competent people', *Academy of Management Executive*, 6(3): 52–65.

American Express (2002) 'International travellers optimistic about travel for 2003', press release, 9 October.

Axtell, C.M., Fleck, S.J. and Turner, N. (2004) 'Virtual teams: collaborating across distance', in C.L. Cooper and I.T. Robertson (eds) *International Review of Industrial and Organizational Psychology*, vol. 19, Chichester: Wiley.

Baan, A. (2004) Personal communication regarding virtual teams at Royal Dutch Shell and other companies.

Bell, B.S. and Kozlowski, S.W.J. (2002) 'A typology of virtual teams: Implications for effective leadership', *Group and Organization Management*, 27: 14–49.

Brewster, C., Harris, H. and Petrovic, J. (2001) 'Globally mobile employees: managing the mix', *Journal of Professional Human Resource Management*, 25: 11–15.

Briscoe, D.R. and Schuler, R.S. (2004) *International Human Resource Management*, 2nd edn, London: Routledge.

Canney Davison, S. and Ekelund, B.Z. (2004) 'Effective team process for global teams', in H.W. Lane, M.L. Maznevski, M.E. Mendenhall and J. McNett (eds) *The Blackwell Handbook of Global Management: A Guide to Managing Complexity*, Oxford: Blackwells.

De Frank, R.S., Konopaske, R. and Ivancevich, J.M. (2000) 'Executive travel stress: perils of the road warrior', *Academy of Management Executive*, 14(2): 58–71.

De Matteo, J.S., Eby, L.T. and Sundtrom, E. (1998) 'Team based rewards: current empirical evidence and directions for future research', in B.M. Staw and L.L. Cummings (eds) *Research in Organizational Behaviour*, vol. 20, Stanford, CT: JAI Press.

DiStefano, J.J. (2003) 'Johannes Van Den Bosch sends an email', in D.C. Thomas (ed.) *Readings and Cases in International Management: A Cross-cultural Perspective*, London: Sage.

DiStefano, J.J. and Maznevski, M.L. (2000) 'Creating value with diverse teams in global management', *Organizational Dynamics*, 29: 45–63.

Dowling, P. and Welch, D. (2004) *International Human Resource Management: Managing People in a Multinational Context*, 4th edn, London: Thomson Learning.

Druskat, V.U. and Wolff, S.B. (2001) 'Building the emotional intelligence of groups', *Harvard Business Review*, 79: 80–91.

Duarte, D.L. and Snyder, N.T. (1999) *Mastering Virtual Teams*, San Francisco, CA: Jossey-Bass.

Duarte, D.L. and Snyder, N.T. (2001) *Mastering Virtual Teams*, 2nd edn, San Francisco, CA: Jossey-Bass.

Evans, P., Pucik, V. and Barsoux, J.L. (2002) *The Global Challenge: Frameworks for International Human Resource Management*, New York: McGraw-Hill/Irwin.

Feldman, D.C. and Thomas, D.C. (1992) 'Career management issues facing expatriates', *Journal of International Business Studies*, 23: 271–93.

Fenwick, M. (2004) 'On international assignments: is expatriation the only way to go?', *Asia Pacific Journal of Human Resources*, 42(3): 365–77.

Finholt, T., Sproull, L. and Kiesler, S. (1990) 'Communication and performance in ad hoc task groups', in J. Galegher, R.E. Kraut and C. Egido (eds) *Intellectual Teamwork: Social and Technological Foundations of Co-operative Work*, Hillsdale, NJ: Lawrence Erlbaum Associates.

Furst, S.A., Reeves, M., Rosen, B. and Blackburn, R.R. (2004) 'Managing the life cycle of virtual teams', *Academy of Management Review*, 18(2): 6–20.

Gibson, C.B. and Cohen, S.G. (eds) (2003) *Virtual Teams that Work. Creating Conditions for Virtual Team Effectiveness*, San Francisco, CA: Jossey-Bass.

Harris, H. (1999) 'The changing world of the expatriate manager', Centre for Research into the

Management of Expatriation, Cranfield: Cranfield School of Management, http://www.som. cranfield.ac.uk/som/research/centres/crème/downloads/changingworld.doc

Harris, H., Brewster, C. and Sparrow, P. (2003) *International Human Resource Management*, London: Chartered Institute of Personnel and Development.

Harvey, M.G. (1997) 'Inpatriation training: the next challenge for international human resource management', *International Journal of Intercultural Relations*, 21(3): 393–428.

Harvey, M.G. and Buckley, M.R. (1997) 'Managing inpatriates: building a global core competency', *Journal of World Business*, 32: 35–52.

Harvey, M.G. and Miceli, N. (1999) 'Exploring inpatriate manager issues: an exploratory empirical study', *International Journal of Intercultural Relation*, 23(2): 339–71.

Harvey, M. and Novicevic, M.N. (2006) 'Development of an efficient architecture for the inpatriation of managers', in M.J. Morley, N. Heraty and D.G. Collings (eds) *International HRM and International Assignments*, Basingstoke: Palgrave.

Harvey, M., Novicevic, M. and Speier, C. (1999a) 'Inpatriate managers: how to increase the probability of success', *Human Resource Management Review*, 9(1): 51–82.

Harvey, M., Speier, C. and Novicevic, M.M. (1999b) 'The role of inpatriation in global staffing', *International Journal of Human Resource Management*, 10(3): 459–76.

Harvey, M.G., Price, M.F., Speier, C. and Novicevic, M.M. (1999c) 'The role of inpatriates in a globalization strategy and challenges associated with the inpatriation process', *Human Resource Planning*, 22(1): 38–50.

Harvey, M.G., Novicevic, M.M. and Speier, C. (2000) 'Strategic global human resource management: the role of inpatriate managers', *Human Resource Management Review*, 10: 153–75.

Harvey, M., Speier, C. and Novicevic, M.M. (2001) 'A Theory-based framework for strategic global human resource staffing policies and practices', *International Journal of Human Resource Management*, 12: 898–915.

Harvey, M., Kiessling, T.S. and Novicevic, M. (2003) 'Staffing marketing positions during global hyper-competitiveness: a market based perspective', *International Journal of Human Resource Management*, 14(2): 223–45.

Hertel, G., Geister, C. and Konradt, U. (2005) 'Managing virtual teams: a review of current empirical research', *Human Resource Management Review*, 15: 69–95.

Jarvenpaa, S.L., Knoll, K. and Leidner, D.E. (1998) 'Is anybody out there? Antecedents of trust in global virtual teams', *Journal of Management Information Systems*, 14: 29–64.

Kayworth, T.R. and Leidner, D.E. (2001) 'Leadership effectiveness in global virtual teams', *Journal of Management Information Systems*, 18: 7–40.

Kiesler, S., Siegel, J. and McGuire, T.W. (1984) 'Social psychological aspects of computer mediated communication', *American Psychologist*, 39: 1123–34.

Kirkman, B.L., Rosen, B., Tesluk, P.E. and Gibson, C.B. (2004) 'The impact of team empowerment on virtual team performance: the moderating role of face-to-face interaction', *Academy of Management Journal*, 47(2): 175–92.

Lawler, E.E. (2003) 'Pay systems for effective teams', in C.B. Gibson and S.G. Cohen (eds) *Virtual Teams that Work: Creating Conditions for Effective Virtual Teams*, San Francisco, CA: Jossey-Bass.

Lee, A.S. (1994) 'Electronic mail as a medium for rich communication: an empirical investigation using hermeneutic interpretation', *MIS Quarterly*, 18: 143–57.

McComb, R. (1999) 'China's Human Resource Odyssey', *China Business Review*, September–October: 30–3.

Mayerhofer, H., Hartmann, L.C., Michelitsch-Riedl, G. and Kollinger, I. (2004) 'Flexpatriate assignments: a neglected issue in global staffing', *International Journal of Human Resource Management*, 15(8): 1371–89.

Mayrhofer, W. and Brewster, C. (1997) 'Ethnocentric staffing policies in European multi-nationals', *International Executive*, 38(6): 749–78.

Mayrhofer, W. and Scullion, H. (2002) 'Female expatriates in international business: empirical evidence from the German clothing industry', *International Journal of Human Resource Management*, 13(5): 815–36.

Maznevski, M.L. and Athanassiou, N.A. (2003) 'Designing the knowledge management infrastructure for virtual teams: building and using social networks and social capital', in C.B. Gibson and S.G. Cohen (eds) *Virtual Teams that Work: Creating Conditions for Virtual Team Effectiveness*, San Francisco, CA: Jossey-Bass.

Maznevski, M.L. and Chudoba, K.M. (2000) 'Bridging space over time: global virtual team dynamics and effectiveness', *Organization Science*, 11: 473–92.

Maznevski, M., Davison, S.C. and Jonsen, K. (2005) 'Global virtual team dynamics and effectiveness', in G. Stahl and I. Bjorkman (eds) *Handbook of Research in International Human Resource Management*, London: Edward Elgar.

Mendez, A. (2003) 'The coordination of globalized R&D activities through project team organization: an exploratory empirical study', *Journal of World Business*, 38(2): 96–109.

Meyerson, D.I., Weick, K.E. and Kramer, R.M. (1996) 'Swift trust and temporary groups', in R.M. Kramer and T.R. Tyler (eds) *Trust in Organisations: Frontiers of Theory and Research*, Thousand Oaks, CA: Sage.

Michailova, S. and Worm, V. (2003) 'Personal networking in Russia and China: Blat and Guanxi', *European Management Journal*, 21(4): 509–19.

Montoya-Weiss, M.M., Massey, A.P. and Song, M. (2001) 'Getting it together: temporal coordination and conflict management in global virtual teams', *Academy of Management Journal*, 44: 1251–62.

Paul, S., Seetharaman, P., Samarah, I. and Mykytyn, P.P. (2004) 'Impact of heterogeneity and collaborative conflict management style on the performance of synchronous global virtual teams', *Information and Management*, 41(3): 303–21.

Petrovic, J. (2000) 'Issues coupled with international assignments', Centre for Research into the Management of Expatriation, Cranfield: Cranfield School of Management, http://www.som.cranfield.ac.uk/som/research/centres/crème/downloads/cronerjune2000.doc.

PriceWaterhouseCoopers (2000) *Managing in a Virtual World: International Non Standard Assignments, Policy and Practice*, PriceWaterhouse Europe.

Reynolds, C. (1997) 'Strategic employment of third country nationals: keys to sustaining the transformation of HR functions', *Human Resource Planning*, 20(1): 33–40.

Roberts, K., Kossek, E. and Ozeki, C. (1998) 'Managing the global workforce: challenges and strategies', *Academy of Management Executive*, 12(4): 93–106.

Schuler, R., Budwar, P.R. and Florkowski, G.W. (2002) 'International human resource management: review and critique', *International Journal of Management Reviews*, 4(1): 41–70.

Scullion, H. and Brewster, C. (2001) 'Managing expatriates: messages from Europe', *Journal of World Business*, 36(4): 346–65.

Shapiro, D.L., Furst, S., Spreitzer, G. and von Glinow, M.A. (2002) 'Transnational teams in the electronic age: are team identity and high performance at risk?', *Journal of Organizational Behaviour*, 23: 455–67.

Tung, R. (2000) 'Human resource management, international', in R. Tung (ed.) *The IEBM Handbook of International Business*, London: International Thomson Business Press.

UNCTAD (2004) *Prospects for FDI Flows, Transnational Corporation Strategies and Promotion Policies: 2004–2007*, GIPA Research Note 1, Geneva: UNCTAD.

Van der Smagt, T. (2000) 'Enhancing virtual teams: social relations vs communication technology', *Industrial Management and Data Systems*, 100: 148–57.

Von Glinow, M.A., Shapiro, D.L. and Brett, J.M. (2004) 'Can we talk, and should we? Managers' Emotional conflict in multicultural teams,' *Academy of Management Review*, 29(4): 578–92.

Warkentin, M.E., Sayeed, L. and Hightower, R. (1997) 'Virtual teams versus face to face teams: an exploratory study of web based conference system', *Decisions Sciences*, 14: 29–64.

Welch, D.E. (2003) 'Globalization of staff movements: beyond cultural adjustment', *Management International Review*, 43(2): 149–69.

Welch, D.E. and Worm, V. (2005) 'International business travellers: a challenge for IHRM', in G. Stahl and I. Björkman (eds) *Handbook of Research in International Human Resource Management*, London: Edward Elgar.

Welch, D.E., Worm, V. and Fenwick, M. (2003) 'Are virtual assignments feasible?', *Management International Review*, Special Issue 1: 89–99.

9 Women in international management

MARGARET LINEHAN

Introduction

The increased participation of women in the workforce has been one of the major changes in the labour force in recent years, and it is anticipated that this trend will continue. Despite growing numbers of women in senior domestic management roles the participation rates of women in international management remains low in all countries. Adler (1995) suggests that probably the single most uncontroversial, indisputable statement one can make about women in management is that there are very few of them. Recent figures show that in the United States 18 per cent of international assignment positions are filled by women (GMAC Global Relocation Services, 2003). In Europe, the number of partaking in international assignments is even lower. During the 1980s the number of female expatriate managers remained at between 2 per cent and 5 per cent of the total expatriate population but by the late 1990s this had increased to 12–15 per cent, which is a significant increase but still less than the presence of women in management would generally warrant (Taylor *et al.*, 2002).

A significant part of the problem is the considerable barriers which still exist for women moving to senior domestic management positions. Izraeli and Adler (1994) in an extensive review of women managers in the global economy showed that despite a growing number of qualified women seeking managerial positions and an emerging cadre of women successfully pursuing managerial careers, the reality remained that the executive suite is still highly resistant to women's entry. Similarly, research suggests that, while organisations may be willing to promote women through their domestic managerial hierarchy, few are prepared to allow women to expand their career horizons through international assignments (Linehan *et al.*, 2003). Such beliefs help create what has been termed the *glass border* (Mandelker, 1994), which supports the *glass ceiling* (Morrison and Von Glinow, 1990).

Burke and Davidson (1994), in attempting to identify specific reasons for women's lack of advancement to senior management positions, suggested that it is important to remember that managerial and professional women live and work in a larger society that is patriarchal, a society in which men have historically had greater access to power, privilege and wealth than women. Similarly, Berthoin-Antal and Izraeli (1993: 63), in their review of women in management worldwide, state that 'probably the single most important hurdle for women in management in all industrialised countries is the persistent stereotype that associates management with being male'. Women in management, and in particular, women in international management encounter more barriers to their career progression than their male counterparts. Formal organisational policies are formed by gender-based societal assumptions regarding the suitability of men or women for international managerial assignments. Formal organisational policies also influence informal processes which may effect the participation of female managers in international management.

Profile of expatriate managers

According to Torrington (1994), there is a small, elite group of genuinely international managers in the world of global business. Torrington distinguishes between international managers and expatriate managers and proposes that this distinction can be summarised as follows: international managers *pass through* foreign countries; expatriates go and *live* in them. Davison and Punnett (1995) noted that gender and race have received relatively little attention in expatriate literature, despite the impact of these and other variables – such as religion, and other distinguishing personal characteristics which frequently arise in expatriate decisions.

Research (GMAC, 2003) with 181 multinationals (77 per cent headquartered in the United States) and operating in more than 130 countries shows that 82 per cent of expatriates are male, 60 per cent of these fall into the 30–49 age group with 65 per cent being married. Similarly, British based organisations surveyed by Harris (1995) revealed that 91 per cent of expatriates were male, and ranged in ages between 31 and 40. Chusmir and Frontczak (1990) also conducted research with 222 American senior male and female expatriate managers in order to compare the perceptions and attitudes of these managers regarding opportunities for women in international business. They concluded that people often expect more of women in management, so women realise they need to be exceptional performers. They suggested that unless the performance of women in management is outstanding, women perceive their opportunities in international management to be more limited. Overall, therefore, it is clear that the profile of the expatriate manager reveals that the majority of such managers are white and male, and are usually accompanied abroad by a spouse.

The international transfer cycle

It has been established from the extant research on international human resource management that male and female managers in domestic managerial positions are not treated similarly by senior management. Because of the relative scarcity of female international managers, comparisons between male and female transfers are more difficult. The international transfer cycle, for male and female managers, however, can be divided into three distinct phases. First, selection for managerial expatriation, second, the assignment period abroad, and third, the re-entry stage.

Stage One

Expatriation does involve a major upheaval for the expatriate managers and their families; while it often proves to be a very positive experience in the long term for all concerned, the immediate transfer is frequently problematic. It is apparent from the extant research that it is much more difficult for female managers to be selected for an international assignment than it is for their male counterparts. The findings from research with women who have completed international assignments, however, illustrates very little evidence of failure. It is important, therefore, to highlight some of the barriers women face as part of the selection process for international assignments. Varma and Stroh (2001) examined reasons why women might not be selected for international assignments. They found that a poor quality relationship between female subordinates and primarily male superiors was a primary cause of the low number of female international managers. Antal and Izraeli (1993) argue that, in the face of uncertainties about the role of expatriates, organisations need certainty in this high-risk area and this leads managers to select others who are most similar to themselves, (males) and, consequently, presumably more likely to be seen as trustworthy and predictable. Similarly, Brewster (1991) notes widespread reliance on personal recommendation for expatriate postings from either a specialist personnel staff member or line managers. This results in more or less predetermined selection interviews which consist more of negotiating the terms of the offer than determining the suitability of the candidate.

Harris and Brewster (1999) also explored the selection processes for international managers in major British-based 'blue-chip' international organisations. They found that the selection process was heavily influenced by informal practices, i.e. word of mouth recommendations were common. This is seen to be particularly problematic for women, given the large percentage of international managers being men. According to Harris and Brewster, the nature of the vacancies reflect a male-type bias, which forces them continually to question their assumptions about women's suitability and, critically, their acceptability in international management positions. These findings confirm prior research by Scullion (1994), who suggested that primarily subjective knowledge of an individual determines who is seen to 'fit in' best with existing organisational norms. Overall, therefore, in practice, international managerial selection tends to be heavily influenced by informal processes and does not reflect the rational, objective policies of formal recruitment and selection theories.

Stage Two

The second stage of the international transfer cycle is the actual assignment period abroad. Studies have established that an international managerial assignment normally extends for a period of three to four years (Borg and Harzing, 1995; Lane and DiStefano, 1992; Linehan, 2000). Borg and Harzing (1995) noted that the first six months abroad are perceived by most expatriates in a similar way. At the beginning of the assignment many things are new and exciting, but after about three months difficulties begin to emerge as the expatriate experiences what has been described as 'culture shock'. Culture shock has been defined as a behavioural pattern associated with powerlessness. Lane and DiStefano (1992) identified symptoms of culture shock as fatigue, tension, anxiety, excessive concern about hygiene, hostility, obsessions about being cheated, withdrawal into work, family, or the expatriate community, or in extreme cases, excessive use of drugs and alcohol. After about five or six months the expatriate starts to adapt to the foreign culture and gradually moves to a more neutral state.

Linehan (2000) found that twenty-eight of the fifty female managers she interviewed were from dual-career couples, and these relocated to facilitate the careers of the female partner, but their male accompanying spouses experienced greater culture shock than themselves. They highlighted the exclusion their partners experienced, for example, not being invited to social gatherings organised by their companies for the (female) partners of other managers. As thirty of the fifty managers were the first females to represent their companies internationally, they did not know if their international experience would be considered valuable by home-country senior management, therefore, they perceived their international assignment as a risk to their future careers. The managers also believed that because of lack of preparation and for the international move, and often having the responsibility for organising a spouse and family, it was a very stressful phase. They also believed that arriving in their new location was generally more stressful personally than professionally. They stated that balancing work and home life was particularly difficult, especially when young children had to be settled into new schools, and arrangements for childcare had to be organised. The managers also believed that in some cases social adjustment was more difficult than organisational adjustment, as in most countries it is not the norm for females to socialise alone, consequently females needed a longer adjusting period than that of their male counterparts.

Overall, it appears that the adjustment period for female international managers takes longer than for their male counterparts because of additional family and home responsibilities. Interestingly, despite the longer adjusting period, when female managers and their families have adjusted to their new locations, female international managers can be as successful or even more successful than their male counterparts.

Stage Three

The third phase of the international career move is the re-entry stage (see Chapter 10 in this volume). According to Handler and Lane (1997), the repatriation process can often be problematic for returning expatriates, their families and their companies. During international assignments, expatriate managers are often 'out of sight' and 'out of mind' to the parent company The re-entry phase is usually haphazard and ill-planned for both male and female managers, but uncertainty regarding re-entry is more difficult for female executives because many female international managers are in a pioneering role (Linehan and Scullion, 2002). Despite the problems associated with repatriation, coming back from an international assignment seldom receives the organisational attention it requires. Until recently, both practitioners and academics tended to assume that repatriation should be easy – after all, the person is 'coming home'. The main reason for this is because repatriation is not expected to be problematic, as all the problems are expected to be connected with going on assignment and getting settled. Repatriation problems, however, are complex because they involve the challenges of personal re-entry and professional re-entry at the same time.

Some of the additional problems experienced by women expatriates at the re-entry stage include tokenism, isolation and exclusion, lack of female role models, and being test cases for future international managers (Linehan and Scullion, 2002). Thirty-one of the thirty-two repatriated female managers in Linehan and Scullion's research indicated that they experienced a loss of status, loss of autonomy and faced major changes in their personal and professional lives when they returned to their home countries. They noted that they went through stages similar to those of culture shock – the first being an excited mood which lasted only a short time, then descending to a low mood, and finally returning to their normal mood. The managers also suggested that the difficulties associated with re-entry are underestimated at present, and that the re-entry process should receive more attention in the future. Research conducted with twenty-seven repatriated female executives in Europe by Collins-O'Sullivan and Linehan (2003) identified specific issues for both married and single women during repatriation. The married women suggested that the extra worry of settling other members of the family added greatly to the already stressful repatriation process. The single women found that when they returned they were in an older age bracket. Many of their former friends were married and had children and were not available to socialise with them. They found that the social network which they used to have had disappeared. The women believed that it was much more difficult for them to break into a new socialising network than it would be for their male counterparts. They expressed a reluctance to go socialising and meeting new people on their own. They believed that this was not a problem which was faced by men. Many of them had not anticipated this problem and found it very difficult to settle again in their home country.

This lack of attention to repatriation may have a long-run impact on the performance of organisations because repatriation difficulties exacerbate problems in attracting international managers, which given the shortages of international managers could constrain the implementation of the companies' internationalisation objectives (Scullion, 2001). In practice, many firms continue to adopt an ad hoc sink or swim attitude towards both employees and their families and many expatriate managers continue to experience the repatriation process as falling far short of expectations (Stroh *et al.*, 2000a). The lack of understanding of the particular needs of female international managers in relation to the repatriation stage is a growing concern in international management. Companies should develop integrated approaches to repatriation for female executives which incorporates both organisational/career issues and individual issues. Companies should regard repatriation as an integral part of the process of expatriation which would involve a fundamental re-examination of the expatriate psychological contract (Guzzo *et al.*, 1994; Rousseau, 1989). In particular, Collins-O'Sullivan and Linehan (2003) suggest that utilising the experiences of female repatriated managers should heighten awareness of female successes in global assignments, increase the future participation rates of women in overseas assignments, and provide role models for potential female international managers. Linehan and Scullion (2002) highlight the importance of closing the gap between expectations and reality for expatriates returning to their parent companies and suggest that multinationals which prepare their female managers for coming home with effective repatriation programmes will have a greater likelihood both of retaining these scarce human resources and of helping them make the difficult adjustment to being home.

The impact of gender on women managers' international careers

The major focus of research on women in management has generally been on women themselves as they arrived in and advanced through organisations. The emphasis has not been on gender aspects per se, but on the implications of gender for the organisation (McGee-Calvert and Ramsey, 1992). According to Marshall (1995), the term 'gender' is gaining breadth of usage. The original connotation referred to the social expectations and roles attributed to or experienced by people based on their biological sex. Gender is now taking on a much broader and more diffuse set of meanings. It has become a general label for talking about women, men, the relationships between them, related aspects of organising, processes through which gender-differentiated behaviour patterns are enacted, and associated issues of power in various guises. Marshall also suggested that the gender aspect of management is not a particularly coherent field, but a highly diverse field.

It has been noted that many researchers refer to the gender of expatriates as male throughout their research. Indeed, Black's (1988) account of work role transitions among American expatriate managers in Japan is derived from an all-male sample and his 1990 treatise on the relationship between personal characteristics and the adjustment of Japanese expatriate managers is based on sixty-seven usable questionnaires returned by male expatriate managers.

Where evidence does exist, however, on the impact of gender in international assignments one of the core arguments is that female expatriates in certain cultures can experience difficulties if they are to play a role that is not 'appropriate' to their perceived role. Adler (1995), however, suggests that the societal and cultural rules governing the behaviour of local women that limit their access to managerial positions and responsibility do not apply to foreign women, and therefore host nationals may in fact be more willing to accept female expatriates playing roles that may be seen as inappropriate for local females. Adler points out that the female international manager has a triple identity. She is a manager, a foreigner and a woman. There are conditions when being a woman will be less conspicuous than her other identities, as local managers see women expatriates as foreigners who happen to be women, not as women who happen to be foreigners. According to Adler, a woman's presence as a manager, rather than a female, is more likely to be seen as uppermost when she is in a senior international position or perceived to be a highly qualified expert in her field.

Similarly, research conducted by Westwood and Leung (1994) with women expatriate managers in Hong Kong revealed that there were no specific barriers or resistances because of their gender. Many of their respondents held the view that, if you were perceived as a competent manager and could do the job, gender was incidental. Local managers were seen as more open-minded and pragmatic than home country senior managers. More recent research conducted by Linehan (2000) with senior female international managers based in Europe suggests that the most difficult hurdle in a female's international career was getting the international assignment in the first place and not, as most had anticipated, gaining the respect of foreigners and succeeding once sent. Similarly, Westwood and Leung's forty-five interviews with women expatriate managers in Hong Kong established that close to half of the respondents said they had no special difficulties because of their gender. Many held the view that, if you were perceived as a competent manager and could do the job, gender was incidental. Westwood and Leung (1994) concluded that the expatriate female managers had a very positive view of their experiences. Problems associated with their gender did not materialise and did not prove any significant impediment to their effective managerial performance in ways that had been anticipated by home-country senior managers. Most women in their study believed that the situation for women managers was better in Hong Kong than in their home countries, and that the worst forms of sexism they encountered came from expatriate, not local males. It seems, therefore, that concerns about women being accepted as expatriate managers arise more from male managers in the home country organisation blaming other cultures for their own prejudices.

In summary, it would appear from Adler's (1987), Westwood and Leung's (1994) and Linehan's (2000) research that women expatriates' performances in overseas assignments, throughout North America, Hong Kong and Europe, are successful and that women are regarded first as managers and second as women.

Women international managers and marital status

According to Izraeli and Zeira (1993), when women's suitability for international assignments is being discussed marital status becomes an issue. They observe that 'stereotypical thinking and the double standard' are evident, whether single or married, the female international's family status is presumed to be problematic. Vinnicombe and Sturges (1995) suggest that some organisations operate a double standard for marriage: they view the married male manager as an asset, with a stable support network at home allowing him to give his undivided attention to his work, but they view the married female manager as a liability, likely to neglect her career at the expense of her family at every possible opportunity. Because of the double standard for marriage many women managers have had little choice but to take this into consideration, and avoid the responsibility of family commitments wherever possible.

Unmarried women

According to Davidson and Cooper (1992), if women managers decide not to marry, they are likely to experience pressure from colleagues who perceive them as an 'oddity', as the stereotype of the 'old maid' still exists. Other potential stressors which are associated with the unattached woman manager are the pressures and strains linked with having to take care of elderly parents and dependants, particularly if they are the 'only daughter'. Davidson and Cooper suggest that single women 'get the rawest deal' in caring for relatives because it often means giving up their social life, having large financial commitments and in some cases having to retire early. It has been suggested that male managers tend to believe that a single woman, away from the social influence of her home country, is more vulnerable to harassment and other dangers than a man.

Married women

In contrast, if a married woman accepts an international assignment, senior home-country managers are concerned with tensions in the family, and the problems associated with dual-career issues. An assumption, often made by senior home-country managers, that women in dual-career marriages do not want an international posting is a further problem for women international managers.

As more women move into international management positions, the 'trailing' or 'accompanying' spouse is increasingly likely to be the male partner, who has to put his own career 'on hold', and some organisations expect dual-career status to generate greater employee hostility to geographical relocation. The failure of the spouse to adjust on a foreign assignment has been highlighted as one of the most common reasons for male expatriate failure and early return from international assignments. Aycan (1997) suggests that spousal support is an important positive influence where the spouse is well adjusted himself or herself.

Research has shown that female managers who marry or live in long-term relationships are more likely than their male counterparts to have partners with professional or managerial careers (Brett *et al.*, 1992; Davidson and Cooper, 1983). This means that more female than male managers must deal with the issues associated with the management of two careers and family life. Spouse-related problems for married females are therefore perceived as being more serious because male partners generally have careers and it is difficult for many men to adjust to the role of secondary bread winner or homemaker, as may be necessary if they cannot work in a foreign location. According to Bielby and Bielby (1988), these roles are more socially acceptable for women, and women, even those with careers, may make the transition to these roles more easily than men. As the majority of international managers is still male, the non-working husband may find himself the lone man in a group of wives. In addition to these concerns, work-permit restrictions by some host countries make it difficult for a spouse to work. In some countries it may be socially unacceptable for the male partner to be the homemaker and the traditional volunteer activities that wives have been encouraged to undertake may not be available or appropriate for males in some countries (Punnett *et al.*, 1992).

Currently most dual-career couples' problems are left up to the couple to resolve, with no help from the parent corporation. According to Handler and Lane (1997), this is problematic because multinationals who ignore policy making on dual-career issues may find it difficult to recruit and maintain high standard international managers. Researchers have suggested that dual-career couple issues should be highlighted as a major expatriate concern and the management of dual-career couples has been identified as one of the five most important human resource challenges for future years (Valcour and Tolbert, 2003). Organisations, however, may no longer be able to assume that the male partner's career will always take precedence, and that the female partner will always subordinate her career aspirations to those of her partner (Napier and Taylor, 2002; Pringle and Mallon, 2003). The failure of organisations to respond to dual-career issues results in costs, not only to the couple but also to their organisations. The willingness of organisations to address dual-career issues may be important for achieving competitive advantage in the future.

Work–family conflict and women international managers

A closely related area concerning the conflicting demands of work and home is where there are children involved in the international move. Work–family conflict is experienced when pressures from the work and family roles are mutually incompatible, such that participation in one role makes it more difficult to participate in the other. Work–family conflict is a major source of pressure for female managers, as females still tend to take on the additional responsibilities for organising family members and the home. Research over time and across cultures continues to document the persistence of inequality in the allocation of household work and family responsibilities, even among couples with 'modern' ideologies and in countries with commitment to gender equality at home and at work (Hochschild, 1989; Lewis and Cooper, 1987; Parasuraman and Greenhaus, 1993).

Hochschild (1989) suggested that because of this uneven distribution of household work, women are said to work a 'second shift' at home in addition to their first shift at work. Hochschild believes that women continue to work this second shift because their job is considered to be of less importance than their husband's job. Similarly, British research carried out by Davidson (1989) reveals that compared to married male managers, married female managers are much more likely to experience higher pressures in respect of career and spouse/partner conflicts, career/home conflicts, and career and marriage/childbearing conflicts.

Berthoin-Antal and Izraeli (1993) also suggest that the work functions and duties performed by managers in all industrialised countries appear to be based on total commitment measured in terms of time spent at the workplace. Career breaks for women managers for child-bearing and child-rearing show incompatibilities with the job of management, which is presumed to be a full-time and continuous job. It is believed that career breaks indicate a lack of commitment and re-entry is problematic.

Lewis and Cooper (1988) also suggested that the dual-career lifestyle becomes more difficult to manage, and parents experience more role conflict and stress than those without children. Hall (1990) noted that fathers have a choice about whether to make their new family status and needs visible, and if they do choose to modify their work schedules they frequently do so in a covert way. For women, on the other hand, Lewis (1994) noted that there is no question about the visibility of motherhood. In so far as they have a choice, it is between making their family needs invisible by conforming to traditional patterns of work, or to modify work schedules, often at considerable cost to career advancement. Women are often forced to make difficult and complex decisions regarding what lifestyle to adopt. Career success is still based on men's traditional work experiences and assumptions about the importance of work to identity. Female career perspectives, choices and priorities, however, do not imply that women's career achievements are any less important than those of men, but some women do not fit the male model of work and careers. As female managers do not always fit the dominant male career model, they are often forced to choose between a career and a family. In choosing an acceptable lifestyle, women face a number of dilemmas, and their choices are more difficult than for their male counterparts because of women's typically stronger linkages to both career and family roles. Women may respond by reducing their employment involvement, which in turn, restricts international career opportunities and advancement.

'Having it all'

Forty-seven of the fifty senior female international managers interviewed by Linehan (2000) believed that it is more difficult for female managers than for their male counterparts to 'have it all', that is, a successful career, a good personal relationship and children. These managers believed that their male counterparts in international management do not have to make the same sacrifices, as it is still generally accepted by organisations and society that the family will move to facilitate the career of the male breadwinner. Twenty-eight managers in Linehan's research, whose families relocated to facilitate their careers, noted that their organising and settling in of their families to new surroundings often proved more difficult than dealing with their new professional lives. Those managers perceived that much of the guilt and conflict experienced by them as female managers were derived from the way parental roles are socially defined. They also believed that such role tensions and constraints are potentially damaging to women's careers. They further perceived that the historical devaluing of women's work means that women tend to be employed in traditional women's occupations which have lower pay, power and prestige – all of which may affect women's career progress. The managers also suggested that gender role identity, particularly in relation to child-bearing and child-rearing does impact on male or female behaviours in relation to occupational expectations. Linehan (2000) concluded that personal relationships, child-bearing and child-rearing conflicts are strong indicators and predictors of the disproportionately low number of females who pursue, or are interested in pursuing, careers in international management.

Do female managers want international careers?

It is clear that international management has long been a masculine preserve in Europe and North America, therefore since the mid-1980s researchers have attempted to ascertain if female managers want international careers. Because of the additional barriers faced by women international managers, particularly in dual-career relationships, Adler (1984) suggests that a belief widely shared is that women do not want to be international managers. According to Berthoin-Antal and Izraeli (1993) such beliefs may discourage female managers from competing with men for international assignments. They conclude that 'women would have to want international assignments much more strongly than men to overcome the multiple dampers on their student-day motivations' (1993: 83). Kanter (1977) also suggests that the minimal participation of women in management may not be due to a lack of motivation, but may be due to blocked opportunities.

According to the International Labour Office, about half the world's workers are in sex-stereotyped occupations. Men still dominate the technical and managerial tasks, while women are concentrated mainly in caring and nurturing occupations and support roles (Economist, 1998). Career theories have been largely built on male models of success and work. Those models are supported by psychoanalytic conceptions of the centrality of work to identity, and by developmental beliefs that maturity and personal empowerment require separation from others. Research by Gallos (1989) established that professional women are capable of aggressively competing and succeeding in the male corporate world, but are prepared to sacrifice their own careers and personal needs in order to support their spouses and assume an accommodative stance in order to avoid confrontations. Hewlett (1986) maintained that there are obvious and logical reasons to expect that women would have their own values for interpreting the world. These include their capacities for childbirth, early-life socialisation differences and social or political pressures for maintaining the traditional feminine role. As a result, women have traditionally been employed in service and care-giving positions, for example, teachers, social workers, nurses and secretaries. Non-traditional career women may also experience external pressures which make life choices difficult for them, as they receive little or no organisational or societal support.

Research by Linehan and Scullion (2001) found that:

- the persistent stereotypical characteristics of a successful international manager are those characteristics which are typically associated with male management
- organisational assumptions and policies regarding the suitability of an individual as an international manager are based on societal assumptions about men and women
- home-country male managers perceive women as being different and not like themselves, so they tend not to select women for expatriate positions.

Linehan and Scullion's findings suggest that female managers would have to be much more determined than men if they want international managerial positions, and they must be prepared to ask for these positions because females are rarely offered such opportunities. In particular, senior home-country male managers believe that entry into a new job requires total involvement and longer than usual hours of work, therefore, the married international manager is likely to be even less available to her family than when working in her own organisation.

All of the European fifty managers interviewed by Linehan (2000) stated that they wanted an international career, but that they often had to persuade senior home-country management to 'take the risk' and give them the opportunity to work abroad. Interestingly, none of the fifty were offered an international career, but they had to ask and repeatedly ask to be sent abroad. They revealed that the wishes and desires of female managers to partake in international managerial positions are equal to those of male managers. The married managers in the research considered themselves to be 'lucky' to be married to spouses who agreed to them pursuing international careers. They believed that due to societal and cultural norms, it is not yet widely acceptable for female managers to have the main career. Similarly, Stroh et al. (2002b) found that US and Canadian women are interested in partaking in international assignments, although there are variations between those with children and those without. Their study also found that home-country organisations were reluctant to ask them to accept an international assignment. Schein et al. (1994) concluded that male attitudes to managerial women are strong, consistent and pervasive and appear to be a global phenomenon, or as Schein suggested, 'think manager equals think male'.

Breaking the glass ceiling and glass border

A review of the relevant research literature in management shows that women face barriers to progression within organisations, barriers which are not faced by their male counterparts. European women, like their United States and Australian counterparts, are confronted by a glass ceiling – a term used to describe a barrier so subtle that it is transparent, yet so strong that it prevents women and minorities from moving up the managerial hierarchy. Schwartz (1989), however, suggests that the metaphor of the glass ceiling is misleading, as 'counterproductive layers of influence on women', such as tradition, socialisation and negative stereotypes, hinder their progression to senior managerial positions. Overcoming 'hidden' or less obvious organisational barriers to managerial equity may be difficult for women to achieve in the near future. In 1992, the Women's Research and Education Institute estimated that it would take seventy-five to one hundred years at the current rate of change in order to attain full economic integration for women at every organisational level.

The specific problems and pressures which have been identified as unique to female managers include:

- burdens of coping with the role of the 'token' woman
- being a test case for future women
- lack of role models and feelings of isolation
- strain of coping with prejudice and sex stereotyping
- overt and indirect discrimination from fellow employees, employers and the organisational structures and climate.

The results of research in the United States, by Kleiman (1992), indicated that women in lower management are likely to encounter the glass ceiling without even advancing into middle management. Kleiman concluded that the height of the glass ceiling has been found to be much lower than first thought. Similarly, O'Leary and Johnson (1991) found that women managers in the United States who reached senior management positions in previously male-dominated areas do so at the cost of isolation and loneliness. An analysis of Linehan's (2000) interview data confirms that both glass ceilings and glass borders are still perceived to exist for women managers, therefore, because of these additional barriers many female managers may choose not to partake in international assignments. The fifty managers interviewed by Linehan (2000), all of whom have reached senior management positions, believe that they need to be as well qualified, or in some cases more qualified, more ambitious, and more mobile than male managers. They suggested, in addition to these traits, they broke through the glass ceiling in their own careers because:

- they persistently asked for their next career move, rather than waiting to be offered the next move
- they were better than their male counterparts at balancing a number of functions at the same time.

The managers suggested that they developed this ability from their childhood experiences and their socialisation as children. They recalled from their childhood socialisation their fathers being singularly focused on work outside the home, whereas their mothers needed to develop the ability to balance a number of different responsibilities. They further believed that even though they had broken through the glass ceiling in their domestic organisations, when they applied for their international career move, they experienced difficulties again. All fifty managers revealed that it is necessary for women to have senior managerial experience in their home organisations before being considered for international managerial positions.

In summary, the barriers which prevent female managers from progressing to senior managerial positions in domestic and international management include:

- the obligation to balance home life and career
- isolation and loneliness
- constant awareness of being a woman in a man's world
- having to prove oneself to others
- having to work harder and to be better than their male counterparts.

It is clear that the glass ceiling in home countries is a contributory factor to the low participation rate of women in international management.

Conclusion

The low participation of women in international management continues to be a cause for concern and will be a key challenge for international human resource managers over the next decade. Given the growing shortages of international managers (Scullion and Paauwe, 2004) and the research which highlights the success of women as expatriates (Caligiuri *et al.*, 1999, Linehan, 2000), the failure to develop effective strategies to promote increased participation of women in international management will become increasingly costly to organisations and will limit the potential supply of international managers. Current human resource management practices primarily reflect the interests of the dominant group (males) in organisations and organisations have not yet succeeded in introducing training and development strategies that effectively meet the needs of women. Women, however, will remain on the periphery of international management unless companies radically transform their international human resource management policies and practices. These practices are, however, often difficult to identify and dismantle as they are embedded in organisational cultures and entrenched in organisational power structures.

In particular, multinationals have a low sense of awareness and a lack of appreciation of the particular needs of female executives in relation to the international transfer process and specifically in relation to repatriation. This lack of attention to repatriation may have a long-run impact on the performance of these organisations because of the problems for repatriate managers and the company. There is also evidence that poor handling of repatriation issues many influence the willingness of future managers to accept foreign assignments.

Female expatriates are further disadvantaged in their careers as few organisations have developed distinctive career models for women. In addition, gender disparity in organisations and family responsibilities often prevent women employees from reaching senior managerial positions. Female managers are often forced to choose between an expatriate career and family, and their choices are more difficult than for their male counterparts because of the linkages that exist between their career and family roles. Finally, existing research has established that female managers are capable of succeeding internationally, and that many of the desired qualities for international management positions are similar for males and females. Efforts, therefore, should be made by organisations to ensure that the outdated attitudes and practices which many female managers encounter be eliminated to enable female managers to achieve their full potential.

References

Adler, N.J. (1984) 'Women do not want international careers and other myths about international management', *Organizational Dynamics*, 13(2): 66–79.

Adler, N.J. (1987) 'Pacific basin managers: a gaijin, not a woman', *Human Resource Management*, 26(2): 169–92.

Adler, N.J. (1995) 'Expatriate women managers', in J. Selman (ed.) *Expatriate Management: New Ideas for International Business*, London: Quorum.

Antal, A. and Izraeli, D. (1993) 'A global comparison of women in management: women managers in their homelands and as expatriates', in E. Fagenson (ed.) *Women in Management: Trends, Issues and Challenges in Managerial Diversity*, Beverly Hills, CA: Sage.

Aycan, Z. (1997) 'Expatriate adjustment as a multifaceted phenomenon: individual and organisational level predictors', *International Journal of Human Resource Management*, 8(3): 434–65.

Berthoin-Antal, A. and Izraeli, D.N. (1993) 'A global comparison of women in management: women managers in their homelands and as expatriates', in E.A. Ferguson (ed.) *Women in Management: Trends, Issues and Challenges in Managerial Diversity*, London: Sage.

Bielby, D.D, and Bielby, W.T. (1988) 'Women and men's commitment to paid work and family: theories, models and hypotheses', *Women and Work: An Annual Review*, 3.

Black, J. S. (1988) 'Work role transitions: a study of American expatriate managers in Japan', *Journal of International Business Studies*, 19(2): 277–94.

Borg, M. and Harzing A.W. (1995) ' Composing an international staff', in A.W. Harzing and J. Van Ruysseveldt (eds) *International Human Resource Management*, London: Sage.

Brett, J.M., Stroh, L.K. and Reilly, A.H. (1992) 'What is it like being a dual career manager in the 1990s?', in S. Zedeck (ed.) *Work, Families and Organizations*, San Francisco, CA: Jossey-Bass.

Brewster, C. (1991) *The Management of Expatriates*, London: Kogan Page.

Burke, R.J. and Davidson, M.J. (1994) 'Women in management: current research issues', in M.J. Davidson and R.J. Burke (eds) *Women in Management: Current Research Issues*, London: Paul Chapman.

Caligiuri, P.M., Joshi, A. and Lazarova, M. (1999) 'Factors influencing the global adjustment of women on global assignments', *International Journal of Human Resource Management*, 10(2): 163–79.

Chusmir, L.H. and Frontczak, N.T. (1990) 'International management opportunities for women: women and men paint different pictures', *International Journal of Management*, 7(3): 295–301.

Collins-O'Sullivan, C. and Linehan, M. (2003) 'The repatriation of female international corporate executives: a qualitative study in a European context', paper presented at Seventh Conference on International Human Resource Management, University of Limerick, Ireland, 4–6 June.

Davidson, M.J. (1989) 'Women managers and stress: profiles of vulnerable individuals', *Clinical Psychology Forum*, 22: 32–4.

Davidson, M.J. and Cooper, C.L. (1992) *Shattering the Glass Ceiling: The Woman Manager*, London: Paul Chapman.

Davidson, M.J. and Cooper, C.L. (eds) (1983) *European Women in Business and Management*, London: Paul Chapman.

Davison, E.D. and Punnett, B.J. (1995) 'International assignments: is there a role for gender and race in decisions', *International Journal of Human Resource Management*, 6(2): 411–41.

Economist (1998) 'Women and work: for better, for worse', *The Economist*, 18 July: 3–16.

Gallos, J.V. (1989) 'Exploring women's development: implications for career theory, practice and research', in M.B. Arthur, D.T. Hall and B.S. Lawrence (eds) *Handbook of Career Theory*, New York: Cambridge University Press.

GMAC Global Relocation Services (2003) *Global Relocation Trends Survey*, Warren, NJ: GMAC Global Relocation Services.

Guzzo, R.A., Noonan, K.A. and Elron, E. (1994) 'Expatriate managers and the psychological contract', *Journal of Applied Psychology*, 79(4): 617–26.

Hall, D.T. (1990) 'Promoting work/family balance: an organisational change approach', *Organizational Dynamics*, 18: 5–18.

Handler, C.A. and Lane, I.M. (1997) 'Career planning and expatriate couples', *Human Resource Management Journal*, 7(3): 67–78.

Harris, H. (1995) 'Women's role in (international) management', in A.W.K. Harzing and J. Van Ruysseveldt (eds) *International Human Resource Management*, London: Sage.

Harris, H. and Brewster, C. (1999) 'The coffee-machine system: how international selection really works', *International Journal of Human Resource Management*, 10(3): 229–51.

Hewlett, S. (1986) *A Lesser Life: The Myth of Women's Liberation in America*, New York: Morrow.

Hochschild, A. (1989) *The Second Shift*, New York: Viking.

Izraeli, D. and Adler, N.J. (eds) (1994) *Competitive Frontiers: Women Managers in a Global Economy*, Oxford: Basil Blackwell.

Izraeli, D. and Zeira, Y. (1993) 'Women managers in international business: a research review and appraisal', *Business and the Contemporary World*, 3: 35–45.

Kanter, R.M. (1977) *Men and Women of the Corporation*, New York: Basic Books.

Kleiman, C. (1992) 'Right stuff can bump against the glass ceiling', *Chicago Tribune*, 6 January: 6.

Lane, H.W. and DiStefano, J.J. (1992) *International Management Behaviour: From Policy to Practice*, Boston, MA: PWS-Kent.

Lewis, S. (1994) 'Role tensions and dual-career couples', in M.J. Davidson and R.J. Burke (eds) *Women in Management: Current Research Issues*, London: Paul Chapman.

Lewis, S. and Cooper, C.L. (1987) 'Stress in dual earner couples and stage in the life cycle', *Journal of Occupational Psychology*, 60: 289–303.

Lewis, S. and Cooper, C.L. (1988) 'The transition to parenthood in two earner couples', *Psychological Medicine*, 18: 477–86.

Linehan, M. (2000) *Senior Female International Managers: Why So Few?*, Aldershot: Ashgate.

Linehan, M. and Scullion, H. (2002) 'Repatriation of female executives: empirical evidence from Europe', *Women in Management Review*, 17(2): 80–8.

Linehan, M., Morley, M.J. and Scullion, H. (2003) 'The management of expatriates: contemporary developments and future challenges', *Journal of Managerial Psychology*, 18(3): 174–84.

McGee-Calvert, L. and Ramsey, V.J. (1992) 'Bringing women's voice to research on women in management: a feminist perspective', *Journal of Management Inquiry*, 1(1): 79–88.

Mandelker, J. (1994) 'Breaking the glass border', *Working Woman*, 19(1): 16.

Marshall, J. (1995) 'Gender and management: a critical review of research', *British Journal of Management*, 6: 53–62.

Morrison, A.M. and Von Glinow, M.A. (1990) 'Women and minorities in management', *American Psychologist*, 45(2): 200–8.

Napier, N. and Taylor, S. (2002) 'Experiences of women professionals abroad: comparisons across Japan, China and Turkey', *International Journal of Human Resource Management*, 13(5): 837–51.

O'Leary, V.E. and Johnson, J.L. (1991) 'Steep ladder, lonely climb', *Women in Management Review and Abstracts*, 6(5): 10–16.

Parasuraman, S.J. and Greenhaus, J.H. (1992) 'Role stressors, social support and well-being among two-career couples', *Journal of Organizational Behaviour*, 13: 339–56.

Pringle, J.K. and Mallon, M. (2003) 'Challenges for the boundaryless career odyssey', *International Journal of Human Resource Management*, 14(5): 839–53.

Punnett, B.J., Crocker, O.I. and Stevens, M.A. (1992) 'The challenge for women expatriates and spouses: some empirical evidence', *International Journal of Human Resource Management*, 3(3): 585–92.

Rousseau, D.M. (1989) 'Psychological and implied contracts in organisations', *Employee Responsibilities and Rights Journal*, 2: 121–39.

Schein, V.E., Mueller, R., Lituchy, T. and Liu, J. (1994) *Think Manager – Think Male: A Global Phenomenon?* Gettysburg College Management Department Working Papers, Gettysburg, PA.

Schwartz, F.N. (1989) 'Management women and the facts of life', *Harvard Business Review*, 67(1): 65–76.

Scullion, H. (1994) 'Staffing policies and strategic control in British multinationals', *International Studies of Management and Organization*, 24(3): 86–104.

Scullion, H. (2001) 'International human resource management', in J. Storey (ed) *Human Resource Management*, London: Thomson.

Scullion, H. and Paauwe, J. (2004) 'International human resource management: recent developments in theory and empirical research', in A.W.K. Harzing and J.V. Van Ruysseveldt (eds) *International Human Resource Management*, London: Sage.

Stroh, L.K., Gregersen, H.B. and Black, J.S. (2000a) 'Triumphs and tragedies: expectations and commitments upon repatriation', *International Journal of Human Resource Management*, 11(4): 1061–81.

Stroh, L.K., Varma, A. and Valy-Durbin, S.J. (2000b) 'Why are women left at home: are they unwilling to go on international assignments?', *Journal of World Business*, 35(3): 241–55.

Taylor, S., Napier, N.K. and Mayrhofer, W. (2002) 'Women in global business: an introduction', *International Journal of Human Resource Management*, 13(5): 739–42.

Torrington, D. (1994) *International Human Resource Management: Think Globally, Act Locally*, London: Prentice Hall.

Valcour, P.M. and Tolbert, P. (2003) 'Gender, family and career in the era of boundarylessness: determinants and effects of intra-and organisational mobility', *International Journal of Human Resource Management*, 14(5): 768–87.

Varma, A. and Stroh, L.K. (2001) 'Different perspectives on selection for international assignments: the impact of LMX and gender', *Cross Cultural Management*, 8(3–4): 85–97.

Vinnicombe, S. and Sturges, J. (1995) 'European women in management', in S. Vinnicombe and N.L. Colwill (eds) *The Essence of Women in Management*, London: Prentice Hall.

Westwood, R.I. and Leung, S.M. (1994) 'The female expatriate manager experience: coping with gender and culture', *International Studies of Management and Organization*, 24(3): 64–85.

Women's Research and Education Institute (WREI) (1992) *The American Woman 1990–1991: A Status Report*, Washington, DC: WREI.

Repatriation: the frequently forgotten phase of an international assignment

MARGARET LINEHAN

Introduction

Much research in international human resource management has focused on the preparation, selection and training of employees for international assignments. An often neglected area is the repatriation phase, and in particular, what happens to the career path of the employee on return. If any aspect of globalisation points out the complexities of international assignments as well as the systemic weakness and lack of planning within the international human resource function, it is repatriation. Repatriation is usually overlooked instead of being seen as the final link in an integrated, circular process that connects good selection, cross-cultural preparation, global career management and completion of the international business objectives (Marmer Solomon, 1995). According to Forster (2000) the biggest single problem encountered by UK companies since the early 1990s has been with the repatriation of employees rather than the management of expatriation. There appears to be differences between US and European multinationals with respect to their policies regarding the guarantee of a re-entry position. Research suggests that 74 per cent of continental European multinationals provided written guarantees of a return position in comparison to 38 per cent of US companies; 50 per cent of UK multinationals provided such guarantees (Conference Board, 1997).

Repatriation usually takes place after a period of about three to five years. An organisation has the opportunity to deepen its management talent base through successful repatriation, but runs the risk of losing this talent, either because it is not well used in the domestic setting or because former expatriates leave the organisation. Generally, the assumption is that since these individuals are returning home – that is, to a familiar way of life – they should have no trouble adapting to either the corporate or the home environment. Experience, however, shows that repatriation is anything but simple. In many cases, the process of adjustment is so difficult that the only solution the expatriates believe they have is to seek employment elsewhere. Research indicates that between 20 per cent and 50 per cent of all expatriates resign – a significantly higher percentage than among non-repatriate executives (Black and Gregersen, 1998; Stroh, 1995). As organisations lose such valuable human resources, they reduce an essential core of internationally astute executives who can effectively formulate and implement global strategy.

Research by Scullion and Starkey (2000) indicated that managing repatriation was more problematic in decentralised multinational organisations due to the less developed career and succession planning systems and the weaker influence of the corporate human resource function. In practice, many organisations continue to adopt an ad-hoc sink or swim attitude towards both employees and their families and many expatriate managers continue to experience the repatriation process as falling far short of expectations (Linehan and Scullion, 2002; Stroh et al., 2000). A survey of one hundred multinational companies (Cendant, 1999) revealed that although almost 70 per cent had a formal repatriation policy, more than half did not measure or track what happened to repatriates on their return home. Adler's (1991) study of North American managers revealed that the effectiveness of expatriates took between six and twelve months to return to an 'acceptable' level following repatriation.

Repatriation problems

The complexity of repatriation varies from organisation to organisation and from employee to employee. Repatriation is also affected by such factors as the number of years spent abroad, the purpose of the international assignment, the foreign location, the age, and the family circumstances of the returning individual. There appears, however, to be a number of problems which are common to most employees.

Adler (1996) summarises the results from a number of studies which indicate that:

- one-fifth of employees who complete an overseas assignment want to leave the company when they return
- less than half of returned expatriate managers receive promotions upon return, in spite of the fact that they were working years in the overseas operation
- two-thirds of returning expatriates believe their overseas assignment had a negative impact on their careers, i.e. out of sight, out of mind
- approximately half of returning employees believed their re-entry position was less satisfying than their overseas assignment.

Similarly, a British study carried out by Johnston (1991) revealed that virtually all repatriated personnel experienced some personal difficulty in reintegration on return to their home organisation.

Other difficulties generally associated with repatriation are readjustment, re-establishment and financial problems.

Readjustment

Readjustment means adjusting to one's native culture again and returning expatriates often experience a second culture shock in the transition from a foreign culture back into one's home culture. It is the experience of facing previously familiar surroundings after living in a different environment for a significant period of time. Repatriation into the domestic organisation and social environment simultaneously has a sudden and profound impact on the individual as well as family members. The expatriate and family members have missed out on many events, fads and trends, and experience social isolation that was not expected, making the problem that much more difficult to deal with by each individual. There is an unanticipated re-entry culture shock or sense of loss and isolation resulting from a lack of current behavioural understanding of the repatriates' home country (Harvey, 1982). Research by Black *et al.* (1992) indicates that 60 per cent of American, 80 per cent of Japanese and 71 per cent of Finnish expatriates experienced some degree of culture shock during repatriation and often the problem is greater for the family than for the repatriate. Organisations often assume, however, that the culture shock of coming home should not be problematic, when, in fact, the challenges of repatriation are generally at least as great as those encountered when going overseas (Harvey, 1989). The main reasons cited for expatriates experiencing 'reverse' culture shock are that, first, expatriates have usually changed their attitudes and behaviour during the course of their international assignment and, second, work and non-work factors at home often change during the international assignment (Gregersen and Black, 1995; Linehan and Scullion, 2002). This means that expatriates often encounter a relatively 'novel' work and non-work environment upon repatriation.

Re-establishment

Re-establishment is finding a suitable position in the organisation on return, but repatriates are not always offered this, which means that if both re-establishment and readjustment are difficult, the re-entry can be very problematic. Employees may take an international assignment without knowing where it will lead careerwise. This may cause anxiety during the assignment, but it can be particularly problematic when an individual does not know what position to expect on returning to the home organisation. Reintegration into the corporate hierarchy is unquestionably the most critical worry confronting returning executives, because it has, or can have, a major impact on the individual's career. It is the area in which a lack of awareness or responsiveness by the company leads to the most bitter frustration on the part of an employee.

Unfortunately, the repatriation reality seems to be that repatriates are more often than not placed in 'holding patterns' without any real job assignment for several months and relatively few receive promotions when returning home (Black *et al.*, 1992; Johnston, 1991). The repatriates may even have to prove themselves all over again to the domestic organisation. There is also the problem of how to keep the repatriate motivated after returning to the domestic organisation. International assignments tend to be professionally challenging, with the foreign manager occupying executive or senior management positions. Overseas, the expatriate was likely to have been in a fairly autonomous position. The expatriate would usually have amassed additional experience from the international assignment such as dealing with foreign customs, cultural problems, interacting in an international environment, and dealing with unexpected situations and problems. The requirement to 'go it alone' in a foreign country has accustomed him or her to the independence not as easily obtained in domestic operations. Specifically, a number of studies have indicated that interviewed repatriates believed that upon repatriation their tasks were extremely mundane, lacking in status and authority when compared to their overseas positions (Forster, 1994; Linehan, 2000).

Financial problems

A further difficulty of repatriation includes financial problems for repatriates. These are the loss of special allowances and premiums and the effect of inflation on housing prices at home. Even though most companies urge their executives to think of the overseas premium as a separate part of their compensation, most companies pay the premium on an ongoing basis as part of an employee's regular pay cheque. Consequently, a family often tends to gradually absorb the extra money into its normal day-to-day spending pattern, becoming accustomed to a higher standard of living than it can have when it is repatriated and no longer receives the premium. The problem of rising home prices is also a concern as many expatriates may have sold their houses when they went abroad and simple cannot afford to buy comparable homes on their return. Black and Gregersen's (1991) research found that most expatriates are provided with better housing conditions during their overseas assignment than they had prior to their departure. While this may make it easier to cope with and adjust to living in a foreign country, it caused problems on repatriation. Providing housing packages that are attractive to expatriates may have positive consequences during the overseas assignment, but it makes it more difficult to avoid a drop in quality of housing conditions and it negatively affects all facets of repatriation adjustment.

Research has shown that failure in both the expatriation and repatriation phase happens in a large number of organisations due to financial misunderstandings (Harvey, 1989). Foreign allowances for education, servants, travel club memberships, etc. may also be lost, thus creating a decline in the family standard of living (Clague and Krupp, 1978). The financial pressures for the repatriated manager are thereby compounded by the disillusionment of family members and their adjusted standard of living. Additionally, when the repatriated manager compares his or her financial position to that of counterparts who did not go on an international assignment the level of financial frustration may increase as the domestic employee does not have to repurchase a home and car at higher prices. The manager who did not take an international assignment may be receiving a higher level of pay due to promotions while the repatriate was on the international assignment (Harvey, 1989). A key factor in the success or failure of international assignments is the initial alignment of expectations between the organisation and the employee (the psychological contract between both parties) and how it evolves over time, which could eventually affect the compensation package. Establishing and maintaining a relationship of mutual loyalty is the best way to ensure that the expatriates' high costs are beneficial to the company, since these are the grounds on which the company can greatly benefit from international assignments.

It is clear, therefore, that repatriates are having difficulties in quickly readjusting and getting back to high levels of motivation and productivity. Thus, from a short-term perspective, these problems of reintegration are costly for both organisations and individuals. From a longer-term perspective, organisations seem not to be fully utilising the skills and experiences which managers are sent overseas to acquire and may be losing many repatriates in the few years subsequent to their return. The costs to organisations of losing repatriates are significant both financially and strategically. No company wants to lose such valued employees. On average, expatriates have more than twelve years of experience with their companies, so that they are often at a stage in their careers when they hold a broad array of significant expectations about such matters as how their skills will be used when they return home (Black and Gregersen, 1991). They may also have specific expectations about the parent company and the work unit in which they will be placed. Many repatriated managers report that if they had been given a choice between coming home to a lateral position or transferring to another overseas location, they would have picked the latter. But they are usually not given the choice.

In summary, various studies suggest that adjusting to one's home culture can be more difficult than adapting to the foreign culture (Adler, 1996; Stroh *et al.*, 2000). According to Tung (1988), European organisations have reported that repatriation may be an equally traumatic experience as expatriation because of problems of reabsorption, both professional and personally. The impact of repatriation on the expatriate and family members may become a significant issue among employees who are considering a foreign assignment if their company does not have a programme for dealing with the complex repatriation dilemma. It is clear that proper career planning is one of the keys to the success of any integration process. If career plans are explicitly spelled out for an employee, then integrating him or her into the home organisation after a successful term overseas should not be difficult. Developing career plans do not require sophisticated staffing expertise, however, adequate financing, continued moral support, and total commitment from top management are required for any well-planned and well-managed repatriate integration programme.

Additional difficulties faced by repatriated female international managers

Few studies have specifically examined the repatriation of the spouses or partners of returning managers despite the fact that 70 per cent of expatriates go abroad and return with their spouse (Hammer et al., 1998). This is even more surprising given the positive relationship between the managers' overall work performance and repatriation adjustment of their spouse (Black and Gregersen, 1991).

There is also a dearth of empirical research which details the repatriation phase for female international managers, presumably because of their relative scarcity. A review of the relevant research literature in international management illustrates that women encounter additional barriers to career progression in comparison to their male counterparts (Caligiuri and Cascio, 1998; Harris, 1995; Linehan, 2000). Two research studies conducted with repatriated female international managers in western Europe indicate that many barriers still remain and suggests that the repatriation phase of the international career move may be even more stressful than expatriation (Linehan and Collins-O'Sullivan, 2003; Linehan and Scullion, 2002). The female repatriated managers in both studies believed that the re-entry phase is usually haphazard and ill planned for both male and female managers. They believed that many of the difficulties experienced at the repatriation stage are similar for both males and females. The managers, however, observed that as females they experienced greater uncertainty regarding re-entry because they do not have female role models or female career paths to follow. The repatriated managers believed that missed promotional opportunities because of being overlooked is, however, a greater risk for female international managers, due to their pioneering role.

Gender

These female executives also highlighted the nature of the additional problems they experienced which were associated with their gender, which they believed their male counterparts would not experience. The interviewees noted that women generally take primary responsibility for organising the family and home, regardless of how many hours they work outside the home, thereby suggesting that women need to be much more organised than their male counterparts: 'when a man is coming back all he has to think about is his job and he usually has a wife at home getting the children to and from school and settling them down' (quoted in Linehan and Scullion, 2002: 84).

Yet, despite the problems associated with repatriation, Linehan and Collins-O'Sullivan's research conducted with twenty-seven female repatriated managers throughout Europe illustrated that only three of the managers received any form of preparation for repatriation. In contrast, however, the majority of interviewees received various forms of preparation for expatriation. The managers suggested that the belief in home country organisations is that employees do not need to be prepared for repatriation. Interestingly, the three managers who did prepare for the repatriation process found it of benefit to them and they believed that it helped to make the process less stressful. The other twenty-four interviewees were very surprised to find that they found the transition so difficult. After living abroad for a number of years they were unprepared both for the changes which had occurred during the time they were away and how these changes impacted on them.

Work–family conflict

The managers interviewed by Linehan and Collins-O'Sullivan (2003) believed that there are extra difficulties for married women returning where there are family and home responsibilities thereby suggesting that the adjustment period for female managers takes longer. They believed that the extra worry of settling other members of the family added greatly to the already stressful repatriation process. They further indicated that preparation for repatriation should also focus on issues which would impact on spouses and children. A primary concern which the managers highlighted was the need to register children in schools prior to the move home. The interviewees suggested that not having been aware of this practical issue caused a large amount of distress and worry for them.

Overall, in relation to work–family conflict the findings of Linehan and Collins-O'Sullivan (2003) suggest that while there are additional problems for women balancing a career with family life, these problems should be expected and planned for. It is not just parents of small children or employees with ageing parents who are struggling with work–family conflict. Many single or childless women are increasingly concerned about leading a balanced life. The managers suggested that women in senior positions should be capable of dealing with any problems which may arise without these pressures affecting their work. There is no standard recipe for creating balance, it does not involve devoting equal amounts of time and energy to work, family and personal life. Instead, bringing work and life into balance is an ongoing process that involves finding the right allocation of time and energy to suit one's needs and values. The women further suggested that work–family conflict is a natural consequence of life which they have to plan for and the various difficulties which arise for family members during the repatriation stage have to be dealt with as they arise. They believed that if women advance to the corporate level then it should be within their capabilities to deal with these additional stressors.

Social networks

Some of the single women also identified issues which they believed impacted on them during the repatriation process because they were female. They stated that on their return they found that their friends had moved on and they suggested that it is harder for them to find a new social network than it is for men. This is something that they had not expected and which they found very difficult to cope with. These women now found that when they returned they were in an older age bracket. Many of their former friends were married and had children and were not available to socialise with them. They found that the social network which they used to have had disappeared. The women believed that it was much more difficult for them to break into a new socialising network than it would be for their male counterparts. They expressed a reluctance to go out socialising and meeting new people on their own. They believed that this was not a problem which was faced by men. Many of them had not anticipated this problem and found it very difficult to settle again in their home country.

Mentors and networks

The findings from both studies indicate that two important factors were the clarity of the repatriation process and the repatriation training received prior to returning to their home countries. The managers expressed that clearer repatriation policies would have a positive impact on work adjustment. They also perceived that training for international managers and their families for the re-entry process, and for any likely problems related to repatriation, should reduce the uncertainty normally associated with re-entry. The managers also believed that if they had the support of mentors or networks during their international assignment the re-entry process might have been easier, as they would have been informed of developments in their home organisations while abroad. Linehan and Scullion (2002) suggest that a mentoring relationship is particularly important at the repatriation stage of the international career move as mentors provide the contact and support from the home organisation which reduces the 'out of sight, out of mind' syndrome. They also suggest that networking may be important for the repatriation of female managers as a significant number of women may not have had mentors. The task for female managers of breaking into this male-dominated 'club' of managers can prove difficult, and this difficulty thereby denies them social support, contacts, opportunities and policy information. All of the interviewees in both studies were aware of 'old boy networks', and the difficulties associated with breaking into these. The interviewees believed that the exclusion of female managers from business and social networks compounds their isolation, which in turn may prevent female managers from building up useful networking relationships which would be advantageous for their repatriation. The managers noted that peer relationships and interpersonal networks provide an additional source of organisational support for managers. The studies also indicate that, given the absence of family and friends while abroad, the benefits provided by formal and informal networking in international management are of greater value when re-entering home country organisations. The female managers believed that networks provide means of 'keeping in touch' with the home organisation and help with future promotional opportunities.

Role models

On a positive note, many of the interviewees in Linehan and Scullion's (2002) research now see themselves as role models, which they believe will positively influence the careers of future female international executives in their organisations. These female executives believed that as role models they are providing support and encouragement, and are helping to reduce isolation for junior female executives. These interviewees believed that if they can show junior female managers that it is possible to combine a successful international career with family life, more female managers may be encouraged to apply for international assignments.

Overall, the lack of understanding of the particular needs of female managers in relation to the repatriation process is a growing concern in international management. Greater attention needs to be directed towards examining in depth the patterns of social and organisational readjustment of returning female managers, their spouses, and families. It has been suggested that more work is needed on the support strategies of highly independent groups that relocate abroad and that the study of group dynamics are rare in the cross-cultural adaptation literature (Adelman, 1988). This suggests that examining the role of social support both within the family unit and various social support networks between the family and others offers a potentially useful framework for understanding in greater depth the dynamics of international repatriation (Hammer *et al.*, 1998).

Career issues on repatriation

Harris *et al.* (2004) note that despite the importance of international assignments, organisations are not yet able to fully evaluate the benefits associated with their use. They suggest that although some organisations have a clear outline of the international assignments' costs, very few, if any, have anything but a vague or unclear picture of their related return on investment. Under this approach, the international assignment is seen as a value-generation process, which contributes to the company's business performance improvement.

Obviously, overseas assignments can be both highly enjoyable and financially lucrative for many employees. For the majority of repatriates, however, the main concern is perhaps the effect of the international assignment on the person's subsequent career development and career path. In other words, did the international assignment have a positive impact on the person's overall career development and subsequent advancement in the organisation? Clague and Krupp (1978) suggested that international assignments should be perceived not just as a means to solve specific job crises overseas, but as an integrated part of the employees' careers. Whether or not the move is intended to be career development for the individual, the assignment out and reassignment back should be considered as part of an integrated whole, preferably prior to the initial move. Both the expatriation assignment and the repatriation move should be examined as parts of an integrated whole, not as two discrete – much less unrelated – events in the individual's career path. Nicholson and West (1988) suggest that while many job relocations are career-enhancing and psychologically rewarding experiences, repatriation is a unique kind of relocation with an equal potential for negative as for positive outcomes. Harris *et al.* (2004) note that although individual repatriates report mainly positive career outcomes, 59 per cent of those who stayed with the same employer had seriously considered leaving. In total, about one-third of the repatriate group they studied had changed their employer. From those, one-third had done so while they were still abroad. The timing indicates that they had changed employer earlier than the average repatriation job negotiations started.

Finding suitable jobs

There is much evidence to suggest that repatriates experience significant problems in finding suitable jobs. Johnston (1991) found that repatriates had to cope with downward mobility and even redundancy. Similarly, research conducted by Forster (1994) with 124 'high-flyers' after their return to Britain illustrated that one in five were unemployed. All were actively seeking work, undergoing retraining or considering moves into other occupations. More than half of Forster's respondents had negative views about the general effects of their return to Britain on their career prospects. One of the main difficulties emerging from Forster's research was the lack of information on repatriation. Little advice was provided by organisations about the possible implications of moves abroad for the career progression of managers after they returned to Britain. Forster (1996) conducted further research in thirty-six British companies and all of these organisations had concerns about the management of repatriation. There were some fears that their preferred candidates for international assignments were starting to turn down offers for such assignments because of the uncertainties surrounding the move. Forster's interviews showed that many of the respondents enjoyed such a high quality of life in their overseas postings that they were very reluctant to return to the United Kingdom particularly as this would mean a drop in salary in many cases. Not only were some staff reluctant to return home, but also those who reported negative outcomes to their assignments were generally unenthusiastic about accepting overseas postings in the future. This pattern is repeated in many American companies, where many do not make any explicit provision for the return of expatriates (Black, 1992).

Linehan (2000) also found that only one of the thirty-two European repatriated managers in her research perceived that she had no problem with the re-entry process. The remaining thirty-one managers believed that re-entry was more difficult than the original move. For example:

> Coming back is as bad if not worse. Going abroad is difficult in that one doesn't know what they are facing, whereas when one is coming back they have a fair idea of what they are coming back to. But, there is the readjustment period when one returns. When I came back from New York to Ireland it took me about six months to settle down again.
>
> (quoted in Linehan, 2000: 142)

The thirty-one managers reported that the re-entry phase is usually unplanned. The above factors, therefore, can have a demotivating effect on the repatriate, and also pose difficulties for organisations to attract potential international managers.

Repatriate turnover

The devaluing of the international experience has been linked to repatriate turnover. Stroh (1995) found that the best predictors or repatriate turnover were whether the company had a career development plan, and whether the company was experiencing problems, such as downsizing. For many European multinationals, the repatriation problem has become more acute in recent years because expansion of foreign operations has often taken place at the same time as rationalisation of domestic operations which means that there are fewer unfilled positions available to repatriates in these organisations (Forster, 2000; Scullion, 2001). Black *et al.* (1992) argue that work adjustment has an important impact on a person's intent to stay with the organisation. They suggest that repatriates frequently evaluate their career expectations based on the treatment they receive on re-entry and often interpret the treatment as a violation of the psychological contract. This perception may arise because of the belief that the person's international performance warrants promotion; that signals were given by the organisation that effective performance in the international assignment would result in career advancement. When the expected promotion does not happen, the repatriate may believe there is no option but to leave the organisation (Linehan, 2000; Welch, 1994).

In summary, when assessing the international assignment there is a need to develop a methodology to measure the assignment in terms of professional development, financial value, and knowledge value for both the repatriate and the organisation which according to Harris *et al.* (2004) is currently the focus of many consultancies operating in the area of international human resource management.

Conclusion

Multinationals have begun to experience difficulty in attracting executives to accept international assignments. One of the contributing factors in this reluctance to go abroad is the ambiguity that surrounds the executive's career on repatriation. Just as multinationals have recognised the need to train executives for international assignments, they must also develop a plan or process for facilitating the re-entry of executives into domestic operations. Re-entry positions signal the importance given to international experience. If the repatriate is promoted or his/her international experience is valued by the home organisation then the international assignment is interpreted as a positive career move. If the repatriated manager, however, does not have a suitable position to return to, or expatriation is seen as 'out of sight, out of mind', other employees may decide that the acceptance of an international assignment is a high-risk decision in terms of future career progression within the organisation.

The increasing empirical and anecdotal evidence illustrates that re-entry to the home country presents new challenges as the repatriate copes with what has been termed *re-entry shock* or *reverse culture shock*. Dowling *et al.* (1999) proposed that given the more profound effect that job-related factors appear to have, re-entry shock is perhaps a more accurate term to describe the readjustment process experienced upon repatriation. Adler (1991) summarised that organisations fail to profit from the potential benefits of employees' overseas assignments. For the organisation to benefit fully from its investment in overseas assignments, both the home organisation and the repatriates need to understand the re-entry transition. Both management and repatriates must identify job skills acquired or enhanced overseas and systematically find ways in which those skills can be integrated and productively used in the home organisation. Management needs to understand the full importance of staying in contact with overseas staff members, of planning for their return, and of recognising the value of their overseas experience. The attitudes of managers who stay at home must be changed, as well as the evaluation and reward schemes.

Without employing 'the best' managers in the global marketplace, many organisations will not be able to effectively compete with major global competitors. If significantly more attention is not focused on the special needs of repatriation, the most capable managers may never take the opportunity afforded by an international assignment. Both the managers and their organisations will be negatively impacted by the decision not to undertake such an international assignment. If approximately one in four repatriates leave their organisation, this represents a substantial financial and human capital loss to the organisation, especially if the skills, knowledge and experience that the individual gains are important to the organisation and scarce in the international or external labour markets (Black and Gregersen, 1991). Organisations, therefore, need to become proactive during the repatriation adjustment stage as they do at the expatriate cross-cultural adjustment stage. Various research studies have illustrated the overall effectiveness of cross-cultural training efforts in helping individuals adapt to working and living in a foreign culture, what is now needed is rigorous research which examines the effectiveness of various re-entry training programmes on the repatriation adjustment of male and female managers.

It is necessary to highlight the importance of closing the gap between expectations and reality for expatriates returning to their parent companies and suggest that multinationals which prepare their managers for coming home with effective repatriation programmes will have a greater likelihood both of retaining these scarce human resources and of helping them make the difficult adjustment to being home. This supports research by Hammer *et al.* (1998) which found that the re-entry variable of expectations was significantly related to re-entry satisfaction for managers and significantly related to re-entry satisfaction and re-entry difficulties for spouses. This is consistent with Martin's (1984) research which suggested that one of the key differences between sojourner acculturation and repatriate acculturation revolves around differences in expectations. Similarly, Hammer *et al.* (1998) argue that re-entry training should focus primarily on helping the expatriate manager and spouse align their expectations with 'the real world' that will be encountered in the home culture both in the work and non-work situation.

References

Adelman, M.B. (1988) 'Cross-cultural adjustment: a theoretical perspective on social support', *International Journal of Intercultural Relations*, 12: 183–203.

Adler, N.J. (1991) *International Dimensions of Organisational Behavior*, 2nd edn, Boston, MA: Kent.

Adler, N.J. (1996) *International Dimensions of Organisational Behavior*, 3rd edn, Boston, MA: Kent.

Black, J.S. (1992) 'Coming home: the relationship of expatriate expectations with repatriation adjustment and job performance', *Human Relations*, 45(2): 113–22.

Black, J.S. and Gregersen, H.B. (1991) 'When Yankee comes home: factors related to expatriate and spouse repatriation adjustment', *Journal of International Business Studies*, 22: 671–94.

Black, J.S. and Gregersen, H.B. (1998) *So You're Going Overseas: A Handbook for Personal and Professional Success*, San Diego, CA: Global.

Black, J.S., Gregersen, H.B. and Mendenhall, M.E. (1992) 'Toward a theoretical framework of repatriation adjustment', *Journal of International Business*, 23(4): 737–60.

Caligiuri, P. and Cascio, W. (1998) 'Can we send her there? Maximising the success of western women on global assignments', *Journal of World Business*, 33(4): 394–416.

Cendant International Assignment Services (1999) *Policies and Practices Survey 1999*, London: Cendant International Assignment Services.

Clague, L. and Krupp, N.B. (1978) 'International personnel: the repatriation problem', *Personnel Administrator*, April: 29–33.

Conference Board (1997) *Managing Expatriates' Return: A Research Report*, Report no. 1148–96-RR, New York: Conference Board.

Dowling, P., Welch, D.E. and Schuler, R.S. (1999) *International Human Resource Management: Managing People in an International Context*, 3rd edn, Cincinatti, OH: South Western College Publishing, ITP.

Forster, N. (1994) 'The forgotten employees? The experiences of expatriate staff returning to the UK', *International Journal of Human Resource Management*, 5(4): 405–27.

Forster, N. (1996) *A Report on the Management of Expatriates in 36 UK Companies*, Cardiff: Cardiff Business School Report.

Forster, N. (2000) 'The myth of the international manager', *International Journal of Human Resource Management*, 11(1): 126–42.

Gregersen, H.B. and Black, J.S. (1995) 'Keeping high performers after international assignments: a key to global executive development', *Journal of International Management*, 1(1): 3–31.

Hammer, M.R., Hart, W. and Rogan, R. (1998) 'Can you go home again? An analysis of the repatriation of corporate managers', *Management International Review*, 38(1): 67–86.

Harris, H. (1995) 'Women's role in (international) management', in A.W.K. Harzing and J. Van Ruysseveldt (eds) *International Human Resource Management*, London: Sage.

Harris, H., Brewster, C. and Sparrow, P. (2004) *International Human Resource Management*, London: Chartered Institute of Personnel Development.

Harvey, M. (1982) 'The other side of foreign assignments: dealing with the repatriation dilemma', *Columbia Journal of World Business*, 17: 53–9.

Harvey, M. (1989) 'Repatriation of corporate executives: an empirical study', *Journal of International Business Studies*, 20: 131–44.

Johnston, J. (1991) 'An empirical study of the repatriation of managers in UK multinationals', *Human Resource Management Journal*, 1(4): 102–9.

Linehan, M. (2000) *Senior Female International Managers: Why So Few?*, Aldershot: Ashgate.

Linehan, M. and Collins-O'Sullivan, C. (2003) 'The repatriation of female international corporate executives: a qualitative study in a European context', paper presented at Seventh Conference on International Human Resource Management, University of Limerick, Ireland, 4–6 June.

Linehan, M. and Scullion, H. (2002) 'Repatriation of female executives: empirical evidence from Europe', Women in Management Review, 17(2): 80–8.

Marmer Solomon, C. (1995) 'Repatriation: up, down or out?', *Personnel Journal*, January: 28–37.

Martin, J.N. (1984) 'The intercultural re-entry: conceptualization and directions for future research', *International Journal of Intercultural Relations*, 8: 115–34.

Nicholson, N. and West, M. (1988) *Managerial Job Change: Men and Women in Transition*, Cambridge: Cambridge University Press.

Scullion, H. (2001) 'International human resource management', in J. Storey (ed.) *Human Resource Management*, London: International Thomson.

Scullion, H. and Starkey, K. (2000) 'In search of the changing role of the corporate human resource function', *International Journal of Human Resource Management*, 11: 1061–81.

Stroh, L.K. (1995) 'Predicting turnover among repatriates: can organisations affect retention rates?', *International Journal of Human Resource Management*, 6(2): 443–56.

Stroh, L.K., Gregersen, H.B. and Black, J.S. (2000) 'Triumphs and tragedies: expectations and commitments upon repatriation', *International Journal of Human Resource Management*, 11: 681–97.

Tung, R. (1988) *The New Expatriates: Managing Human Resources Abroad*, Cambridge, MA: Ballinger.

Welch, D. (1994) 'Determinants of international human resource management approaches and activities: a suggested framework', *Journal of Management Studies*, 31(2): 139–64.

Index